بسم الله الرحمن الرحيم

In the Name of Allah, the Most Generous, the Most Merciful

Islam in English Press: for accessible guides to Islamic knowledge.

The Source of Islamic Spirituality
Commentary on Surah 17
The Night Journey – Surah Isrāa' / Bani Isra'il

By Ayatollah Sayyid Fadhel Hosseini Milani
Recorded and edited by Amar Hegedüs.

Acknowledgements: Islam in English Press would like to thank Hasan Ghazi for his valuable contribution to the Qur'anic quotations, Arabic alphabet and his unstinting support during the preparation of this work.

First published in 2004 by Islam in English Press
P. O. Box 2842, London W6 9ZH.

ISBN 0-9541585-1-2

A catalogue of this book can be found in The British Library.

First published in this edition 2004.

Artwork by Kristine Hatch.

Printed and bound in Finland.

The Source of Islamic Spirituality

Commentary on Surah 17

The Night Journey – Surah Isrāa' / Bani Isra'il

Ayatollah Sayyid Fadhel Hosseini Milani

Recorded and edited by Amar Hegedüs

ISLAM IN ENGLISH PRESS

Contents

Editor's Note

In the name of Allah, the Most Generous, the Most Merciful

Although it may appear obvious that the Qur'an is Allah's revelation in the Arabic language, it must be emphasised that the Qur'an is in Arabic. No interpretation, elucidation, exposition, explanation, or rendition may ever claim to be anything other than an attempt to clarify the meaning of that Arabic.

Words used in one endeavour sometimes acquire specific significance and meanings which differ from their meaning and significance in common usage. For example, in the English language a mouse may be any of a number of small rodents typically resembling diminutive rats with a pointed snout, rather small ears, elongated body and slender, hairless or sparsely haired tail. In another context the word 'mouse' designates a small lead weight fastened to a string which is used to pull window sash cords into place over pulleys in the jambs of the frame. In the context of information technology a mouse designates the device by which the cursor may easily be moved around a computer screen.

The same applies to many words used in the Qur'an. For example, the root word 'Wilayah' is used in the Qur'an as a noun 124 times and as a verb 112 times. According to *Mufradatu'l-Qur'an*, the distinguished Qur'anic lexicon, the word 'Wilayah' is used to describe things so close, one to the other, that their identities almost appear seamlessly fused. Depending on how it is used, the word may describe a special or spiritual affinity, an intimacy and friendship, or having a responsibility for. In all its usages, 'Wilayah' and its derivatives imply that subjects are of the same variety or type and in such close personal contact as to provide them with contiguity.

The word 'Wilayah' thus has the connotation of 'assistance', the word 'Walayah', of 'being in charge' or 'the person in authority of a certain matter' even though both meanings convey 'being in charge and having authority'. The renowned Lexicon of Islamic Terms – *Mufradatu'l-Qur'an* – provides examples of such word usage. From the word 'Wilayah' many other words are derived. Some words such as 'Mawla' can, with the sanction of the original word, and depending on their situational and syntactical context, have as many as 27 different usages. Such derivatives are applied to the material and abstract, as well as the physical and mental. Originally used in a physical sense they were later, by comparison with what had been visualised or abstracted from the perceived meaning, or from its material and tangible associations, also used with abstract meanings.

This work is the critical explanation and interpretation of Ayatollah Sayyid Fadhel Hosseini Milani, a renowned Muslim scholar who has a profound knowledge of Arabic and the ethical-religious concepts in the Qur'an.

Amar Hegedüs

Foreword

In the Name of Allah, the Most Generous, the Most Merciful

The Prophet Ibrahim ﷺ is considered the father of monotheism and the first guide to the rational understanding of the Almighty and His attributes and creation. The prophets who came after him, particularly Mūsa, 'Isa and Muḥammad ﷺ, taught the same lessons he did but in greater detail.

Despite this, in what nowadays appears to be the teaching of Judaism, greater accent is placed on what has been manifest and rather less on the unseen. In contrast, Christianity teaches its adherents to align themselves to the unseen, which is claimed to have greater significance than that which has been manifest. It is only Islam that promotes a balance between these two aspects. While human beings do not need to be reminded of their physical needs, many ignore the spiritual dimensions that link the physical to the unseen.

Many surahs of the Qur'an promote these issues, but Surah 17 is particularly inspiring in establishing a balance not only between body and spirit, but also between the mundane and the celestial.

What is the 'Night Journey'? Did the Prophet ﷺ physically ascend to the sublime or was his a spiritual journey? Was it a physical manifestation or a vision? Is it possible for a human being to defy gravity and effect space travel? What proof is there that such an amazing journey ever took place? All these matters need to be questioned – and answered.

The ascent of the Prophet ﷺ illustrates the potential of a purified soul, to be elevated to levels from which it may pass beyond time and space and become acquainted with that which is beyond the physical senses.

Moving from the title of 'Night Journey – Surah Isrāa' to the title of 'The Children of Isra'il – Bani Isra'il', necessitates investigation of the historical background of the Jewish community and its links to tyranny and corruption, for it is through that study that we are able to connect the present to the past and learn the lessons of history.

Since this world is a domain in which Divine and Satanic powers oppose and challenge each other, every human being is given the choice to elect the side to which they wish to ally themselves. Each side employs its own means of influence to either guide or mislead. The former is an invitation to illumination, the latter to darkness. The former may elevate them from the level of brute animal to the highest possible status, the latter may beguile them into the abyss of all abysses.

In this Surah, Allah details the ways and means that Satan – Shaytan – uses to mislead. We have felt it necessary to exemplify those means with examples from contemporary socio-political issues, despite these not being the primary subject matter of this study. Importantly however, it is in the socio-ethical teachings of this Surah that Divine Revelation provides solutions to our inescapable social problems.

Last but not least are the Most Beautiful Names of our Almighty Creator and the part these play in the establishment of Muslim personality.

This work is a humble attempt to provide clear answers to the above issues. In dealing with them the reader is offered a comprehensive picture of both social and spiritual aspects of the Faith of Islam. This is not intended to be an arcane theoretical work but rather one in which practical contributions for the human conduct of daily life is made.

Let us pray that Allah Almighty will enlighten our hearts and illumine our way to Him.

Dr. Sayyid Fadhel
فاضل الحسيني الميلاني
Hosseini Milani

Conventions

Throughout this book you will see colophons of the Arabic terms of respect used by Muslims:

صلى الله عليه وآله وسلم **Sallalahu Alayhi wa alihi wa Salaam**
May Allah's greetings and blessings be upon him and his progeny
(used immediately after referring to the Prophet Muhammad)

عليها السلام **Alayha al-Salaam** – Peace be upon her
(used immediately after referring to Khadijah, Fatimah, Zaynab and Maryam)

عليه السلام **Alayhi al-Salaam** – May Allah bless him
(used immediately after referring to a **single** Imam or Prophet)

عليهما السلام **Alayhima al-Salaam** – May Allah bless them
(used immediately after referring to **two** Imams or **two** Prophets)

عليهم السلام **Alayhum al-Salaam** – May Allah bless them
(used immediately after referring to **three or more** Imams or Prophets)

رحمه الله **Rahimahu Allah** – May Allah grant him mercy
(used immediately after referring to a single deceased and respected **person**)

رحمهم الله **Rahimahum Allah** – May Allah grant them mercy
(used immediately after referring to deceased and respected **people**)

قدس سره **Quddisa Sirroh** – May his soul be blessed
(used immediately after referring to a single deceased and respected **scholar**)

قدس سرهما **Quddisa Sirrohuma** – May their souls be blessed
(used immediately after referring to deceased and respected **scholars**)

رضي الله عنه **Radi Allahu anhu** – May Allah be pleased with him
(used after referring to a respected companion of the Prophet or the Imams)

سُورَةُ الإِسْرَاءِ

بِسْمِ ٱللَّهِ ٱلرَّحْمَٰنِ ٱلرَّحِيمِ

سُبْحَٰنَ ٱلَّذِىٓ أَسْرَىٰ بِعَبْدِهِۦ لَيْلًا مِّنَ ٱلْمَسْجِدِ ٱلْحَرَامِ
إِلَى ٱلْمَسْجِدِ ٱلْأَقْصَا ٱلَّذِى بَٰرَكْنَا حَوْلَهُۥ لِنُرِيَهُۥ مِنْ ءَايَٰتِنَآ إِنَّهُۥ
هُوَ ٱلسَّمِيعُ ٱلْبَصِيرُ ١ وَءَاتَيْنَا مُوسَى ٱلْكِتَٰبَ وَجَعَلْنَٰهُ
هُدًى لِّبَنِىٓ إِسْرَٰٓءِيلَ أَلَّا تَتَّخِذُوا۟ مِن دُونِى وَكِيلًا ٢
ذُرِّيَّةَ مَنْ حَمَلْنَا مَعَ نُوحٍ إِنَّهُۥ كَانَ عَبْدًا شَكُورًا ٣
وَقَضَيْنَآ إِلَىٰ بَنِىٓ إِسْرَٰٓءِيلَ فِى ٱلْكِتَٰبِ لَتُفْسِدُنَّ فِى ٱلْأَرْضِ
مَرَّتَيْنِ وَلَتَعْلُنَّ عُلُوًّا كَبِيرًا ٤ فَإِذَا جَآءَ وَعْدُ أُولَىٰهُمَا بَعَثْنَا
عَلَيْكُمْ عِبَادًا لَّنَآ أُو۟لِى بَأْسٍ شَدِيدٍ فَجَاسُوا۟ خِلَٰلَ ٱلدِّيَارِ
وَكَانَ وَعْدًا مَّفْعُولًا ٥ ثُمَّ رَدَدْنَا لَكُمُ ٱلْكَرَّةَ عَلَيْهِمْ
وَأَمْدَدْنَٰكُم بِأَمْوَٰلٍ وَبَنِينَ وَجَعَلْنَٰكُمْ أَكْثَرَ نَفِيرًا ٦
إِنْ أَحْسَنتُمْ أَحْسَنتُمْ لِأَنفُسِكُمْ وَإِنْ أَسَأْتُمْ فَلَهَا فَإِذَا جَآءَ
وَعْدُ ٱلْءَاخِرَةِ لِيَسُۥٓـُٔوا۟ وُجُوهَكُمْ وَلِيَدْخُلُوا۟ ٱلْمَسْجِدَ
كَمَا دَخَلُوهُ أَوَّلَ مَرَّةٍ وَلِيُتَبِّرُوا۟ مَا عَلَوْا۟ تَتْبِيرًا ٧

عَسَىٰ رَبُّكُمْ أَن يَرْحَمَكُمْ ۚ وَإِنْ عُدتُّمْ عُدْنَا ۘ وَجَعَلْنَا جَهَنَّمَ لِلْكَٰفِرِينَ
حَصِيرًا ﴿٨﴾ إِنَّ هَٰذَا ٱلْقُرْءَانَ يَهْدِى لِلَّتِى هِىَ أَقْوَمُ وَيُبَشِّرُ
ٱلْمُؤْمِنِينَ ٱلَّذِينَ يَعْمَلُونَ ٱلصَّٰلِحَٰتِ أَنَّ لَهُمْ أَجْرًا كَبِيرًا ﴿٩﴾
وَأَنَّ ٱلَّذِينَ لَا يُؤْمِنُونَ بِٱلْءَاخِرَةِ أَعْتَدْنَا لَهُمْ عَذَابًا أَلِيمًا ﴿١٠﴾
وَيَدْعُ ٱلْإِنسَٰنُ بِٱلشَّرِّ دُعَآءَهُۥ بِٱلْخَيْرِ ۖ وَكَانَ ٱلْإِنسَٰنُ عَجُولًا ﴿١١﴾
وَجَعَلْنَا ٱلَّيْلَ وَٱلنَّهَارَ ءَايَتَيْنِ ۖ فَمَحَوْنَآ ءَايَةَ ٱلَّيْلِ وَجَعَلْنَآ ءَايَةَ
ٱلنَّهَارِ مُبْصِرَةً لِّتَبْتَغُوا۟ فَضْلًا مِّن رَّبِّكُمْ وَلِتَعْلَمُوا۟ عَدَدَ
ٱلسِّنِينَ وَٱلْحِسَابَ ۚ وَكُلَّ شَىْءٍ فَصَّلْنَٰهُ تَفْصِيلًا ﴿١٢﴾ وَكُلَّ
إِنسَٰنٍ أَلْزَمْنَٰهُ طَٰٓئِرَهُۥ فِى عُنُقِهِۦ ۖ وَنُخْرِجُ لَهُۥ يَوْمَ ٱلْقِيَٰمَةِ كِتَٰبًا
يَلْقَىٰهُ مَنشُورًا ﴿١٣﴾ ٱقْرَأْ كِتَٰبَكَ كَفَىٰ بِنَفْسِكَ ٱلْيَوْمَ عَلَيْكَ حَسِيبًا
﴿١٤﴾ مَّنِ ٱهْتَدَىٰ فَإِنَّمَا يَهْتَدِى لِنَفْسِهِۦ ۖ وَمَن ضَلَّ فَإِنَّمَا يَضِلُّ
عَلَيْهَا ۚ وَلَا تَزِرُ وَازِرَةٌ وِزْرَ أُخْرَىٰ ۗ وَمَا كُنَّا مُعَذِّبِينَ حَتَّىٰ نَبْعَثَ
رَسُولًا ﴿١٥﴾ وَإِذَآ أَرَدْنَآ أَن نُّهْلِكَ قَرْيَةً أَمَرْنَا مُتْرَفِيهَا فَفَسَقُوا۟ فِيهَا
فَحَقَّ عَلَيْهَا ٱلْقَوْلُ فَدَمَّرْنَٰهَا تَدْمِيرًا ﴿١٦﴾ وَكَمْ أَهْلَكْنَا مِنَ
ٱلْقُرُونِ مِنۢ بَعْدِ نُوحٍ ۗ وَكَفَىٰ بِرَبِّكَ بِذُنُوبِ عِبَادِهِۦ خَبِيرًۢا بَصِيرًا ﴿١٧﴾

مَّن كَانَ يُرِيدُ ٱلْعَاجِلَةَ عَجَّلْنَا لَهُۥ فِيهَا مَا نَشَآءُ لِمَن نُّرِيدُ ثُمَّ
جَعَلْنَا لَهُۥ جَهَنَّمَ يَصْلَىٰهَا مَذْمُومًا مَّدْحُورًا ١٨ وَمَنْ أَرَادَ
ٱلْءَاخِرَةَ وَسَعَىٰ لَهَا سَعْيَهَا وَهُوَ مُؤْمِنٌ فَأُو۟لَٰٓئِكَ كَانَ
سَعْيُهُم مَّشْكُورًا ١٩ كُلًّا نُّمِدُّ هَٰٓؤُلَآءِ وَهَٰٓؤُلَآءِ مِنْ عَطَآءِ
رَبِّكَ ۚ وَمَا كَانَ عَطَآءُ رَبِّكَ مَحْظُورًا ٢٠ ٱنظُرْ كَيْفَ فَضَّلْنَا
بَعْضَهُمْ عَلَىٰ بَعْضٍ ۚ وَلَلْءَاخِرَةُ أَكْبَرُ دَرَجَٰتٍ وَأَكْبَرُ تَفْضِيلًا
٢١ لَّا تَجْعَلْ مَعَ ٱللَّهِ إِلَٰهًا ءَاخَرَ فَتَقْعُدَ مَذْمُومًا مَّخْذُولًا ٢٢
۞ وَقَضَىٰ رَبُّكَ أَلَّا تَعْبُدُوٓا۟ إِلَّآ إِيَّاهُ وَبِٱلْوَٰلِدَيْنِ إِحْسَٰنًا ۚ إِمَّا
يَبْلُغَنَّ عِندَكَ ٱلْكِبَرَ أَحَدُهُمَآ أَوْ كِلَاهُمَا فَلَا تَقُل لَّهُمَآ
أُفٍّ وَلَا تَنْهَرْهُمَا وَقُل لَّهُمَا قَوْلًا كَرِيمًا ٢٣ وَٱخْفِضْ
لَهُمَا جَنَاحَ ٱلذُّلِّ مِنَ ٱلرَّحْمَةِ وَقُل رَّبِّ ٱرْحَمْهُمَا كَمَا رَبَّيَانِى
صَغِيرًا ٢٤ رَّبُّكُمْ أَعْلَمُ بِمَا فِى نُفُوسِكُمْ ۚ إِن تَكُونُوا۟ صَٰلِحِينَ
فَإِنَّهُۥ كَانَ لِلْأَوَّٰبِينَ غَفُورًا ٢٥ وَءَاتِ ذَا ٱلْقُرْبَىٰ حَقَّهُۥ
وَٱلْمِسْكِينَ وَٱبْنَ ٱلسَّبِيلِ وَلَا تُبَذِّرْ تَبْذِيرًا ٢٦ إِنَّ ٱلْمُبَذِّرِينَ
كَانُوٓا۟ إِخْوَٰنَ ٱلشَّيَٰطِينِ ۖ وَكَانَ ٱلشَّيْطَٰنُ لِرَبِّهِۦ كَفُورًا ٢٧

وَإِمَّا تُعۡرِضَنَّ عَنۡهُمُ ٱبۡتِغَآءَ رَحۡمَةٖ مِّن رَّبِّكَ تَرۡجُوهَا فَقُل لَّهُمۡ قَوۡلٗا
مَّيۡسُورٗا ٢٨ وَلَا تَجۡعَلۡ يَدَكَ مَغۡلُولَةً إِلَىٰ عُنُقِكَ وَلَا تَبۡسُطۡهَا
كُلَّ ٱلۡبَسۡطِ فَتَقۡعُدَ مَلُومٗا مَّحۡسُورًا ٢٩ إِنَّ رَبَّكَ يَبۡسُطُ ٱلرِّزۡقَ
لِمَن يَشَآءُ وَيَقۡدِرُۚ إِنَّهُۥ كَانَ بِعِبَادِهِۦ خَبِيرَۢا بَصِيرٗا ٣٠ وَلَا تَقۡتُلُوٓاْ
أَوۡلَٰدَكُمۡ خَشۡيَةَ إِمۡلَٰقٖۖ نَّحۡنُ نَرۡزُقُهُمۡ وَإِيَّاكُمۡۚ إِنَّ قَتۡلَهُمۡ كَانَ
خِطۡـٔٗا كَبِيرٗا ٣١ وَلَا تَقۡرَبُواْ ٱلزِّنَىٰٓۖ إِنَّهُۥ كَانَ فَٰحِشَةٗ وَسَآءَ
سَبِيلٗا ٣٢ وَلَا تَقۡتُلُواْ ٱلنَّفۡسَ ٱلَّتِي حَرَّمَ ٱللَّهُ إِلَّا بِٱلۡحَقِّۗ وَمَن
قُتِلَ مَظۡلُومٗا فَقَدۡ جَعَلۡنَا لِوَلِيِّهِۦ سُلۡطَٰنٗا فَلَا يُسۡرِف فِّي
ٱلۡقَتۡلِۖ إِنَّهُۥ كَانَ مَنصُورٗا ٣٣ وَلَا تَقۡرَبُواْ مَالَ ٱلۡيَتِيمِ إِلَّا بِٱلَّتِي
هِيَ أَحۡسَنُ حَتَّىٰ يَبۡلُغَ أَشُدَّهُۥۚ وَأَوۡفُواْ بِٱلۡعَهۡدِۖ إِنَّ ٱلۡعَهۡدَ كَانَ
مَسۡـُٔولٗا ٣٤ وَأَوۡفُواْ ٱلۡكَيۡلَ إِذَا كِلۡتُمۡ وَزِنُواْ بِٱلۡقِسۡطَاسِ ٱلۡمُسۡتَقِيمِۚ
ذَٰلِكَ خَيۡرٞ وَأَحۡسَنُ تَأۡوِيلٗا ٣٥ وَلَا تَقۡفُ مَا لَيۡسَ لَكَ بِهِۦ عِلۡمٌۚ
إِنَّ ٱلسَّمۡعَ وَٱلۡبَصَرَ وَٱلۡفُؤَادَ كُلُّ أُوْلَٰٓئِكَ كَانَ عَنۡهُ مَسۡـُٔولٗا ٣٦
وَلَا تَمۡشِ فِي ٱلۡأَرۡضِ مَرَحًاۖ إِنَّكَ لَن تَخۡرِقَ ٱلۡأَرۡضَ وَلَن تَبۡلُغَ
ٱلۡجِبَالَ طُولٗا ٣٧ كُلُّ ذَٰلِكَ كَانَ سَيِّئُهُۥ عِندَ رَبِّكَ مَكۡرُوهٗا ٣٨

ذَٰلِكَ مِمَّآ أَوْحَىٰٓ إِلَيْكَ رَبُّكَ مِنَ ٱلْحِكْمَةِ ۗ وَلَا تَجْعَلْ مَعَ ٱللَّهِ إِلَٰهًا
ءَاخَرَ فَتُلْقَىٰ فِى جَهَنَّمَ مَلُومًا مَّدْحُورًا ﴿٣٩﴾ أَفَأَصْفَىٰكُمْ رَبُّكُم
بِٱلْبَنِينَ وَٱتَّخَذَ مِنَ ٱلْمَلَٰٓئِكَةِ إِنَٰثًا ۚ إِنَّكُمْ لَتَقُولُونَ قَوْلًا عَظِيمًا ﴿٤٠﴾
وَلَقَدْ صَرَّفْنَا فِى هَٰذَا ٱلْقُرْءَانِ لِيَذَّكَّرُوا۟ وَمَا يَزِيدُهُمْ إِلَّا نُفُورًا ﴿٤١﴾
قُل لَّوْ كَانَ مَعَهُۥٓ ءَالِهَةٌ كَمَا يَقُولُونَ إِذًا لَّٱبْتَغَوْا۟ إِلَىٰ ذِى ٱلْعَرْشِ سَبِيلًا
﴿٤٢﴾ سُبْحَٰنَهُۥ وَتَعَٰلَىٰ عَمَّا يَقُولُونَ عُلُوًّا كَبِيرًا ﴿٤٣﴾ تُسَبِّحُ لَهُ ٱلسَّمَٰوَٰتُ
ٱلسَّبْعُ وَٱلْأَرْضُ وَمَن فِيهِنَّ ۚ وَإِن مِّن شَىْءٍ إِلَّا يُسَبِّحُ بِحَمْدِهِۦ وَلَٰكِن
لَّا تَفْقَهُونَ تَسْبِيحَهُمْ ۗ إِنَّهُۥ كَانَ حَلِيمًا غَفُورًا ﴿٤٤﴾ وَإِذَا قَرَأْتَ
ٱلْقُرْءَانَ جَعَلْنَا بَيْنَكَ وَبَيْنَ ٱلَّذِينَ لَا يُؤْمِنُونَ بِٱلْءَاخِرَةِ حِجَابًا
مَّسْتُورًا ﴿٤٥﴾ وَجَعَلْنَا عَلَىٰ قُلُوبِهِمْ أَكِنَّةً أَن يَفْقَهُوهُ وَفِىٓ ءَاذَانِهِمْ
وَقْرًا ۚ وَإِذَا ذَكَرْتَ رَبَّكَ فِى ٱلْقُرْءَانِ وَحْدَهُۥ وَلَّوْا۟ عَلَىٰٓ أَدْبَٰرِهِمْ نُفُورًا
﴿٤٦﴾ نَّحْنُ أَعْلَمُ بِمَا يَسْتَمِعُونَ بِهِۦٓ إِذْ يَسْتَمِعُونَ إِلَيْكَ وَإِذْ هُمْ نَجْوَىٰٓ
إِذْ يَقُولُ ٱلظَّٰلِمُونَ إِن تَتَّبِعُونَ إِلَّا رَجُلًا مَّسْحُورًا ﴿٤٧﴾ ٱنظُرْ
كَيْفَ ضَرَبُوا۟ لَكَ ٱلْأَمْثَالَ فَضَلُّوا۟ فَلَا يَسْتَطِيعُونَ سَبِيلًا ﴿٤٨﴾
وَقَالُوٓا۟ أَءِذَا كُنَّا عِظَٰمًا وَرُفَٰتًا أَءِنَّا لَمَبْعُوثُونَ خَلْقًا جَدِيدًا ﴿٤٩﴾

۞ قُلْ كُونُوا۟ حِجَارَةً أَوْ حَدِيدًا ﴿٥٠﴾ أَوْ خَلْقًا مِّمَّا يَكْبُرُ فِى
صُدُورِكُمْ ۚ فَسَيَقُولُونَ مَن يُعِيدُنَا ۖ قُلِ ٱلَّذِى فَطَرَكُمْ أَوَّلَ مَرَّةٍ ۚ
فَسَيُنْغِضُونَ إِلَيْكَ رُءُوسَهُمْ وَيَقُولُونَ مَتَىٰ هُوَ ۖ قُلْ عَسَىٰٓ أَن
يَكُونَ قَرِيبًا ﴿٥١﴾ يَوْمَ يَدْعُوكُمْ فَتَسْتَجِيبُونَ بِحَمْدِهِۦ
وَتَظُنُّونَ إِن لَّبِثْتُمْ إِلَّا قَلِيلًا ﴿٥٢﴾ وَقُل لِّعِبَادِى يَقُولُوا۟ ٱلَّتِى هِىَ
أَحْسَنُ ۚ إِنَّ ٱلشَّيْطَـٰنَ يَنزَغُ بَيْنَهُمْ ۚ إِنَّ ٱلشَّيْطَـٰنَ كَانَ لِلْإِنسَـٰنِ
عَدُوًّا مُّبِينًا ﴿٥٣﴾ رَّبُّكُمْ أَعْلَمُ بِكُمْ ۖ إِن يَشَأْ يَرْحَمْكُمْ أَوْ إِن يَشَأْ
يُعَذِّبْكُمْ ۚ وَمَآ أَرْسَلْنَـٰكَ عَلَيْهِمْ وَكِيلًا ﴿٥٤﴾ وَرَبُّكَ أَعْلَمُ
بِمَن فِى ٱلسَّمَـٰوَٰتِ وَٱلْأَرْضِ ۗ وَلَقَدْ فَضَّلْنَا بَعْضَ ٱلنَّبِيِّـۧنَ عَلَىٰ بَعْضٍ ۖ
وَءَاتَيْنَا دَاوُۥدَ زَبُورًا ﴿٥٥﴾ قُلِ ٱدْعُوا۟ ٱلَّذِينَ زَعَمْتُم مِّن دُونِهِۦ فَلَا
يَمْلِكُونَ كَشْفَ ٱلضُّرِّ عَنكُمْ وَلَا تَحْوِيلًا ﴿٥٦﴾ أُو۟لَـٰٓئِكَ ٱلَّذِينَ
يَدْعُونَ يَبْتَغُونَ إِلَىٰ رَبِّهِمُ ٱلْوَسِيلَةَ أَيُّهُمْ أَقْرَبُ وَيَرْجُونَ
رَحْمَتَهُۥ وَيَخَافُونَ عَذَابَهُۥٓ ۚ إِنَّ عَذَابَ رَبِّكَ كَانَ مَحْذُورًا ﴿٥٧﴾
وَإِن مِّن قَرْيَةٍ إِلَّا نَحْنُ مُهْلِكُوهَا قَبْلَ يَوْمِ ٱلْقِيَـٰمَةِ
أَوْ مُعَذِّبُوهَا عَذَابًا شَدِيدًا ۚ كَانَ ذَٰلِكَ فِى ٱلْكِتَـٰبِ مَسْطُورًا ﴿٥٨﴾

وَمَا مَنَعَنَآ أَن نُّرْسِلَ بِٱلْـَٔايَٰتِ إِلَّآ أَن كَذَّبَ بِهَا ٱلْأَوَّلُونَ ۚ
وَءَاتَيْنَا ثَمُودَ ٱلنَّاقَةَ مُبْصِرَةً فَظَلَمُوا۟ بِهَا ۚ وَمَا نُرْسِلُ بِٱلْـَٔايَٰتِ
إِلَّا تَخْوِيفًا ﴿٥٩﴾ وَإِذْ قُلْنَا لَكَ إِنَّ رَبَّكَ أَحَاطَ بِٱلنَّاسِ ۚ وَمَا
جَعَلْنَا ٱلرُّءْيَا ٱلَّتِىٓ أَرَيْنَٰكَ إِلَّا فِتْنَةً لِّلنَّاسِ وَٱلشَّجَرَةَ ٱلْمَلْعُونَةَ
فِى ٱلْقُرْءَانِ ۚ وَنُخَوِّفُهُمْ فَمَا يَزِيدُهُمْ إِلَّا طُغْيَٰنًا كَبِيرًا ﴿٦٠﴾
وَإِذْ قُلْنَا لِلْمَلَٰٓئِكَةِ ٱسْجُدُوا۟ لِءَادَمَ فَسَجَدُوٓا۟ إِلَّآ إِبْلِيسَ
قَالَ ءَأَسْجُدُ لِمَنْ خَلَقْتَ طِينًا ﴿٦١﴾ قَالَ أَرَءَيْتَكَ هَٰذَا ٱلَّذِى
كَرَّمْتَ عَلَىَّ لَئِنْ أَخَّرْتَنِ إِلَىٰ يَوْمِ ٱلْقِيَٰمَةِ لَأَحْتَنِكَنَّ
ذُرِّيَّتَهُۥٓ إِلَّا قَلِيلًا ﴿٦٢﴾ قَالَ ٱذْهَبْ فَمَن تَبِعَكَ مِنْهُمْ فَإِنَّ
جَهَنَّمَ جَزَآؤُكُمْ جَزَآءً مَّوْفُورًا ﴿٦٣﴾ وَٱسْتَفْزِزْ مَنِ ٱسْتَطَعْتَ
مِنْهُم بِصَوْتِكَ وَأَجْلِبْ عَلَيْهِم بِخَيْلِكَ وَرَجِلِكَ وَشَارِكْهُمْ
فِى ٱلْأَمْوَٰلِ وَٱلْأَوْلَٰدِ وَعِدْهُمْ ۚ وَمَا يَعِدُهُمُ ٱلشَّيْطَٰنُ إِلَّا
غُرُورًا ﴿٦٤﴾ إِنَّ عِبَادِى لَيْسَ لَكَ عَلَيْهِمْ سُلْطَٰنٌ ۚ وَكَفَىٰ
بِرَبِّكَ وَكِيلًا ﴿٦٥﴾ رَّبُّكُمُ ٱلَّذِى يُزْجِى لَكُمُ ٱلْفُلْكَ
فِى ٱلْبَحْرِ لِتَبْتَغُوا۟ مِن فَضْلِهِۦٓ ۚ إِنَّهُۥ كَانَ بِكُمْ رَحِيمًا ﴿٦٦﴾

وَإِذَا مَسَّكُمُ ٱلضُّرُّ فِى ٱلْبَحْرِ ضَلَّ مَن تَدْعُونَ إِلَّآ إِيَّاهُ ۖ فَلَمَّا نَجَّىٰكُمْ
إِلَى ٱلْبَرِّ أَعْرَضْتُمْ ۚ وَكَانَ ٱلْإِنسَٰنُ كَفُورًا ٦٧ أَفَأَمِنتُمْ أَن يَخْسِفَ
بِكُمْ جَانِبَ ٱلْبَرِّ أَوْ يُرْسِلَ عَلَيْكُمْ حَاصِبًا ثُمَّ لَا تَجِدُوا۟ لَكُمْ
وَكِيلًا ٦٨ أَمْ أَمِنتُمْ أَن يُعِيدَكُمْ فِيهِ تَارَةً أُخْرَىٰ فَيُرْسِلَ
عَلَيْكُمْ قَاصِفًا مِّنَ ٱلرِّيحِ فَيُغْرِقَكُم بِمَا كَفَرْتُمْ ۙ ثُمَّ لَا تَجِدُوا۟
لَكُمْ عَلَيْنَا بِهِۦ تَبِيعًا ٦٩ ۞ وَلَقَدْ كَرَّمْنَا بَنِىٓ ءَادَمَ وَحَمَلْنَٰهُمْ
فِى ٱلْبَرِّ وَٱلْبَحْرِ وَرَزَقْنَٰهُم مِّنَ ٱلطَّيِّبَٰتِ وَفَضَّلْنَٰهُمْ عَلَىٰ
كَثِيرٍ مِّمَّنْ خَلَقْنَا تَفْضِيلًا ٧٠ يَوْمَ نَدْعُوا۟ كُلَّ أُنَاسٍۭ
بِإِمَٰمِهِمْ ۖ فَمَنْ أُوتِىَ كِتَٰبَهُۥ بِيَمِينِهِۦ فَأُو۟لَٰٓئِكَ يَقْرَءُونَ
كِتَٰبَهُمْ وَلَا يُظْلَمُونَ فَتِيلًا ٧١ وَمَن كَانَ فِى هَٰذِهِۦٓ
أَعْمَىٰ فَهُوَ فِى ٱلْءَاخِرَةِ أَعْمَىٰ وَأَضَلُّ سَبِيلًا ٧٢ وَإِن كَادُوا۟
لَيَفْتِنُونَكَ عَنِ ٱلَّذِىٓ أَوْحَيْنَآ إِلَيْكَ لِتَفْتَرِىَ عَلَيْنَا غَيْرَهُۥ ۖ
وَإِذًا لَّٱتَّخَذُوكَ خَلِيلًا ٧٣ وَلَوْلَآ أَن ثَبَّتْنَٰكَ لَقَدْ كِدتَّ
تَرْكَنُ إِلَيْهِمْ شَيْـًٔا قَلِيلًا ٧٤ إِذًا لَّأَذَقْنَٰكَ ضِعْفَ
ٱلْحَيَوٰةِ وَضِعْفَ ٱلْمَمَاتِ ثُمَّ لَا تَجِدُ لَكَ عَلَيْنَا نَصِيرًا ٧٥

وَإِن كَادُوا۟ لَيَسْتَفِزُّونَكَ مِنَ ٱلْأَرْضِ لِيُخْرِجُوكَ مِنْهَا ۖ
وَإِذًا لَّا يَلْبَثُونَ خِلَٰفَكَ إِلَّا قَلِيلًا ٧٦ سُنَّةَ مَن قَدْ
أَرْسَلْنَا قَبْلَكَ مِن رُّسُلِنَا ۖ وَلَا تَجِدُ لِسُنَّتِنَا تَحْوِيلًا ٧٧ أَقِمِ
ٱلصَّلَوٰةَ لِدُلُوكِ ٱلشَّمْسِ إِلَىٰ غَسَقِ ٱلَّيْلِ وَقُرْءَانَ ٱلْفَجْرِ ۖ إِنَّ
قُرْءَانَ ٱلْفَجْرِ كَانَ مَشْهُودًا ٧٨ وَمِنَ ٱلَّيْلِ فَتَهَجَّدْ بِهِۦ
نَافِلَةً لَّكَ عَسَىٰٓ أَن يَبْعَثَكَ رَبُّكَ مَقَامًا مَّحْمُودًا ٧٩ وَقُل رَّبِّ
أَدْخِلْنِى مُدْخَلَ صِدْقٍ وَأَخْرِجْنِى مُخْرَجَ صِدْقٍ وَٱجْعَل لِّى مِن
لَّدُنكَ سُلْطَٰنًا نَّصِيرًا ٨٠ وَقُلْ جَآءَ ٱلْحَقُّ وَزَهَقَ ٱلْبَٰطِلُ ۚ
إِنَّ ٱلْبَٰطِلَ كَانَ زَهُوقًا ٨١ وَنُنَزِّلُ مِنَ ٱلْقُرْءَانِ مَا هُوَ شِفَآءٌ
وَرَحْمَةٌ لِّلْمُؤْمِنِينَ ۙ وَلَا يَزِيدُ ٱلظَّٰلِمِينَ إِلَّا خَسَارًا ٨٢ وَإِذَآ
أَنْعَمْنَا عَلَى ٱلْإِنسَٰنِ أَعْرَضَ وَنَـَٔا بِجَانِبِهِۦ ۖ وَإِذَا مَسَّهُ ٱلشَّرُّ كَانَ يَـُٔوسًا
٨٣ قُلْ كُلٌّ يَعْمَلُ عَلَىٰ شَاكِلَتِهِۦ فَرَبُّكُمْ أَعْلَمُ بِمَنْ هُوَ أَهْدَىٰ
سَبِيلًا ٨٤ وَيَسْـَٔلُونَكَ عَنِ ٱلرُّوحِ ۖ قُلِ ٱلرُّوحُ مِنْ أَمْرِ رَبِّى
وَمَآ أُوتِيتُم مِّنَ ٱلْعِلْمِ إِلَّا قَلِيلًا ٨٥ وَلَئِن شِئْنَا لَنَذْهَبَنَّ
بِٱلَّذِىٓ أَوْحَيْنَآ إِلَيْكَ ثُمَّ لَا تَجِدُ لَكَ بِهِۦ عَلَيْنَا وَكِيلًا ٨٦

إِلَّا رَحْمَةً مِّن رَّبِّكَ ۚ إِنَّ فَضْلَهُۥ كَانَ عَلَيْكَ كَبِيرًا ﴿٨٧﴾ قُل
لَّئِنِ ٱجْتَمَعَتِ ٱلْإِنسُ وَٱلْجِنُّ عَلَىٰٓ أَن يَأْتُوا۟ بِمِثْلِ هَٰذَا ٱلْقُرْءَانِ
لَا يَأْتُونَ بِمِثْلِهِۦ وَلَوْ كَانَ بَعْضُهُمْ لِبَعْضٍ ظَهِيرًا ﴿٨٨﴾ وَلَقَدْ
صَرَّفْنَا لِلنَّاسِ فِى هَٰذَا ٱلْقُرْءَانِ مِن كُلِّ مَثَلٍ فَأَبَىٰٓ أَكْثَرُ ٱلنَّاسِ
إِلَّا كُفُورًا ﴿٨٩﴾ وَقَالُوا۟ لَن نُّؤْمِنَ لَكَ حَتَّىٰ تَفْجُرَ لَنَا مِنَ
ٱلْأَرْضِ يَنۢبُوعًا ﴿٩٠﴾ أَوْ تَكُونَ لَكَ جَنَّةٌ مِّن نَّخِيلٍ وَعِنَبٍ
فَتُفَجِّرَ ٱلْأَنْهَٰرَ خِلَٰلَهَا تَفْجِيرًا ﴿٩١﴾ أَوْ تُسْقِطَ ٱلسَّمَآءَ كَمَا
زَعَمْتَ عَلَيْنَا كِسَفًا أَوْ تَأْتِىَ بِٱللَّهِ وَٱلْمَلَٰٓئِكَةِ قَبِيلًا ﴿٩٢﴾
أَوْ يَكُونَ لَكَ بَيْتٌ مِّن زُخْرُفٍ أَوْ تَرْقَىٰ فِى ٱلسَّمَآءِ وَلَن نُّؤْمِنَ
لِرُقِيِّكَ حَتَّىٰ تُنَزِّلَ عَلَيْنَا كِتَٰبًا نَّقْرَؤُهُۥ ۗ قُلْ سُبْحَانَ رَبِّى هَلْ
كُنتُ إِلَّا بَشَرًا رَّسُولًا ﴿٩٣﴾ وَمَا مَنَعَ ٱلنَّاسَ أَن يُؤْمِنُوٓا۟ إِذْ جَآءَهُمُ
ٱلْهُدَىٰٓ إِلَّآ أَن قَالُوٓا۟ أَبَعَثَ ٱللَّهُ بَشَرًا رَّسُولًا ﴿٩٤﴾ قُل لَّوْ كَانَ
فِى ٱلْأَرْضِ مَلَٰٓئِكَةٌ يَمْشُونَ مُطْمَئِنِّينَ لَنَزَّلْنَا عَلَيْهِم
مِّنَ ٱلسَّمَآءِ مَلَكًا رَّسُولًا ﴿٩٥﴾ قُلْ كَفَىٰ بِٱللَّهِ
شَهِيدًۢا بَيْنِى وَبَيْنَكُمْ ۚ إِنَّهُۥ كَانَ بِعِبَادِهِۦ خَبِيرًۢا بَصِيرًا ﴿٩٦﴾

وَمَن يَهْدِ ٱللَّهُ فَهُوَ ٱلْمُهْتَدِ ۖ وَمَن يُضْلِلْ فَلَن تَجِدَ لَهُمْ أَوْلِيَآءَ
مِن دُونِهِۦ ۖ وَنَحْشُرُهُمْ يَوْمَ ٱلْقِيَٰمَةِ عَلَىٰ وُجُوهِهِمْ عُمْيًا وَبُكْمًا
وَصُمًّا ۖ مَّأْوَىٰهُمْ جَهَنَّمُ ۖ كُلَّمَا خَبَتْ زِدْنَٰهُمْ سَعِيرًا ٩٧
ذَٰلِكَ جَزَآؤُهُم بِأَنَّهُمْ كَفَرُوا۟ بِـَٔايَٰتِنَا وَقَالُوٓا۟ أَءِذَا كُنَّا عِظَٰمًا
وَرُفَٰتًا أَءِنَّا لَمَبْعُوثُونَ خَلْقًا جَدِيدًا ٩٨ ۞ أَوَلَمْ يَرَوْا۟ أَنَّ ٱللَّهَ
ٱلَّذِى خَلَقَ ٱلسَّمَٰوَٰتِ وَٱلْأَرْضَ قَادِرٌ عَلَىٰٓ أَن يَخْلُقَ مِثْلَهُمْ
وَجَعَلَ لَهُمْ أَجَلًا لَّا رَيْبَ فِيهِ فَأَبَى ٱلظَّٰلِمُونَ إِلَّا كُفُورًا ٩٩
قُل لَّوْ أَنتُمْ تَمْلِكُونَ خَزَآئِنَ رَحْمَةِ رَبِّىٓ إِذًا لَّأَمْسَكْتُمْ خَشْيَةَ
ٱلْإِنفَاقِ ۚ وَكَانَ ٱلْإِنسَٰنُ قَتُورًا ١٠٠ وَلَقَدْ ءَاتَيْنَا مُوسَىٰ تِسْعَ
ءَايَٰتٍۭ بَيِّنَٰتٍ ۖ فَسْـَٔلْ بَنِىٓ إِسْرَٰٓءِيلَ إِذْ جَآءَهُمْ فَقَالَ لَهُۥ فِرْعَوْنُ
إِنِّى لَأَظُنُّكَ يَٰمُوسَىٰ مَسْحُورًا ١٠١ قَالَ لَقَدْ عَلِمْتَ مَآ أَنزَلَ
هَٰٓؤُلَآءِ إِلَّا رَبُّ ٱلسَّمَٰوَٰتِ وَٱلْأَرْضِ بَصَآئِرَ وَإِنِّى لَأَظُنُّكَ
يَٰفِرْعَوْنُ مَثْبُورًا ١٠٢ فَأَرَادَ أَن يَسْتَفِزَّهُم مِّنَ ٱلْأَرْضِ
فَأَغْرَقْنَٰهُ وَمَن مَّعَهُۥ جَمِيعًا ١٠٣ وَقُلْنَا مِنۢ بَعْدِهِۦ لِبَنِىٓ إِسْرَٰٓءِيلَ
ٱسْكُنُوا۟ ٱلْأَرْضَ فَإِذَا جَآءَ وَعْدُ ٱلْـَٔاخِرَةِ جِئْنَا بِكُمْ لَفِيفًا ١٠٤

وَبِٱلْحَقِّ أَنزَلْنَٰهُ وَبِٱلْحَقِّ نَزَلَ ۗ وَمَآ أَرْسَلْنَٰكَ إِلَّا مُبَشِّرًا وَنَذِيرًا ١٠٥
وَقُرْءَانًا فَرَقْنَٰهُ لِتَقْرَأَهُۥ عَلَى ٱلنَّاسِ عَلَىٰ مُكْثٍ وَنَزَّلْنَٰهُ تَنزِيلًا ١٠٦
قُلْ ءَامِنُوا۟ بِهِۦٓ أَوْ لَا تُؤْمِنُوٓا۟ ۚ إِنَّ ٱلَّذِينَ أُوتُوا۟ ٱلْعِلْمَ مِن قَبْلِهِۦٓ إِذَا يُتْلَىٰ
عَلَيْهِمْ يَخِرُّونَ لِلْأَذْقَانِ سُجَّدًا ١٠٧ وَيَقُولُونَ سُبْحَٰنَ رَبِّنَآ إِن كَانَ
وَعْدُ رَبِّنَا لَمَفْعُولًا ١٠٨ وَيَخِرُّونَ لِلْأَذْقَانِ يَبْكُونَ وَيَزِيدُهُمْ
خُشُوعًا ۩ ١٠٩ قُلِ ٱدْعُوا۟ ٱللَّهَ أَوِ ٱدْعُوا۟ ٱلرَّحْمَٰنَ ۖ أَيًّا مَّا تَدْعُوا۟ فَلَهُ
ٱلْأَسْمَآءُ ٱلْحُسْنَىٰ ۚ وَلَا تَجْهَرْ بِصَلَاتِكَ وَلَا تُخَافِتْ بِهَا وَٱبْتَغِ
بَيْنَ ذَٰلِكَ سَبِيلًا ١١٠ وَقُلِ ٱلْحَمْدُ لِلَّهِ ٱلَّذِى لَمْ يَتَّخِذْ وَلَدًا وَلَمْ يَكُن
لَّهُۥ شَرِيكٌ فِى ٱلْمُلْكِ وَلَمْ يَكُن لَّهُۥ وَلِىٌّ مِّنَ ٱلذُّلِّ ۖ وَكَبِّرْهُ تَكْبِيرًۢا ١١١

Surah 17 – Al-Isrāa’ سُورَةُ الإِسۡرَاءِ

The name al-Isrāa’ refers to Allah’s beloved Prophet Muḥammad ﷺ being elevated towards the sublime. This is recorded as having occurred on the 27th night of Rajab in the year which preceded Hijrah – his migration from Makkah to Madinah.

1) Glory be to Him who transported His servant [Muḥammad] by night from the Holy Mosque, to see his Lord’s signs in the blessed environment of the Farthest Mosque. Truly He is All-Hearing, All-Seeing.

سُبْحَٰنَ ٱلَّذِىٓ أَسْرَىٰ بِعَبْدِهِۦ لَيْلًا مِّنَ ٱلْمَسْجِدِ ٱلْحَرَامِ
إِلَى ٱلْمَسْجِدِ ٱلْأَقْصَا ٱلَّذِى بَٰرَكْنَا حَوْلَهُۥ لِنُرِيَهُۥ مِنْ ءَايَٰتِنَآ ۚ إِنَّهُۥ
هُوَ ٱلسَّمِيعُ ٱلْبَصِيرُ ﴿١﴾

2) We gave Mūsa [Moses] the book of guidance for the Children of Isra’il [the Torah – Tawrāt – and told them], ‘Do not seek [guidance and protection] from any but Me’.

وَءَاتَيْنَا مُوسَى ٱلْكِتَٰبَ وَجَعَلْنَٰهُ
هُدًى لِّبَنِىٓ إِسْرَٰٓءِيلَ أَلَّا تَتَّخِذُوا۟ مِن دُونِى وَكِيلًا ﴿٢﴾

3) You are the offspring of those We delivered [in the Ark] with Nūh [Noah], a truly grateful servant.

ذُرِّيَّةَ مَنْ حَمَلْنَا مَعَ نُوحٍ ۚ إِنَّهُۥ كَانَ عَبْدًا شَكُورًا ﴿٣﴾

4) In that book We told the Children of Isra’il, ‘You are certain to become exceedingly arrogant and will establish tyrannical regimes on two occasions’.

وَقَضَيْنَآ إِلَىٰ بَنِىٓ إِسْرَٰٓءِيلَ فِى ٱلْكِتَٰبِ لَتُفْسِدُنَّ فِى ٱلْأَرْضِ
مَرَّتَيْنِ وَلَتَعْلُنَّ عُلُوًّا كَبِيرًا ﴿٤﴾

5) On the first, We fulfilled Our warning by sending an invincible force to overwhelm you, enter your dwellings and ravage your nation.

فَإِذَا جَآءَ وَعۡدُ أُولَىٰهُمَا بَعَثۡنَا
عَلَيۡكُمۡ عِبَادٗا لَّنَآ أُوْلِي بَأۡسٖ شَدِيدٖ فَجَاسُواْ خِلَٰلَ ٱلدِّيَارِۚ
وَكَانَ وَعۡدٗا مَّفۡعُولٗا ٥

6) Later, We sanctioned your victory, extended your resources, increased your offspring and expanded your numbers.

ثُمَّ رَدَدۡنَا لَكُمُ ٱلۡكَرَّةَ عَلَيۡهِمۡ
وَأَمۡدَدۡنَٰكُم بِأَمۡوَٰلٖ وَبَنِينَ وَجَعَلۡنَٰكُمۡ أَكۡثَرَ نَفِيرًا ٦

7) [We gave you freedom of choice.] If you do good, it is you who will reap its benefit and, if you are evil, it is you who will suffer its effect.
On the second occasion We fulfilled Our warning, and sent a force to defeat and humiliate you, to enter the Temple as your earlier vanquisher had before and to lay waste all that was conquered.

إِنۡ أَحۡسَنتُمۡ أَحۡسَنتُمۡ لِأَنفُسِكُمۡۖ وَإِنۡ أَسَأۡتُمۡ فَلَهَاۚ فَإِذَا جَآءَ
وَعۡدُ ٱلۡأٓخِرَةِ لِيَسُـُٔواْ وُجُوهَكُمۡ وَلِيَدۡخُلُواْ ٱلۡمَسۡجِدَ
كَمَا دَخَلُوهُ أَوَّلَ مَرَّةٖ وَلِيُتَبِّرُواْ مَا عَلَوۡاْ تَتۡبِيرًا ٧

8) It may be that your Lord will show you mercy, but when you return to disobedience His chastisement will follow. In the afterlife, Hell will confine all those who reject faith.

عَسَىٰ رَبُّكُمۡ أَن يَرۡحَمَكُمۡۚ وَإِنۡ عُدتُّمۡ عُدۡنَاۚ وَجَعَلۡنَا جَهَنَّمَ لِلۡكَٰفِرِينَ
حَصِيرًا ٨

9) This Qur'an guides human beings towards ethical and principled behaviour and confirms that those who believe and do good will receive generous rewards.

إِنَّ هَٰذَا ٱلۡقُرۡءَانَ يَهۡدِي لِلَّتِي هِيَ أَقۡوَمُ وَيُبَشِّرُ
ٱلۡمُؤۡمِنِينَ ٱلَّذِينَ يَعۡمَلُونَ ٱلصَّٰلِحَٰتِ أَنَّ لَهُمۡ أَجۡرٗا كَبِيرٗا ٩

10) And it warns of the painful torment that awaits those who deny the 'hereafter'.

وَأَنَّ ٱلَّذِينَ لَا يُؤْمِنُونَ بِٱلْءَاخِرَةِ أَعْتَدْنَا لَهُمْ عَذَابًا أَلِيمًا ﴿١٠﴾

11) Human beings frequently pray for things that are bad for them, in the mistaken belief that they are asking for something good. They are often hasty [in their judgements].

وَيَدْعُ ٱلْإِنسَٰنُ بِٱلشَّرِّ دُعَآءَهُۥ بِٱلْخَيْرِ ۖ وَكَانَ ٱلْإِنسَٰنُ عَجُولًا ﴿١١﴾

12) Night and day are but signs of Our Omnipotence. The night cloaked in darkness [so that you can rest], the day illuminated [so that you can] seek the bounty of your Lord and calculate the passage of time. All is made clear [for you].

وَجَعَلْنَا ٱلَّيْلَ وَٱلنَّهَارَ ءَايَتَيْنِ ۖ فَمَحَوْنَآ ءَايَةَ ٱلَّيْلِ وَجَعَلْنَآ ءَايَةَ
ٱلنَّهَارِ مُبْصِرَةً لِّتَبْتَغُوا۟ فَضْلًا مِّن رَّبِّكُمْ وَلِتَعْلَمُوا۟ عَدَدَ
ٱلسِّنِينَ وَٱلْحِسَابَ ۚ وَكُلَّ شَىْءٍ فَصَّلْنَٰهُ تَفْصِيلًا ﴿١٢﴾

13) We have tied the destiny of human beings around their own necks and will, on the 'Day of Resurrection', produce an open record for them.

وَكُلَّ
إِنسَٰنٍ أَلْزَمْنَٰهُ طَٰٓئِرَهُۥ فِى عُنُقِهِۦ ۖ وَنُخْرِجُ لَهُۥ يَوْمَ ٱلْقِيَٰمَةِ كِتَٰبًا
يَلْقَىٰهُ مَنشُورًا ﴿١٣﴾

14) [And will tell them] 'Read, and let your soul be its own judge'.

ٱقْرَأْ كِتَٰبَكَ كَفَىٰ بِنَفْسِكَ ٱلْيَوْمَ عَلَيْكَ حَسِيبًا

﴿١٤﴾

15) Those who seek Allah's guidance benefit their souls. Those who go astray suffer the consequences themselves. Each has its own burden to bear. But We do not punish those to whom We have not sent a Messenger [with warnings].

مَّنِ ٱهْتَدَىٰ فَإِنَّمَا يَهْتَدِى لِنَفْسِهِۦ ۖ وَمَن ضَلَّ فَإِنَّمَا يَضِلُّ
عَلَيْهَا ۚ وَلَا تَزِرُ وَازِرَةٌ وِزْرَ أُخْرَىٰ ۗ وَمَا كُنَّا مُعَذِّبِينَ حَتَّىٰ نَبْعَثَ
رَسُولًا ﴿١٥﴾

16) [When this has been done], if communities reject guidance and lose themselves in immoderate behaviour, We warn them to return to obedience before [if they decline to desist] We determine to destroy them completely.

وَإِذَآ أَرَدۡنَآ أَن نُّهۡلِكَ قَرۡيَةً أَمَرۡنَا مُتۡرَفِيهَا فَفَسَقُواْ فِيهَا
فَحَقَّ عَلَيۡهَا ٱلۡقَوۡلُ فَدَمَّرۡنَٰهَا تَدۡمِيرٗا ١٦

17) And We have destroyed many generations since Nūh's time! Only your Lord sees and fully comprehends His creatures' sins.

وَكَمۡ أَهۡلَكۡنَا مِنَ
ٱلۡقُرُونِ مِنۢ بَعۡدِ نُوحٖۗ وَكَفَىٰ بِرَبِّكَ بِذُنُوبِ عِبَادِهِۦ خَبِيرَۢا بَصِيرٗا ١٧

18) Some seek only to indulge in the instant pleasures of this fleeting life. And We readily grant as much of those to whichever of them We please, but in the end, they are consigned to endure the suffering and disgrace of hell.

مَّن كَانَ يُرِيدُ ٱلۡعَاجِلَةَ عَجَّلۡنَا لَهُۥ فِيهَا مَا نَشَآءُ لِمَن نُّرِيدُ ثُمَّ
جَعَلۡنَا لَهُۥ جَهَنَّمَ يَصۡلَىٰهَا مَذۡمُومٗا مَّدۡحُورٗا ١٨

19) However, true believers – those who strive for [the good of] the life to come – will find favour with their Lord.

وَمَنۡ أَرَادَ
ٱلۡأٓخِرَةَ وَسَعَىٰ لَهَا سَعۡيَهَا وَهُوَ مُؤۡمِنٞ فَأُوْلَٰٓئِكَ كَانَ
سَعۡيُهُم مَّشۡكُورٗا ١٩

20) But it is possible for the former, as well as the latter [hedonists as well as believers], to draw benefit from Divine Generosity without constraint.

كُلّٗا نُّمِدُّ هَٰٓؤُلَآءِ وَهَٰٓؤُلَآءِ مِنۡ عَطَآءِ
رَبِّكَۚ وَمَا كَانَ عَطَآءُ رَبِّكَ مَحۡظُورًا ٢٠

21) Observe how [on earth], some receive more and achieve higher status than others – but positions in the hereafter will be superior and levels of excellence incomparably greater.

ٱنظُرْ كَيْفَ فَضَّلْنَا
بَعْضَهُمْ عَلَىٰ بَعْضٍ ۚ وَلَلْءَاخِرَةُ أَكْبَرُ دَرَجَٰتٍ وَأَكْبَرُ تَفْضِيلًا
﴿٢١﴾

22) Worship no Divinity other than Allah so that you are not reproved and forsaken.

لَّا تَجْعَلْ مَعَ ٱللَّهِ إِلَٰهًا ءَاخَرَ فَتَقْعُدَ مَذْمُومًا مَّخْذُولًا ﴿٢٢﴾

23) For your Lord has ordered you not to worship any except Him. He also commanded you to be good to your parents. Should either or both of them reach old age and need care, do not behave irritably or reproach and reject them but always respond to them gently.

۞ وَقَضَىٰ رَبُّكَ أَلَّا تَعْبُدُوٓا۟ إِلَّآ إِيَّاهُ وَبِٱلْوَٰلِدَيْنِ إِحْسَٰنًا ۚ إِمَّا
يَبْلُغَنَّ عِندَكَ ٱلْكِبَرَ أَحَدُهُمَآ أَوْ كِلَاهُمَا فَلَا تَقُل لَّهُمَآ
أُفٍّ وَلَا تَنْهَرْهُمَا وَقُل لَّهُمَا قَوْلًا كَرِيمًا ﴿٢٣﴾

24) Treat them with humility and tenderness praying, 'Lord be merciful to them, as they were to me when I was little'.

وَٱخْفِضْ
لَهُمَا جَنَاحَ ٱلذُّلِّ مِنَ ٱلرَّحْمَةِ وَقُل رَّبِّ ٱرْحَمْهُمَا كَمَا رَبَّيَانِى
صَغِيرًا ﴿٢٤﴾

25) Your Lord is aware of what is in your heart and how you behave [towards His Creation]. He is All-Forgiving to those who repent.

رَّبُّكُمْ أَعْلَمُ بِمَا فِى نُفُوسِكُمْ ۚ إِن تَكُونُوا۟ صَٰلِحِينَ
فَإِنَّهُۥ كَانَ لِلْأَوَّٰبِينَ غَفُورًا ﴿٢٥﴾

26) Give close relatives what they are entitled to, and be generous to travellers in need and the poor; however, do not fritter your wealth away.

وَءَاتِ ذَا ٱلْقُرْبَىٰ حَقَّهُۥ
وَٱلْمِسْكِينَ وَٱبْنَ ٱلسَّبِيلِ وَلَا تُبَذِّرْ تَبْذِيرًا ﴿٢٦﴾

27) Those who squander resources are, like Satan, ungrateful to the Lord [for what He has provided].

إِنَّ ٱلْمُبَذِّرِينَ
كَانُوٓا۟ إِخْوَٰنَ ٱلشَّيَٰطِينِ ۖ وَكَانَ ٱلشَّيْطَٰنُ لِرَبِّهِۦ كَفُورًا ﴿٢٧﴾

28) But if [your current situation is such that you are not able to assist people], because you yourself are in need of your Lord's support, decline their request with kind words and compassion.

وَإِمَّا تُعْرِضَنَّ عَنْهُمُ ٱبْتِغَآءَ رَحْمَةٍ مِّن رَّبِّكَ تَرْجُوهَا فَقُل لَّهُمْ قَوْلًا
مَّيْسُورًا ﴿٢٨﴾

29) Do not be miserly and worthy of reproach, nor be so generous that you become destitute.

وَلَا تَجْعَلْ يَدَكَ مَغْلُولَةً إِلَىٰ عُنُقِكَ وَلَا تَبْسُطْهَا
كُلَّ ٱلْبَسْطِ فَتَقْعُدَ مَلُومًا مَّحْسُورًا ﴿٢٩﴾

30) Your Lord sees and is aware of His servants' needs. He showers some with abundance, yet limits the resources of others as He wills.

إِنَّ رَبَّكَ يَبْسُطُ ٱلرِّزْقَ
لِمَن يَشَآءُ وَيَقْدِرُ ۚ إِنَّهُۥ كَانَ بِعِبَادِهِۦ خَبِيرًۢا بَصِيرًا ﴿٣٠﴾

31) Do not let fear of poverty induce you to murder your children, for We will provide for both you and for them. It is wicked to kill them.

وَلَا تَقْتُلُوٓا۟
أَوْلَٰدَكُمْ خَشْيَةَ إِمْلَٰقٍ ۖ نَّحْنُ نَرْزُقُهُمْ وَإِيَّاكُمْ ۚ إِنَّ قَتْلَهُمْ كَانَ
خِطْـًٔا كَبِيرًا ﴿٣١﴾

32) Do not have sexual relationships outside marriage because that is improper and withholds honour.

وَلَا تَقْرَبُوا۟ ٱلزِّنَىٰٓ ۖ إِنَّهُۥ كَانَ فَٰحِشَةً وَسَآءَ
سَبِيلًا ﴿٣٢﴾

33) Do not take life [which Allah has decreed sacred], other than in the legitimate pursuit of justice. The heirs of those who have been unjustly slain are authorised to extract lawful retribution, but not more than that.

وَلَا تَقْتُلُوا۟ ٱلنَّفْسَ ٱلَّتِى حَرَّمَ ٱللَّهُ إِلَّا بِٱلْحَقِّ ۗ وَمَن
قُتِلَ مَظْلُومًا فَقَدْ جَعَلْنَا لِوَلِيِّهِۦ سُلْطَـٰنًا فَلَا يُسْرِف فِّى
ٱلْقَتْلِ ۖ إِنَّهُۥ كَانَ مَنصُورًا ٣٣

34) Safeguard the property of orphans until they have attained maturity. Remain true to your word for you are accountable.

وَلَا تَقْرَبُوا۟ مَالَ ٱلْيَتِيمِ إِلَّا بِٱلَّتِى
هِىَ أَحْسَنُ حَتَّىٰ يَبْلُغَ أَشُدَّهُۥ ۚ وَأَوْفُوا۟ بِٱلْعَهْدِ ۖ إِنَّ ٱلْعَهْدَ كَانَ
مَسْـُٔولًا ٣٤

35) [Be just!] Always give full measure and weigh with accurate scales, for to do so is better for you in the long run.

وَأَوْفُوا۟ ٱلْكَيْلَ إِذَا كِلْتُمْ وَزِنُوا۟ بِٱلْقِسْطَاسِ ٱلْمُسْتَقِيمِ ۚ
ذَٰلِكَ خَيْرٌ وَأَحْسَنُ تَأْوِيلًا ٣٥

36) Remembering that you are [ultimately] accountable [for your actions], use [your faculties] of sight, hearing and intellect to appraise [the value of] advice before you follow it.

وَلَا تَقْفُ مَا لَيْسَ لَكَ بِهِۦ عِلْمٌ ۚ
إِنَّ ٱلسَّمْعَ وَٱلْبَصَرَ وَٱلْفُؤَادَ كُلُّ أُو۟لَـٰٓئِكَ كَانَ عَنْهُ مَسْـُٔولًا ٣٦

37) Do not strut the earth in triumph and arrogance. You can neither tear it apart nor match the grandeur of its mountains.

وَلَا تَمْشِ فِى ٱلْأَرْضِ مَرَحًا ۖ إِنَّكَ لَن تَخْرِقَ ٱلْأَرْضَ وَلَن تَبْلُغَ
ٱلْجِبَالَ طُولًا ٣٧

38) Avoid these evils for the wickedness of such things is odious in the sight of your Lord.

كُلُّ ذَٰلِكَ كَانَ سَيِّئُهُۥ عِندَ رَبِّكَ مَكْرُوهًا ٣٨

39) These are but examples of the wisdom your Lord revealed to you, but [even more importantly] worship Allah only, or face being cast, guilty and rejected, into Hell.

ذَٰلِكَ مِمَّآ أَوۡحَىٰٓ إِلَيۡكَ رَبُّكَ مِنَ ٱلۡحِكۡمَةِۗ وَلَا تَجۡعَلۡ مَعَ ٱللَّهِ إِلَٰهًا
ءَاخَرَ فَتُلۡقَىٰ فِي جَهَنَّمَ مَلُومٗا مَّدۡحُورًا ٣٩

40) Has your Lord given you sons but created daughters in the form of Angels for Himself? This is certainly a monstrous claim you make!

أَفَأَصۡفَىٰكُمۡ رَبُّكُم
بِٱلۡبَنِينَ وَٱتَّخَذَ مِنَ ٱلۡمَلَٰٓئِكَةِ إِنَٰثًاۚ إِنَّكُمۡ لَتَقُولُونَ قَوۡلًا عَظِيمٗا ٤٠

41) Despite Our repeated explanation of its various aspects, this Qur'an has not increased any awareness in them, other than their own aversion to it.

وَلَقَدۡ صَرَّفۡنَا فِي هَٰذَا ٱلۡقُرۡءَانِ لِيَذَّكَّرُواْ وَمَا يَزِيدُهُمۡ إِلَّا نُفُورٗا ٤١

42) Say [O Muḥammad]: If there are other divinities, as they assert, they would have been able to manifest the [nature] of the Lord of the Throne.

قُل لَّوۡ كَانَ مَعَهُۥٓ ءَالِهَةٞ كَمَا يَقُولُونَ إِذٗا لَّٱبۡتَغَوۡاْ إِلَىٰ ذِي ٱلۡعَرۡشِ سَبِيلٗا
٤٢

43) All praise is due to Him for He is immeasurably exalted, beyond their comprehension.

سُبۡحَٰنَهُۥ وَتَعَٰلَىٰ عَمَّا يَقُولُونَ عُلُوّٗا كَبِيرٗا ٤٣

44) All creatures in the seven heavens and the earth below extol their Lord. All glorify Him even if we are unable to understand their praises. He is Most-Tolerant, Most-Forgiving.

تُسَبِّحُ لَهُ ٱلسَّمَٰوَٰتُ
ٱلسَّبۡعُ وَٱلۡأَرۡضُ وَمَن فِيهِنَّۚ وَإِن مِّن شَيۡءٍ إِلَّا يُسَبِّحُ بِحَمۡدِهِۦ وَلَٰكِن
لَّا تَفۡقَهُونَ تَسۡبِيحَهُمۡۚ إِنَّهُۥ كَانَ حَلِيمًا غَفُورٗا ٤٤

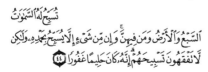

45) When [O Muḥammad] you recite the Qur’an, We insert invisible barriers between you and those who do not believe in the life to come.

وَإِذَا قَرَأْتَ
ٱلْقُرْءَانَ جَعَلْنَا بَيْنَكَ وَبَيْنَ ٱلَّذِينَ لَا يُؤْمِنُونَ بِٱلْـَٔاخِرَةِ حِجَابًا
مَّسْتُورًا ﴿٤٥﴾

46) We lay veils over their hearts to prevent them understanding, and heaviness over their ears to prevent their hearing. For, when you refer to there being no divinity other than Allah, they turn away in dislike.

وَجَعَلْنَا عَلَىٰ قُلُوبِهِمْ أَكِنَّةً أَن يَفْقَهُوهُ وَفِىٓ ءَاذَانِهِمْ
وَقْرًا ۚ وَإِذَا ذَكَرْتَ رَبَّكَ فِى ٱلْقُرْءَانِ وَحْدَهُۥ وَلَّوْا۟ عَلَىٰٓ أَدْبَـٰرِهِمْ نُفُورًا
﴿٤٦﴾

47) When they listen to you, We know very well what they listen for and that behind your back they say, ‘If you follow him, you will be led by one possessed’.

نَّحْنُ أَعْلَمُ بِمَا يَسْتَمِعُونَ بِهِۦٓ إِذْ يَسْتَمِعُونَ إِلَيْكَ وَإِذْ هُمْ نَجْوَىٰٓ
إِذْ يَقُولُ ٱلظَّـٰلِمُونَ إِن تَتَّبِعُونَ إِلَّا رَجُلًا مَّسْحُورًا ﴿٤٧﴾

48) Observe [O Prophet] what they identify you with, for they are so far astray they will never find their way [to truth].

ٱنظُرْ
كَيْفَ ضَرَبُوا۟ لَكَ ٱلْأَمْثَالَ فَضَلُّوا۟ فَلَا يَسْتَطِيعُونَ سَبِيلًا ﴿٤٨﴾

49) They ask, ‘When we [have perished and] are bones reduced to dust, shall we really be raised up and given a new existence?’

وَقَالُوٓا۟ أَءِذَا كُنَّا عِظَـٰمًا وَرُفَـٰتًا أَءِنَّا لَمَبْعُوثُونَ خَلْقًا جَدِيدًا ﴿٤٩﴾

50) Tell them, ‘Even if you have turned into stone or iron’.

۞ قُلْ كُونُوا۟ حِجَارَةً أَوْ حَدِيدًا ﴿٥٠﴾

51) 'Or any other substance which you cannot even conceive of being brought to life, even then, you will still be restored to life.' And if they ask, 'Who can bring us to life?' Tell them, 'The one who first created you'. Then, when they shake their heads and ask, 'And when will that be?' Tell them, 'It may well be soon'.

أَوْ خَلْقًا مِّمَّا يَكْبُرُ فِي
صُدُورِكُمْ ۚ فَسَيَقُولُونَ مَن يُعِيدُنَا ۖ قُلِ ٱلَّذِى فَطَرَكُمْ أَوَّلَ مَرَّةٍ ۚ
فَسَيُنْغِضُونَ إِلَيْكَ رُءُوسَهُمْ وَيَقُولُونَ مَتَىٰ هُوَ ۖ قُلْ عَسَىٰٓ أَن
يَكُونَ قَرِيبًا ﴿٥١﴾

52) On the day that He summons you, you will respond with His praises and will think that you have only been [in your grave] a short while.

يَوْمَ يَدْعُوكُمْ فَتَسْتَجِيبُونَ بِحَمْدِهِۦ
وَتَظُنُّونَ إِن لَّبِثْتُمْ إِلَّا قَلِيلًا ﴿٥٢﴾

53) And tell My servants to conduct themselves with circumspection, for Satan is ever ready to provoke discord. He is the declared enemy of humanity.

وَقُل لِّعِبَادِى يَقُولُوا۟ ٱلَّتِى هِىَ
أَحْسَنُ ۚ إِنَّ ٱلشَّيْطَـٰنَ يَنزَغُ بَيْنَهُمْ ۚ إِنَّ ٱلشَّيْطَـٰنَ كَانَ لِلْإِنسَـٰنِ
عَدُوًّا مُّبِينًا ﴿٥٣﴾

54) Your Lord has perfect awareness [of what you deserve and do not deserve] and grants mercy or punishment as He pleases. Therefore [O Muḥammad], We have not made you responsible for their actions.

رَّبُّكُمْ أَعْلَمُ بِكُمْ ۖ إِن يَشَأْ يَرْحَمْكُمْ أَوْ إِن يَشَأْ
يُعَذِّبْكُمْ ۚ وَمَآ أَرْسَلْنَـٰكَ عَلَيْهِمْ وَكِيلًا ﴿٥٤﴾

55) Moreover, your Lord has perfect awareness of all who are in the heavens and on the earth; We endowed certain Prophets more highly than others and gave the Zabūr [Psalms] to Dawūd [David].

وَرَبُّكَ أَعْلَمُ
بِمَن فِى ٱلسَّمَـٰوَٰتِ وَٱلْأَرْضِ ۗ وَلَقَدْ فَضَّلْنَا بَعْضَ ٱلنَّبِيِّـۧنَ عَلَىٰ بَعْضٍ ۖ
وَءَاتَيْنَا دَاوُۥدَ زَبُورًا ﴿٥٥﴾

56) Tell them, 'Call on those other than Him whom you imagine to be divine; they have neither the power to alleviate your distress nor to remove it'.

قُلِ ٱدْعُوا۟ ٱلَّذِينَ زَعَمْتُم مِّن دُونِهِۦ فَلَا
يَمْلِكُونَ كَشْفَ ٱلضُّرِّ عَنكُمْ وَلَا تَحْوِيلًا ٥٦

57) Those they call upon, seek to approach their Lord themselves. Even those who are nearest, long for His mercy and dread His punishment. The Lord's chastisement is to be truly feared.

أُو۟لَٰٓئِكَ ٱلَّذِينَ
يَدْعُونَ يَبْتَغُونَ إِلَىٰ رَبِّهِمُ ٱلْوَسِيلَةَ أَيُّهُمْ أَقْرَبُ وَيَرْجُونَ
رَحْمَتَهُۥ وَيَخَافُونَ عَذَابَهُۥٓ ۚ إِنَّ عَذَابَ رَبِّكَ كَانَ مَحْذُورًا ٥٧

58) There is not a population whom We will not severely punish or who will not perish before the Day of Resurrection. This is documented in the Book of Records.

وَإِن مِّن قَرْيَةٍ إِلَّا نَحْنُ مُهْلِكُوهَا قَبْلَ يَوْمِ ٱلْقِيَٰمَةِ
أَوْ مُعَذِّبُوهَا عَذَابًا شَدِيدًا ۚ كَانَ ذَٰلِكَ فِى ٱلْكِتَٰبِ مَسْطُورًا ٥٨

59) Nothing stood in the way of Our sending Ayat [signs], even though former generations treated them with contempt. When We sent the she camel as a clear sign to the Thamud people, they mistreated her. But We never send signs other than as warnings.

وَمَا مَنَعَنَآ أَن نُّرْسِلَ بِٱلْءَايَٰتِ إِلَّآ أَن كَذَّبَ بِهَا ٱلْأَوَّلُونَ ۚ
وَءَاتَيْنَا ثَمُودَ ٱلنَّاقَةَ مُبْصِرَةً فَظَلَمُوا۟ بِهَا ۚ وَمَا نُرْسِلُ بِٱلْءَايَٰتِ
إِلَّا تَخْوِيفًا ٥٩

60) We informed you [O Prophet] that the Lord encompasses humankind [within His Knowledge and Omnipotence]. We did not institute the vision We showed you in your dream, nor the accursed tree in the Qur'an, other than as a trial for people. Yet despite Our instilling fear in them their transgressions increase.

وَإِذْ قُلْنَا لَكَ إِنَّ رَبَّكَ أَحَاطَ بِٱلنَّاسِ ۚ وَمَا
جَعَلْنَا ٱلرُّءْيَا ٱلَّتِىٓ أَرَيْنَٰكَ إِلَّا فِتْنَةً لِّلنَّاسِ وَٱلشَّجَرَةَ ٱلْمَلْعُونَةَ
فِى ٱلْقُرْءَانِ ۚ وَنُخَوِّفُهُمْ فَمَا يَزِيدُهُمْ إِلَّا طُغْيَٰنًا كَبِيرًا ٦٠

61) When We ordered the angels to bow down in respect to Adam, all prostrated themselves. But [the Jinn] Iblis retorted, 'Is it appropriate that I prostrate myself before a creature You created out of clay?'

وَإِذْ قُلْنَا لِلْمَلَٰٓئِكَةِ ٱسْجُدُوا۟ لِءَادَمَ فَسَجَدُوٓا۟ إِلَّآ إِبْلِيسَ
قَالَ ءَأَسْجُدُ لِمَنْ خَلَقْتَ طِينًا ﴿٦١﴾

62) Iblis then added, 'Grant me Your authority until the Day of Resurrection and I will surely reduce to subjection almost all the offspring of that creature which You have honoured above me'.

قَالَ أَرَءَيْتَكَ هَٰذَا ٱلَّذِى
كَرَّمْتَ عَلَىَّ لَئِنْ أَخَّرْتَنِ إِلَىٰ يَوْمِ ٱلْقِيَٰمَةِ لَأَحْتَنِكَنَّ
ذُرِّيَّتَهُۥٓ إِلَّا قَلِيلًا ﴿٦٢﴾

63) Allah then ordered, 'Go with those who follow you to reap the rewards of Gehennam [Hell]. An ample recompense for all of you'.

قَالَ ٱذْهَبْ فَمَن تَبِعَكَ مِنْهُمْ فَإِنَّ
جَهَنَّمَ جَزَآؤُكُمْ جَزَآءً مَّوْفُورًا ﴿٦٣﴾

64) Proposition and entice as much as you like. Attack people [with all the forces at your disposal] on horse or on foot, conspire with them to procure wealth and children, and make promises to them [as you will]. Satan's promises are deceptive!

وَٱسْتَفْزِزْ مَنِ ٱسْتَطَعْتَ
مِنْهُم بِصَوْتِكَ وَأَجْلِبْ عَلَيْهِم بِخَيْلِكَ وَرَجِلِكَ وَشَارِكْهُمْ
فِى ٱلْأَمْوَٰلِ وَٱلْأَوْلَٰدِ وَعِدْهُمْ ۚ وَمَا يَعِدُهُمُ ٱلشَّيْطَٰنُ إِلَّا
غُرُورًا ﴿٦٤﴾

65) But you will not hold sway over My servants, for your Lord will protect them.

إِنَّ عِبَادِى لَيْسَ لَكَ عَلَيْهِمْ سُلْطَٰنٌ ۚ وَكَفَىٰ
بِرَبِّكَ وَكِيلًا ﴿٦٥﴾

66) It is your Lord who powers ships across the seas for you so that you may obtain His Bounty. He is always Merciful to you.

رَّبُّكُمُ ٱلَّذِى يُزْجِى لَكُمُ ٱلْفُلْكَ
فِى ٱلْبَحْرِ لِتَبْتَغُوا۟ مِن فَضْلِهِۦٓ ۚ إِنَّهُۥ كَانَ بِكُمْ رَحِيمًا ٦٦

67) And whenever danger threatens you at sea, all those to whom you appeal abandon you other than Him; but as soon as He returns you safely to shore, you ignore Him. Human beings are truly thankless creatures.

وَإِذَا مَسَّكُمُ ٱلضُّرُّ فِى ٱلْبَحْرِ ضَلَّ مَن تَدْعُونَ إِلَّآ إِيَّاهُ ۖ فَلَمَّا نَجَّىٰكُمْ
إِلَى ٱلْبَرِّ أَعْرَضْتُمْ ۚ وَكَانَ ٱلْإِنسَٰنُ كَفُورًا ٦٧

68) Can you rest assured that He will not cause you to be buried under a landslide or caught in a sandstorm? Then you would have no one to protect you.

أَفَأَمِنتُمْ أَن يَخْسِفَ
بِكُمْ جَانِبَ ٱلْبَرِّ أَوْ يُرْسِلَ عَلَيْكُمْ حَاصِبًا ثُمَّ لَا تَجِدُوا۟ لَكُمْ
وَكِيلًا ٦٨

69) Can you be certain that your ingratitude will not result in His sending you back to sea, to perish in a raging tempest? Who would you then find to support you other than Us?

أَمْ أَمِنتُمْ أَن يُعِيدَكُمْ فِيهِ تَارَةً أُخْرَىٰ فَيُرْسِلَ
عَلَيْكُمْ قَاصِفًا مِّنَ ٱلرِّيحِ فَيُغْرِقَكُم بِمَا كَفَرْتُمْ ۙ ثُمَّ لَا تَجِدُوا۟
لَكُمْ عَلَيْنَا بِهِۦ تَبِيعًا ٦٩

70) We truly honoured the Children of Adam, carried them over land and sea, sustained them with wholesome things and preferred them to most of Our other creation.

۞ وَلَقَدْ كَرَّمْنَا بَنِىٓ ءَادَمَ وَحَمَلْنَٰهُمْ
فِى ٱلْبَرِّ وَٱلْبَحْرِ وَرَزَقْنَٰهُم مِّنَ ٱلطَّيِّبَٰتِ وَفَضَّلْنَٰهُمْ عَلَىٰ
كَثِيرٍ مِّمَّنْ خَلَقْنَا تَفْضِيلًا ٧٠

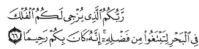

71) On the Day in which all human beings are summoned by their Imams, those given records in their right hand will read them [joyously] without suffering the slightest discomfort.

يَوۡمَ نَدۡعُواْ كُلَّ أُنَاسٍ
بِإِمَٰمِهِمۡ فَمَنۡ أُوتِيَ كِتَٰبَهُۥ بِيَمِينِهِۦ فَأُوْلَٰٓئِكَ يَقۡرَءُونَ
كِتَٰبَهُمۡ وَلَا يُظۡلَمُونَ فَتِيلًا ﴿٧١﴾

72) However, those who were blind in this life, will be raised blind in the Hereafter, even further astray from the Path [of Truth].

وَمَن كَانَ فِى هَٰذِهِۦۤ
أَعۡمَىٰ فَهُوَ فِى ٱلۡأٓخِرَةِ أَعۡمَىٰ وَأَضَلُّ سَبِيلًا ﴿٧٢﴾

73) They strove hard to beguile you away from what We revealed to you, and to get you to fabricate something quite different in Our name. They would then certainly have accepted you in friendship.

وَإِن كَادُواْ
لَيَفۡتِنُونَكَ عَنِ ٱلَّذِىٓ أَوۡحَيۡنَآ إِلَيۡكَ لِتَفۡتَرِىَ عَلَيۡنَا غَيۡرَهُۥ
وَإِذًا لَّٱتَّخَذُوكَ خَلِيلًا ﴿٧٣﴾

74) And had We not entrenched you in faith, you might well have inclined to them a little.

وَلَوۡلَآ أَن ثَبَّتۡنَٰكَ لَقَدۡ كِدتَّ
تَرۡكَنُ إِلَيۡهِمۡ شَيۡـًٔا قَلِيلًا ﴿٧٤﴾

75) In which case, We would have made you bear a double [punishment] in life and a double [chastisement] after death, with no one to support you against Us.

إِذًا لَّأَذَقۡنَٰكَ ضِعۡفَ
ٱلۡحَيَوٰةِ وَضِعۡفَ ٱلۡمَمَاتِ ثُمَّ لَا تَجِدُ لَكَ عَلَيۡنَا نَصِيرًا ﴿٧٥﴾

76) Then they tried to banish you and drive you off the land. Had that succeeded they would not have remained there [safely] for long.

وَإِن كَادُواْ لَيَسۡتَفِزُّونَكَ مِنَ ٱلۡأَرۡضِ لِيُخۡرِجُوكَ مِنۡهَا
وَإِذًا لَّا يَلۡبَثُونَ خِلَٰفَكَ إِلَّا قَلِيلًا ﴿٧٦﴾

77) This was Our practice when We sent Messengers before you, and you will observe that Our practice has not altered.

سُنَّةَ مَن قَدْ
أَرْسَلْنَا قَبْلَكَ مِن رُّسُلِنَا ۖ وَلَا تَجِدُ لِسُنَّتِنَا تَحْوِيلًا ﴿٧٧﴾

78) Establish prayer when the sun begins to descend from its summit [at noon], and at the darkening of the night and the recitation of the Qur'an at dawn. For the [recital] at dawn is witnessed.

أَقِمِ
ٱلصَّلَوٰةَ لِدُلُوكِ ٱلشَّمْسِ إِلَىٰ غَسَقِ ٱلَّيْلِ وَقُرْءَانَ ٱلْفَجْرِ ۖ إِنَّ
قُرْءَانَ ٱلْفَجْرِ كَانَ مَشْهُودًا ﴿٧٨﴾

79) And forsake sleep for [part] of the night in order to offer additional prayers, for your Lord may well raise you to an honourable position.

وَمِنَ ٱلَّيْلِ فَتَهَجَّدْ بِهِۦ
نَافِلَةً لَّكَ عَسَىٰٓ أَن يَبْعَثَكَ رَبُّكَ مَقَامًا مَّحْمُودًا ﴿٧٩﴾

80) And pray, 'Lord, make me worthy to carry out everything I undertake and worthy of everything I complete and grant me Your support'.

وَقُل رَّبِّ
أَدْخِلْنِى مُدْخَلَ صِدْقٍ وَأَخْرِجْنِى مُخْرَجَ صِدْقٍ وَٱجْعَل لِّى مِن
لَّدُنكَ سُلْطَٰنًا نَّصِيرًا ﴿٨٠﴾

81) And say, 'Truth has flourished and overcome falsehood, for all falsehood must ultimately be defeated'.

وَقُلْ جَآءَ ٱلْحَقُّ وَزَهَقَ ٱلْبَٰطِلُ ۚ
إِنَّ ٱلْبَٰطِلَ كَانَ زَهُوقًا ﴿٨١﴾

82) Our revelations of the Qur'an are sources of healing and mercy for those who believe, but sources of pain and loss for those who are unjust.

وَنُنَزِّلُ مِنَ ٱلْقُرْءَانِ مَا هُوَ شِفَآءٌ
وَرَحْمَةٌ لِّلْمُؤْمِنِينَ وَلَا يَزِيدُ ٱلظَّـٰلِمِينَ إِلَّا خَسَارًا ٨٢

83) When Our favours make lives agreeable, human beings frequently turn away in disdain; yet when ill-fortune afflicts them they frequently despair.

وَإِذَآ
أَنْعَمْنَا عَلَى ٱلْإِنسَـٰنِ أَعْرَضَ وَنَـَٔا بِجَانِبِهِۦ وَإِذَا مَسَّهُ ٱلشَّرُّ كَانَ يَـُٔوسًا
٨٣

84) Say [O Muḥammad], 'Everyone's behaviour accords with their own beliefs; but the Lord knows best whose path is true'.

قُلْ كُلٌّ يَعْمَلُ عَلَىٰ شَاكِلَتِهِۦ فَرَبُّكُمْ أَعْلَمُ بِمَنْ هُوَ أَهْدَىٰ
سَبِيلًا ٨٤

85) When they ask you [O Muḥammad] about the spirit, tell them, 'The spirit is at the command of my Lord and He has revealed only a little knowledge of it'.

وَيَسْـَٔلُونَكَ عَنِ ٱلرُّوحِ قُلِ ٱلرُّوحُ مِنْ أَمْرِ رَبِّى
وَمَآ أُوتِيتُم مِّنَ ٱلْعِلْمِ إِلَّا قَلِيلًا ٨٥

86) And if We willed, We could certainly erase what We have revealed to you. Then you would have no one to petition Us on your behalf.

وَلَئِن شِئْنَا لَنَذْهَبَنَّ
بِٱلَّذِىٓ أَوْحَيْنَآ إِلَيْكَ ثُمَّ لَا تَجِدُ لَكَ بِهِۦ عَلَيْنَا وَكِيلًا ٨٦

87) [You have only been spared] by the Mercy of your Lord. His favours to you are indeed great.

إِلَّا رَحْمَةً مِّن رَّبِّكَ إِنَّ فَضْلَهُۥ كَانَ عَلَيْكَ كَبِيرًا ٨٧

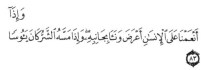

88) Say [O Muḥammad], 'If both humankind and jinn laboured to produce the like of this Qur'an they could not succeed, even if they managed to successfully co-operate with each other'.

قُل
لَّئِنِ ٱجْتَمَعَتِ ٱلْإِنسُ وَٱلْجِنُّ عَلَىٰٓ أَن يَأْتُوا۟ بِمِثْلِ هَٰذَا ٱلْقُرْءَانِ
لَا يَأْتُونَ بِمِثْلِهِۦ وَلَوْ كَانَ بَعْضُهُمْ لِبَعْضٍ ظَهِيرًا ﴿٨٨﴾

89) Although We have provided them with multifaceted explanations in this Qur'an, most human beings are ungrateful and reject it.

وَلَقَدْ
صَرَّفْنَا لِلنَّاسِ فِى هَٰذَا ٱلْقُرْءَانِ مِن كُلِّ مَثَلٍ فَأَبَىٰٓ أَكْثَرُ ٱلنَّاسِ
إِلَّا كُفُورًا ﴿٨٩﴾

90) And they say, 'We will not believe you [O Muḥammad] until you make a spring of water gush forth for us from this [arid] land.

وَقَالُوا۟ لَن نُّؤْمِنَ لَكَ حَتَّىٰ تَفْجُرَ لَنَا مِنَ
ٱلْأَرْضِ يَنۢبُوعًا ﴿٩٠﴾

91) Or until you have a garden of palms and vines and make rivers suddenly surge through it.

أَوْ تَكُونَ لَكَ جَنَّةٌ مِّن نَّخِيلٍ وَعِنَبٍ
فَتُفَجِّرَ ٱلْأَنْهَٰرَ خِلَٰلَهَا تَفْجِيرًا ﴿٩١﴾

92) Or you cause, as you threaten, the heaven to shatter and drop upon us; or you bring Allah and the angels face to face before us.

أَوْ تُسْقِطَ ٱلسَّمَآءَ كَمَا
زَعَمْتَ عَلَيْنَا كِسَفًا أَوْ تَأْتِىَ بِٱللَّهِ وَٱلْمَلَٰٓئِكَةِ قَبِيلًا ﴿٩٢﴾

93) Or you have a house of gold, or ascend into the heavens; and we will not believe you have been there unless you bring back a book which we may read.' Say then [O Muḥammad], 'Glory to my Lord. I am only a mortal who has been sent as a Messenger'.

أَوْ يَكُونَ لَكَ بَيْتٌ مِّن زُخْرُفٍ أَوْ تَرْقَىٰ فِي ٱلسَّمَآءِ وَلَن نُّؤْمِنَ
لِرُقِيِّكَ حَتَّىٰ تُنَزِّلَ عَلَيْنَا كِتَٰبًا نَّقْرَؤُهُۥ ۗ قُلْ سُبْحَانَ رَبِّي هَلْ
كُنتُ إِلَّا بَشَرًا رَّسُولًا ﴿٩٣﴾

94) And when guidance came to them, nothing would have prevented them from accepting it other than their saying, 'Would Allah have sent a mortal as His Messenger?'

وَمَا مَنَعَ ٱلنَّاسَ أَن يُؤْمِنُوٓا۟ إِذْ جَآءَهُمُ
ٱلْهُدَىٰٓ إِلَّآ أَن قَالُوٓا۟ أَبَعَثَ ٱللَّهُ بَشَرًا رَّسُولًا ﴿٩٤﴾

95) Say to them, 'Had there been angels walking at peace on earth, We would have sent an angel to them as Our Messenger'.

قُل لَّوْ كَانَ
فِي ٱلْأَرْضِ مَلَٰٓئِكَةٌ يَمْشُونَ مُطْمَئِنِّينَ لَنَزَّلْنَا عَلَيْهِم
مِّنَ ٱلسَّمَآءِ مَلَكًا رَّسُولًا ﴿٩٥﴾

96) Say, 'Allah suffices as witness between us, He sees and knows what is in His servants' hearts'.

قُلْ كَفَىٰ بِٱللَّهِ
شَهِيدًۢا بَيْنِي وَبَيْنَكُمْ ۚ إِنَّهُۥ كَانَ بِعِبَادِهِۦ خَبِيرًۢا بَصِيرًا ﴿٩٦﴾

97) And whoever Allah guides is indeed guided aright, and those whom He lets go astray can find no one except Him to protect them. We shall assemble them on the Day of Resurrection upon their faces, blind, deaf and dumb; their destination Gehennam [Hell], and whenever the blaze dies down, We shall again increase its intensity.

وَمَن يَهْدِ ٱللَّهُ فَهُوَ ٱلْمُهْتَدِ ۖ وَمَن يُضْلِلْ فَلَن تَجِدَ لَهُمْ أَوْلِيَآءَ
مِن دُونِهِۦ ۖ وَنَحْشُرُهُمْ يَوْمَ ٱلْقِيَٰمَةِ عَلَىٰ وُجُوهِهِمْ عُمْيًا وَبُكْمًا
وَصُمًّا ۖ مَّأْوَىٰهُمْ جَهَنَّمُ ۖ كُلَّمَا خَبَتْ زِدْنَٰهُمْ سَعِيرًا ﴿٩٧﴾

98) That will be their recompense for disbelieving Our signs and questioning, 'When we [have perished] and our bones reduced to dust, shall we really be raised up and given a new existence?'

ذَٰلِكَ جَزَآؤُهُم بِأَنَّهُمۡ كَفَرُواْ بِـَٔايَٰتِنَا وَقَالُوٓاْ أَءِذَا كُنَّا عِظَٰمٗا
وَرُفَٰتًا أَءِنَّا لَمَبۡعُوثُونَ خَلۡقٗا جَدِيدٗا ٩٨

99) Can they not see that Allah, who created the heavens and the earth, is able to recreate their like? There is no doubt that He decreed an appointed time for them; but those who are unjust refuse to accept anything other than disbelief.

۞ أَوَلَمۡ يَرَوۡاْ أَنَّ ٱللَّهَ
ٱلَّذِي خَلَقَ ٱلسَّمَٰوَٰتِ وَٱلۡأَرۡضَ قَادِرٌ عَلَىٰٓ أَن يَخۡلُقَ مِثۡلَهُمۡ
وَجَعَلَ لَهُمۡ أَجَلٗا لَّا رَيۡبَ فِيهِ فَأَبَى ٱلظَّٰلِمُونَ إِلَّا كُفُورٗا ٩٩

100) Say [to them] 'Even if you possessed the [limitless] treasuries of my Lord's mercy, you would hoard it for horror of spending; people are always grudging'.

قُل لَّوۡ أَنتُمۡ تَمۡلِكُونَ خَزَآئِنَ رَحۡمَةِ رَبِّيٓ إِذٗا لَّأَمۡسَكۡتُمۡ خَشۡيَةَ
ٱلۡإِنفَاقِۚ وَكَانَ ٱلۡإِنسَٰنُ قَتُورٗا ١٠٠

101) And We gave Mūsa [Moses] nine clear proofs [of Allah's sovereignty]. Ask the Children of Isra'il. When he came to them, Fir'awn [Pharaoh] said to him, 'Mūsa [Moses], I think you are possessed'.

وَلَقَدۡ ءَاتَيۡنَا مُوسَىٰ تِسۡعَ
ءَايَٰتِۭ بَيِّنَٰتٖۖ فَسۡـَٔلۡ بَنِيٓ إِسۡرَٰٓءِيلَ إِذۡ جَآءَهُمۡ فَقَالَ لَهُۥ فِرۡعَوۡنُ
إِنِّي لَأَظُنُّكَ يَٰمُوسَىٰ مَسۡحُورٗا ١٠١

102) Mūsa [Moses] said, 'You know very well that no one except the Lord of the heavens and the earth has sent these signs as clear proofs [to you]. [If you cannot see this] you are surely doomed'.

قَالَ لَقَدۡ عَلِمۡتَ مَآ أَنزَلَ
هَٰٓؤُلَآءِ إِلَّا رَبُّ ٱلسَّمَٰوَٰتِ وَٱلۡأَرۡضِ بَصَآئِرَ وَإِنِّي لَأَظُنُّكَ
يَٰفِرۡعَوۡنُ مَثۡبُورٗا ١٠٢

103) At this, Fir'awn [Pharaoh] resolved to expel them from his realm, but We drowned him and those who accompanied him.

فَأَرَادَ أَن يَسْتَفِزَّهُم مِّنَ ٱلْأَرْضِ
فَأَغْرَقْنَٰهُ وَمَن مَّعَهُۥ جَمِيعًا ١٠٣

104) After that, We said to the Children of Isra'il, 'Dwell in that land. And when the promised day arrives We will gather your dispersed people together'.

وَقُلْنَا مِنۢ بَعْدِهِۦ لِبَنِىٓ إِسْرَٰٓءِيلَ
ٱسْكُنُوا۟ ٱلْأَرْضَ فَإِذَا جَآءَ وَعْدُ ٱلْـَٔاخِرَةِ جِئْنَا بِكُمْ لَفِيفًا ١٠٤

105) We revealed [the Qur'an] to guide you to truth and it has brought the truth! We sent you only as an encouragement and as a warning.

وَبِٱلْحَقِّ أَنزَلْنَٰهُ وَبِٱلْحَقِّ نَزَلَ ۗ وَمَآ أَرْسَلْنَٰكَ إِلَّا مُبَشِّرًا وَنَذِيرًا ١٠٥

106) We revealed the Qur'an in stages and organised it so that sections may be regularly recited.

وَقُرْءَانًا فَرَقْنَٰهُ لِتَقْرَأَهُۥ عَلَى ٱلنَّاسِ عَلَىٰ مُكْثٍ وَنَزَّلْنَٰهُ تَنزِيلًا ١٠٦

107) Tell them, 'Believe in it or not. Those who already innately knew [the truth] prostrated themselves as soon as the Qur'an's message was conveyed to them'.

قُلْ ءَامِنُوا۟ بِهِۦٓ أَوْ لَا تُؤْمِنُوٓا۟ ۚ إِنَّ ٱلَّذِينَ أُوتُوا۟ ٱلْعِلْمَ مِن قَبْلِهِۦٓ إِذَا يُتْلَىٰ
عَلَيْهِمْ يَخِرُّونَ لِلْأَذْقَانِ سُجَّدًا ١٠٧

108) Saying, 'Glory to our Lord! His covenant must be fulfilled'.

وَيَقُولُونَ سُبْحَٰنَ رَبِّنَآ إِن كَانَ
وَعْدُ رَبِّنَا لَمَفْعُولًا ١٠٨

109) Humbled and with tears in their eyes, they prostrated themselves.

وَيَخِرُّونَ لِلْأَذْقَانِ يَبْكُونَ وَيَزِيدُهُمْ
خُشُوعًا ۩ ١٠٩

110) Say to them [O Muḥammad], 'Pray to Allah or to The All-Merciful, no matter which you choose, the Most Beautiful Names are all His. And do not be loud in your prayer, nor hushed but be moderate'.

قُلِ ادْعُوا اللَّهَ أَوِ ادْعُوا الرَّحْمَٰنَ ۖ أَيًّا مَّا تَدْعُوا فَلَهُ
الْأَسْمَاءُ الْحُسْنَىٰ ۚ وَلَا تَجْهَرْ بِصَلَاتِكَ وَلَا تُخَافِتْ بِهَا وَابْتَغِ
بَيْنَ ذَٰلِكَ سَبِيلًا ١١٠

111) And say, 'Praise be to Allah who has no son, no one to share His sovereignty with, and who needs no aid. So extol Him and His limitless greatness'.

وَقُلِ الْحَمْدُ لِلَّهِ الَّذِي لَمْ يَتَّخِذْ وَلَدًا وَلَمْ يَكُن
لَّهُ شَرِيكٌ فِي الْمُلْكِ وَلَمْ يَكُن لَّهُ وَلِيٌّ مِّنَ الذُّلِّ ۖ وَكَبِّرْهُ تَكْبِيرًا ١١١

IN THE NAME OF ALLAH, THE MOST GENEROUS, THE MOST MERCIFUL

Commentary

Contents

This Surah which consists of 111 ayat, 109 revealed at Makkah, is known by two names. The first, 'Isrāa' – Ascension – refers to the Holy Prophet's physical journey from Makkah to Jerusalem, and his ascension from there towards the Sublime. The Prophet's ascension, considered one of his greatest miracles, is also referred to as his 'Night Journey'. The second name, 'Bani Isra'il' – The Children of Isra'il, indicates that they also are the subject matter of this Surah. Overall, this Surah refers to the following issues:

1) The Prophet's Night Journey
2) 'Arrogance' of the Children of Isra'il
3) Comprehensive guidance of the Qur'an
4) Benefits of Divine guidance
5) Everyone benefits from Allah's unrestricted generosity
6) Socio-ethical ordinances
7) Allah's 'Oneness'
8) The Restoration of life
9) The Accursed Tree
10) Satan's enmity towards humankind
11) Arguments regarding the existence of God
12) The Dignity of humankind
13) Daily Prayer
14) The Spirit
15) Validation of the Message
16) Outrageous Makkan demands
17) Revelation in stages
18) Allah's Most Beautiful Names

1 The Prophet's Night Journey

The Surah begins with the glorification – 'subḥan' – of Allah Almighty, an exaltation which refutes all notion of the Almighty having human qualities. Although Muslims frequently use the phrase 'Subḥan Allah' to express surprise, this is not the case here:

> **1. Glory be to Him who transported His servant [Muḥammad] by night from the Holy Mosque, to see his Lord's signs in the blessed environment of the Farthest Mosque. Truly He is All-Hearing, All-Seeing.**

The Holy Mosque is Al-Masjid al-Haram in Makkah and the Farthest Mosque is the mosque Al-Quds al-Sharif in Jerusalem, also known as Al-Masjid al-Aqsa. This latter is referred to as being within the 'blessed environment' which permitted Muḥammad ﷺ to see his Lord's Signs. Certain commentators conclude that because Al-Masjid al-Aqsa and Al-Masjid al-Haram are only a few hundred miles apart, the adjective 'farthest', indicates that the 'blessed environment' refers to the most distant heaven. For those commentators, the Prophet's journey to Jerusalem has no meaning if the purpose of the Night Journey was to present the wonders and glory of Allah's Kingdom. They argue that, if Allah had selected an earthly place to disclose these, He would surely have chosen Al-Masjid al-Haram.

However, signs of Divine Judgement seen by the Prophet ﷺ in Jerusalem included the periodic destructions of the temple in Jerusalem which were the result of the arrogance of the 'chosen people'.

The Prophet's great companion, Ibn Abbas, ؓ claimed that the 'blessed environment' referred to Palestine and Jordan – blessed by rivers, fruit, vegetables, prophets and righteousness. Yakut al-Hamawi in his book, *The Encyclopaedia of Cities – Mujam al-Buldan,* suggests that the 'blessed environment' refers to the land of Sham which includes Jordan, Palestine, Syria and Lebanon, because in another ayah Allah tells us,

> Between them [the people of Sheba in Yemen] and the cities on which We poured Our blessings and located prominent positions, measured distances need to be travelled . . .
>
> Qur'an 34:18

Measured distances is a reference to the ancient spice road, the main route for pilgrims from the Yemen to Makkah, which followed the western coast of Arabia, through Amman and Damascus.

A Brief History of Jerusalem

Jerusalem has been known by a number of names throughout history. The earliest mentioned in the Torah was Shalim, thought to be an abbreviation for 'The City of Peace' – Yuroshalim. When the ancient inhabitants of Canaan settled there, they referred to it as Urshalim. This name was established 900 years before David – Dawūd ﷺ. Later, Jerusalem came to be known as 'The Dry Land' – Zion.

The term 'zionism', first used by Nathan Birnbaum in 1890, was later used to describe the utopian dream of Theodor Herzl (1860–1904), who implemented the systematic transference of Jews from Europe to Palestine. This term was readily adopted by Isra'ili politicians who were determined to establish their government in Palestine. Although the term 'zionist' is, thus, modern, it relates to 'Zion', a revered concept of Judaism in that it refers to a desire to return to Zion, symbol of Jerusalem and, by extension, the whole land. Those interested in further reading on zionism in the English language, may refer to the excellent books, *The Bible and Colonialism: A Moral Critique* (ISBN 1-85075-815-8) and *Zionism and the State of Israel: A Moral Enquiry* (ISBN 0-415-20462-3) both by Michael Prior, CM. Dr Prior is Head of the Department of Theology and Religious Studies at St Mary's University College, University of Surrey.

However, since its Islamic conquest, Jerusalem has been known to Muslims as: 'The Sacred Home' – Al-Quds, Al-Quds al-Sharif, Al-Bayt al-Muqaddas and Bayt al-Maqdis.

Al-Quds, the first Qiblah in Islam

After his ascension to the heavens, when worship – 'ṣalat' – was enjoined, the Prophet ﷺ faced the direction of Bayt al-Maqdis in al-Quds whenever he prayed. He continued this practice until, 17 months after his migration to Madinah, revelation guided him to face the direction of the Ka'abah instead. Thus, Bayt al-Maqdis was the qiblah for Muslims until Allah Almighty revealed the following,

> We see the turning of your face to the heavens, now We shall turn you towards a Qiblah that will please you. Turn then your face in the direction of the sacred mosque.
>
> Qur'an 2:144

When Allah Almighty informed the Prophet ﷺ of this change of qiblah, He warned him,

> The fools amongst people will say, 'What has made them turn away from the direction they used to face?' Say, 'To Allah belongs both the East and the West. He guides whomever He wills to the straight path'.
>
> Qur'an 2:142

Key to Al-Masjid al-Aqsa

1) Minaret Bab al-Ghawanimah
2) Minaret al-Asbat
3) Dome of Sulayman – Qubbat Sulayman
4) Dome of those who love the Prophet – Qubbat Ushshaq an-Nabi
5) Throne of Sulayman – Kursi Sulayman
6) Dome of the Spirits – Qubbat al-Arwah
7) Dome of the Hebronite – Qubbat al-Khalili
8) Golden Gate – Al-Bab al-Zahabi
9) Dome of the Ascension – Qubbat al-Mi'raj
10) Dome of The Prophet – Qubbat al-Nabi (aka Qubbat Jibra'il)
11) Dome of the Rock – Qubbat al-Sakhra
12) Dome of the Chain – Qubbat al-Silsila
13) Minaret al-Silsila
14) Fountain of Qait Bey – Sabil Qait Bey
15) Pool of Raranj – Hawḍ al-Raranj
16) Fountain of Qassim Pasha – Sabil Qassim Pasha
17) Dome of Moses – Qubbat Mūsa
18) Dais of Burhan al-Din – Minbar Burhan al-Din
19) Al-Buraq wall
20) Al-Kas
21) Dome of Yusuf Agha – Qubbat Yusuf Agha
22) Al-Jami' Al-Aqsa
23) Entrance to underground Masjid Marwan
24) New entrance to underground Masjid Marwan
25) Islamic museum
26) Minaret al-Fakhriyyah
27) Al Zawiya al-Khunthaniya

Al-Masjid al-Aqsa consultant – Muhsin Kilby

Al-Masjid al-Aqsa

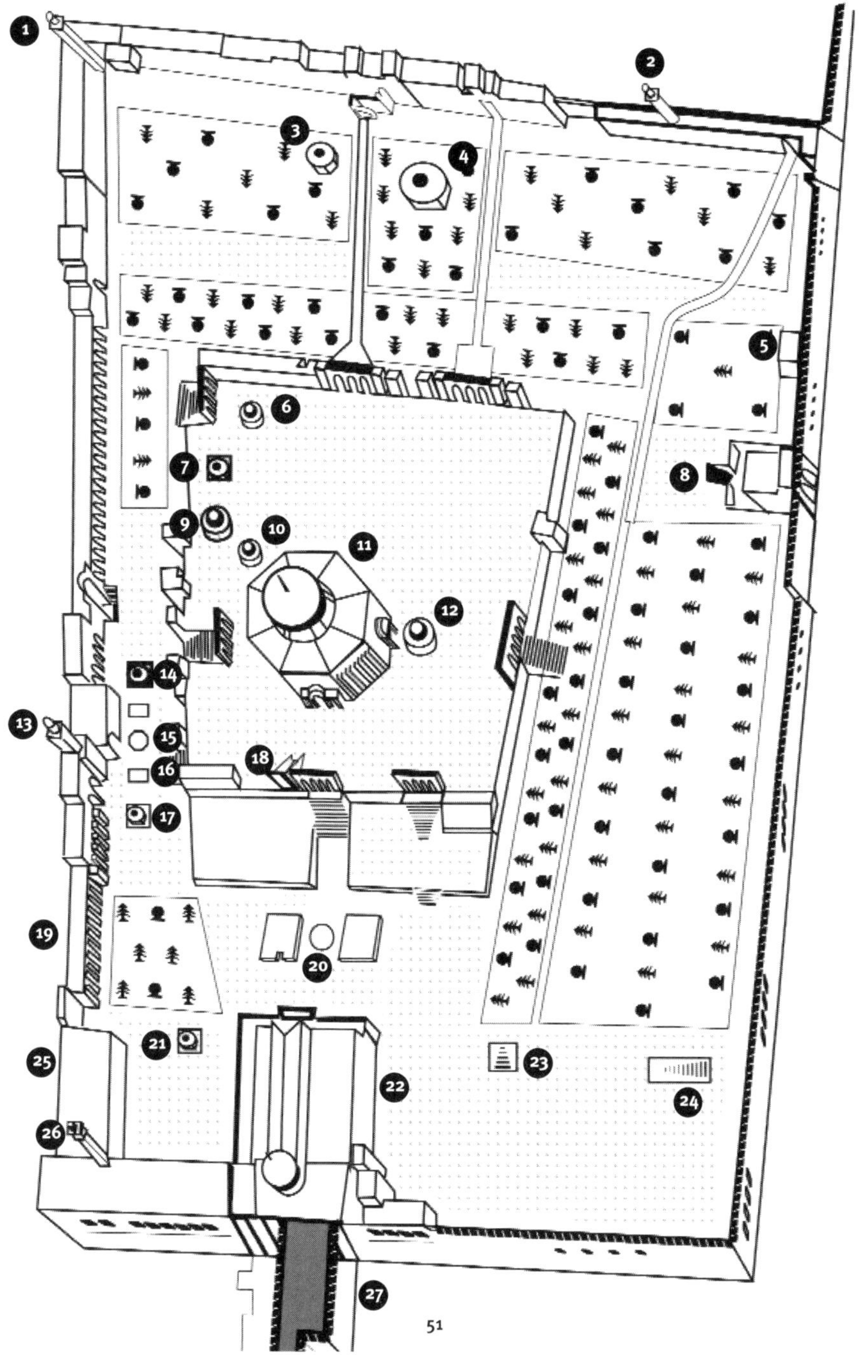

The 'Farthest Mosque' – Al-Aqsa – is located towards the south-east of the city with buildings and annexes covering 141 acres (57ha) of Mount Moriah. This location was neglected from the fifth century CE, until the time of the Caliph Umar ibn al-Khatab, who ordered the rock to be cleaned and a mosque, capable of accommodating 3,000 worshippers, to be built there.

Since 1929, Zionists have tried to extend their access and control of the area adjacent to the 56-ft-long (17-m) and 65-ft-high (20-m) Al-Buraq section of its outer wall, venerated by Muslims because, on the 'Night Journey', the Messenger of Allah ﷺ is said to have tethered his mount 'Buraq' there. Jews refer to this section as 'The Wailing Wall'. Their actions distressed Palestinian Muslims to the extent that, on 23 August, 1929, a demonstration held to counter such action, led to a legal ruling to uphold Palestinian rights and prevent Zionist incursion. However, since 1948, the Isra'ili state has demolished much of the Muslim infrastructure surrounding this area.

The purpose of the Night Journey is affirmed in Surah 53, in which Allah Almighty refers to the Lote Tree at the utmost boundary near the Garden of Abode,

> His [Muḥammad's] sight never swerved or went awry. For he truly saw the signs of his Lord.
>
> Qur'an 53:17-18

Although Karamites (followers of Muḥammad ibn Keram, an anthropomorphist who limited the nature of Allah Almighty by claiming He literally sat upon His throne) and the Juhamiyyah (followers of Juham ibn Safwan who espoused pre-destination) only regard this as a spiritual journey, the Imamiyyah (Muslims who follow the teaching and authentic Qur'anic commentary of the Prophet's progeny), the Zaydiyyah (Muslims who contend that Zayd ibn 'Ali ibn Ḥusayn, and not his brother Muḥammad al-Baqir ؑ, was appointed Imam after their father's death) and the Mu'tazilites (distinguished from Asha'rites by their exercise of intellectual reasoning in the interpretation of theological and jurisprudential issues), all believe this journey to have been both spiritual and physical.

The Night Journey was neither vision nor dream. The terms 'ascension' and 'descension' are employed to illustrate movement of the cognitive self through various spheres of finite creation, toward the 'absolute' and, from there, back down again to the lowest level of finite matter. On the basis of what Allah tells us in Qur'an 55:33, human beings may cross the boundaries of the heavens and the earth when Allah grants them the authority and power to do so. There can be no valid interpretation, other than that the Prophet Muḥammad ﷺ visited the heavens, met all the earlier prophets, saw both paradise and hell, and comprehended Allah's absolute omnipotent authority in full. We need not doubt his physical ascension in a state of wakefulness, once we accept that it is not proper to ascribe our own limited human abilities and faculties to Allah Almighty.

In certain traditions reported by 'the error-free Imams', two journeys are referred to in Surah 53:13,

> Indeed he [Muḥammad] saw him [Jibra'il] on his second descent.
>
> Allamah Muhammad Husayn Tabatabai, Tafsīr Al-Mizan, Vol. 13, p.31

When the Prophet ﷺ spoke of his Night Journey, those who did not believe him to be a prophet regarded it with great suspicion. Abu Jahl (a prominent disbeliever at the time of the Prophet ﷺ) told his associates that they now had a perfect opportunity to prove him a liar. They asked questions regarding the pillars and chandeliers in the Farthest Mosque, to which the Prophet ﷺ responded but – knowing that they could not possibly know whether or not his answers were accurate – also said, 'Another sign to convince you is that on my way back I saw a caravan due to arrive here tomorrow'. He described it in detail, including information on how and where the caravan had lost a camel at one place and water at another.

Disbelievers who eagerly awaited the caravan's arrival the following morning were amazed to discover everything occurred exactly as the Prophet ﷺ had described.

2   'Arrogance' of the Children of Isra'il

2. We gave Mūsa [Moses] the book of guidance for the Children of Isra'il [the Torah – Tawrāt – and told them], 'Do not seek [guidance and protection] from any but Me'.

3. You are the offspring of those We delivered [in the Ark] with Nūh [Noah], a truly grateful servant.

4. In that book We told the Children of Isra'il, 'You are certain to become exceedingly arrogant and will establish tyrannical regimes on two occasions'.

5. On the first, We fulfilled Our warning by sending an invincible force to overwhelm you, enter your dwellings and ravage your nation.

6. Later, We sanctioned your victory, extended your resources, increased your offspring and expanded your numbers.

7. [We gave you freedom of choice.] If you do good, it is you who will reap its benefit and, if you are evil, it is you who will suffer its effect.

On the second occasion We fulfilled Our warning, and sent a force to defeat and humiliate you, to enter the Temple as your earlier vanquisher had before, and to lay waste all that was conquered.

8. It may be that your Lord will show you mercy, but when you return to disobedience His chastisement will follow. In the afterlife, Hell will confine all those who reject faith.

These seven ayat show how the will of Allah affects human society; how He guides human beings to the path of obedience and realisation of His Oneness; how they may then, with complete freedom, achieve happiness and bounty in this life, as well as in the life hereafter. If they adhere to His guidelines and behave decently, the fruit of their actions will be paradise. If they do not and behave badly, the fruit they will reap will be His chastisement.

Here, Allah presents the arrogance and mischief of the Children of Isra'il as an example. He ordered them to follow the guidance He sent down to Mūsa 🕊 in His Divine Book, the *Tawrāt*. Instead, on two noteworthy occasions they deliberately rebelled against the Lord.

They behaved outrageously arrogantly in the land, in the full knowledge that Allah had clearly stated He would punish those who make mischief.

The ayah – 'We gave Mūsa a book of guidance for the Children of Isra'il [the *Torah – Tawrāt* and told them] "Do not [seek guidance and protection] from any but Me" ' – seems to be an appropriate point to determine what is meant by the term 'exceedingly arrogant' used in this Surah. In doing this we have included references to the Biblical and Gospel texts, as well as to Christian and Jewish scholarship.

Arrogance of the Sages

The arrogance of the Sages is illustrated by their confounding the actual form of the Sacred Scripture of Judaism, that is Divine Revelation, with their own accretions.

Jews refer to 'Mattan Torah' – the giving of the Torah to Mūsa عليه السلام – for when he descended Mount Sinai he brought the revelation which they refer to as 'Torah'. However, while Exodus 20 suggests that the Ten Commandments might have constituted the complete Revelation at Sinai, certain Jewish commentators understand that other laws were also revealed at that time. However, in the 5th century BCE, the term 'Torah' started to be applied to all five books of the Pentateuch, and today the Hebrew Bible lists 'Torah' as the Five Books of Moses – *Genesis, Exodus, Leviticus, Numbers* and *Deuteronomy.*

As the current 'Torah' does not specify what was revealed to Mūsa عليه السلام, the Sages – a general term for Rabbis and other Jewish teachers of the 2nd century BCE to the 7th century CE – argued that the Torah comprised the Written Torah – 'torah she-bikhav' – as well as their own traditional exegesis of the Torah or Oral Torah – 'torah she-be'al peh' – which they claim to have 'equal authority'.

Thus, in addition to what are referred to as The Five Books of Moses, certain Jews consider the Torah to be the product of generations of inspired prophets, priests and teachers, starting at the time of Mūsa عليه السلام and manifesting its present form in the 6th or 5th centuries BCE.

The Sages declared that from the day that the First Temple was destroyed by the Babylonians in 586 BCE, revelation would no longer be brought by prophets, but that everything that needed to be revealed would thereafter be revealed through them. They insisted that Rabbinic teachings, even those of which they were not yet aware, had been given to Mūsa عليه السلام at Mount Sinai. The outrageous arrogance of the Sages is illustrated by the classic tale in which God's contribution to a legal debate is cast out by their fine oratory and argument. God, they report, is overjoyed that His clever children managed to defeat Him. (*Etz Hayim,* p.1398)

The most outrageous effect of this is that the writings, which condone the oppression, marginalisation, exploitation and genocide of the indigenous peoples of Judaism's 'Promised Land', are today accepted as constituting Divine revelation.

To search for original biblical texts is to discover manuscripts produced hundreds of years after the 'original' was written. Available manuscripts often vary; some verses appear only in a few manuscripts, handwriting is not always legible and scribes made occasional copying mistakes. There are also wide differences in spelling, punctuation, layout of poetry, etc., in some of the added notes of clarification called 'masorah' that gave rise to what are referred to as 'masoretic texts', or Bibles which accord with the masorah. Even so, there remain areas of disagreement and too great a number of details for the masorah to address. In addition, masoretic notes are often vague, written in shorthand, and sometimes cite conflicting textual evidence.

Some biblical scholars have tried to refine the texts they found, but each began with a different set of manuscripts produced by scribes of varying and uncertain reliability. Each used different methodologies to resolve textual problems and thus arrived at different conclusions as to what the 'best' text is. The result is that many Jews now accept the Bible as a text which continually evolves and changes to justify the accuracy of their tradition.

Scholars have demonstrated: that texts were edited to reflect political attitudes with evidence that both practices and sanctuaries connected with the earlier religion of Canaan were deliberately marginalised; that prophetic books contain many passages of uncertain meaning; that scholars have made conjectural improvements of their own; that the as-yet-imperfect understanding of the language of the Bible, or apparent disorder of the Hebrew text, makes accurate translation of many passages impossible.

The first known scribe to produce a complete manuscript of the Bible from previously independently preserved books was Aaron ben Moses Ben-Asher (who lived in Tiberias, *c.* 930 CE). Two generations later, Samuel ben Jacob (Egypt, 1010 CE) who spent ten years composing his Bible codex, noted on its completion in 1010 CE that he had copied several manuscripts into one volume including the text of Aaron ben Moses Ben-Asher. This oldest complete Hebrew Bible lay undiscovered by historians and Bible editors until 1840. Referred to as the Leningrad Codex, it has been repeatedly edited by teams of religious and academic Christian and Jewish scholars. One group, led by Rudolph Kittel, made it the base for a critical edition, *Biblia Hebraica Kittel* (BHK, 1937); another revised that edition to produce *Biblia Hebraica Stutgartensia* (BHS, 1967–77). Those who have computerised it now refer to it as the *Michigan-Claremont-Westminster* (MCW) electronic BHS.

In the third century BCE when the Hebrew and Aramaic vernacular of the Jewish population of Alexandria, then under Hellenic influence, was replaced by spoken Greek, a translation of the Bible in Greek was made for them. This is known as the *Septuagint* – Latin for 'seventy' – because it was imagined that 72 people, six elders from each of the 12 tribes of Israel, had undertaken that work. A short time later, when Aramaic had become the spoken language of the Jews to the north and east of Judea, Aramaic translations, known as the 'Targums', were produced. The *Septuagint* and the Targums are claimed to be the oldest and most influential translations of the Bible because virtually every Christian translation followed the translation method of the *Septuagint* and, generally, its renderings of the Hebrew.

The Church adopted the *Septuagint* as its Bible in the 1st century CE and translated it into the languages of the various Christian communities. When Greek gave way to the Latin of the Roman Empire, a Latin translation of the Scripture became the recognised Bible of the Church. In 340–420 CE, Father Jerome produced the official Latin version known as the *Vulgate*, or Bible in the language of the common people. Protestant scholars later translated the Bible into various languages. In the sixteenth century the two most famous translations started to appear: Martin Luther's version in German (1526) and 85 years later William Tyndale's in English, known as the *King James Version* (1611).

Contemporary scholars of semantic analysis do not place reliance on indirect evidence of translated texts which they regard merely as rough-and-ready guides to fumbling first steps, and never a reliable basis for discussion. When we read a text in the original we tend almost unconsciously to read into it concepts fostered by our own mother tongue, and to transmute many, if not all, of its key terms into equivalent terms in our own native language. (*See* Morris R Cohen's, *A Preface to Logic* (London, 1946 p. 16)).

For those who seek Jewish scholarly information regarding their Holy Scriptures – Tanakh – we recommend the following:

1) *Hebrew–English Tanakh* (Bible), comprising the *Torah* – The Five Books of Moses, Nevi'im – The Prophets and Kethuvim – The Writings. © 2000 New York, The Jewish Publication Society.

The prefaces to both the 1999 and 1985 editions are included and provide invaluable historic information.

2) *Etz Hayim* – Torah and Commentary. © 2001 The Rabbinical Assembly of The United Synagogue of Conservative Judaism, New York, The Jewish Publication Society.

This includes 41 topical essays, each written by a rabbi or scholar affiliated with the Conservative Movement. Taken as a whole, these essays provide a comprehensive introduction to the central themes of the Torah and their context in Judaism.

For further historical information on the subject, we recommend *Ancient Israel: Its Life and Institutions* by Fr Roland de Vaux, which, according to *The Times Literary Supplement*, 'covers every aspect of Israel's way of life. Every page is replete with learning'.

Started in 2002, *Holy Land Studies* (ISSN 1474-9475 – a Continuum imprint of the Sheffield Academic Press) draws expertise from virtually every relevant discipline: history, culture, politics, religion, archaeology, sociology, etc., to address the issues concerned with 'not only the region's need for peace and stability, but in virtue of the land's unique importance, in traditional eschatologies'. This is edited by Michael Prior, the Christian scholar uniquely known for his moral critiques of biblical texts.

The response to all of the above means that increasing numbers of people now question the assertions made repeatedly over the ages, that the text of the Torah represents Divine Revelation and gives Divine permission for the ethnic cleansing of the people of Palestine.

Biblical reference to the Children of Isra'il

Among many biblical references to the insolent pride of the Children of Isra'il, we find the following,

> Hear, O heavens, and give ear, O earth: for the Lord hath spoken, I have nourished and brought up children, and they have rebelled against me. The ox knoweth his owner, and the ass his master's crib: *but* Israel doth not know, my people doth not consider. Ah sinful nation, a people laden with iniquity, a seed of evildoers, children that are corrupters: they have forsaken the Lord, they have provoked the Holy One of Israel unto anger, they are gone away backward. Why should ye be stricken any more? Ye will revolt more and more: the whole head is sick, and the whole heart faint. From the sole of the foot even unto the head *there* is no soundness in it; *but* wounds, and bruises, and putrefying sores: they have not been closed, neither bound up, neither mollified with ointment. Your country *is* desolate, your cities *are* burned with fire: your land, strangers devour it in your presence, and *it is* desolate, as overthrown by strangers.
>
> Isaiah 1:2–7

When a subject named Naboth refused to sell his vineyard to the king, the king's wife brought false charges against him and had him stoned:

> And the word of the Lord came to Elijah the Tishbite saying, . . . go down to meet Ahab king of Israel, . . . *he* is in the vineyard of Naboth, whither he is gone down to possess it. And thou shalt speak to him, saying, 'Thus saith the Lord, Hast thou killed, and also taken possession?'
>
> 1 Kings 21:17–19

> But there was none like unto Ahab, which did sell himself to work wickedness in the sight of the Lord . . .
>
> 1 Kings 21:25

> Declare this in the house of Jacob, and publish it in Judah, saying, Hear now this, O foolish people, and without understanding; which have eyes, and see not; which have ears and hear not. Fear ye not me? saith the Lord: Will ye not tremble at my presence, which have placed the sand *for* the bound of the sea by a perpetual decree, that it cannot pass: and though the waves thereof toss themselves, yet can they not prevail; though they roar, yet can they not pass over it? But this people have a revolting and a rebellious heart, they are revolted and gone. Neither say they in their heart, Let us now fear the Lord our God, that giveth rain, both the former and the latter, in his season: he reserveth unto us the appointed weeks of the harvest. Your iniquities have turned away these *things*, and your sins have withholden good *things* from you. For among my people are found wicked *men*: they lay wait, as he that setteth snares; they set a trap, they catch men. As a cage is full of birds, so *are* their houses full of deceit: therefore they are become great, and waxen rich. They are waxen fat, they shine: yea, they overpass the deeds of the wicked: they judge not the cause, the cause of the fatherless, yet they prosper; and the right of the needy do they not judge. Shall I not visit for these *things*? saithth the Lord: shall not my soul be avenged on such a nation as this?
>
> Jeremiah 5:20–29

Chastisement of overbearing tribal rulers fighting to control the land

A severe chastisement occurred after the reign of Solomon (d. *c.* 928 BCE) when the kingdom was split by a realignment of Jewish tribes who then chose to wage war on one another for control of all the land. For half a century this struggle depleted the resources of both Isra'il in the north and Judah in the south and allowed the Egyptian King Shishak to control the major trade routes. When Judah was about to be conquered by Isra'il, its king, assisted by his powerful northern neighbour Aram-Damascus, overcame Isra'il. However, over the subsequent 30 years Isra'il won back its land.

Victory encouraged autocratic authority to ever greater assumed superiority and injustice until the Assyrian conquests of Syria and Palestine overshadowed the territorial conflict of Isra'il and Judah. They were only saved because Assyria focused its attention on Aram-Damascus.

However, as their economic progress and military strength recovered, the rulers of both Isra'il and Judah resumed their territorial ambitions. Isra'il and Aram-Damascus, unable to obtain Judah's support in a new anti-Syrian alliance, entered Jerusalem to install their own representative on the throne. Against the advice of the Prophet Isaiah, Judah turned to the powerful Assyrian King, Tiglath-Pilezer III, who took the opportunity to invade and divide

Isra'il into three administrative areas. Further rebellion in Isra'il resulted in the succeeding kings – Shalmaneser V, and his successor, Sargon II – administering Isra'il as an Assyrian province. Despite Judah not being administered by the Assyrians, it too rebelled against them after Sargon II died. His successor, Sennacherib, waited four years before mounting a punitive expedition. His forces entered Judah in 701 BCE, captured 46 towns and demanded the surrender of Jerusalem. No record exists of how the campaign ended, but even though Judah's submission was complete, Jerusalem was apparently not destroyed.

In 633 BCE, when the Assyrian King Ashur-Banipal died, the Assyrian empire crumbled and Judah, under Josiah, began again to expand. Within 20 years, Isra'il and Judah had been united under this powerful ruler. Strife with Egypt and Babylon continued until Pharaoh Nech II gained victory to rule Judah for four years via his puppet, King Jehoiakim. When the Neo-Babylonian ruler Nebuchadnezzar conquered Judah in 597 BCE, he exiled its aristocrats and craftsmen to Babylon and left his puppet, King Zedekiah, to rule. A rebellion ensued which resulted in one city after another being sacked throughout Judah. Jerusalem, captured in 587 BCE, was razed to the ground. The citizens who survived and who were not farmers, were exiled to Babylon. Devastation was complete, and the area remained in ruins for years.

In 332 BCE Alexander the Great conquered Palestine. At his death in 323 BCE, his leading generals, Ptolemy and Seleucus, struggled for control over the conquered lands. Ptolemy acquired Egypt, Palestine and part of Syria, a domination which lasted from 301 until 200 BCE when the Seleucid king Antiochus III (223–187 BCE), gained mastery over the entire area. That kingdom ended when the last great Seleucid king, Antiochus Sidetes, died in 129 BCE.

The Roman commander Pompey arrived in Syria in 64 BCE, at a time of political instability in what was by then referred to as Judea. It was inevitable that one or other of the disputing parties would sooner or later appeal to him for support; thus, by 63 BCE, the whole of Judea was absorbed by the Roman republic. Julius Caesar, who ruled there between 45 and 44 BCE, permitted the walls of Jerusalem to be rebuilt and restored the port of Jaffa to Judea. However, when the Parthians attacked the Romans in Syria, the Jews took the opportunity to revolt against Roman rule. Rome ultimately routed the Parthians and in 37 BCE regained Jerusalem. Even so, they took considerable pains to respect the religious feelings of the Jews and granted Agrippa (Herod's grandson) great influence in Rome. They bestowed on him the title King Agrippa I and granted him the right to rule Judea until his death (in 44 CE).

Allah explains in Ayah 6 how, after He had abased and humiliated the Children of Isra'il, they repented and rectified their behaviour. It is a rule that those who undertake good deeds benefit themselves, and those who commit evil harm themselves. And it is also apparent from Ayah 6 that the Children of Isra'il repented and were released from captivity and further humiliation and gradually were able again to increase their wealth and offspring.

Arrogance of the Pharisees

At a certain time of Jewish history a segment of society known as Pharisees – a religious party or school of up to 7,000 Jews – had become a major force and held great political power. Christian sources report them as ambitious, arrogant, proudly self-righteous and only interested in promoting their own material ends. While there are numerous reports in the Gospels of Jesus – 'Isa 🕮 – castigating the Pharisees, we only include a few from the Gospel according to St Matthew:

13 But woe unto you, scribes and Pharisees, hypocrites! for ye shut up the kingdom of heaven against men: for ye neither go in *yourselves*, neither suffer ye them that are entering to go in.

14 Woe unto you, scribes and Pharisees, hypocrites! for ye devour widows, houses, and for a pretence make long prayer: therefore ye shall receive the greater damnation.

15 Woe unto you, scribes and Pharisees, hypocrites! for ye compass sea and land to make one proselyte, and when he is made, ye make him twofold more the child of hell than yourselves.

23 Woe unto you, scribes and Pharisees, hypocrites! for ye pay tithe of mint and anise and cummin and have omitted the weightier *matters* of the law, judgment, mercy, and faith: these ought ye to have done, and not to leave the other undone.

24 *Ye* blind guides, which strain at a gnat, and swallow a camel.

25 Woe unto you, scribes and Pharisees, hypocrites! for ye make clean the outside of the cup and of the platter, but within they are full of extortion and excess.

27 Woe unto you, scribes and Pharisees, hypocrites! for ye are like unto whited sepulchres, which indeed appear beautiful outward, but are within full of dead *men's* bones, and of all uncleanness.

28 Even so ye also outwardly appear righteous unto men, but within ye are full of hypocrisy and iniquity.

29 Woe unto you, scribes and Pharisees, hypocrites! because ye build the tombs of the prophets, and garnish the sepulchres of the righteous,

30 And say, If we had been in the days of our fathers, we would not have been partakers with them in the blood of the prophets.

Matthew Chapter 23

The Pharisees encouraged 'zealot' action with laments that Judea was now only one of the many provinces under Rome and no longer an independent nation of 'chosen people'. They roused antagonisms over a foreign army being based on Judean soil, over Roman support for ethnic Greek and Syrian citizens, about being obliged to honour loan contracts and being taxed by Rome. As a consequence, zealots set administrative archives alight in an attempt to destroy the contractual evidence of loan contracts, terrorised the upper classes and waged guerrilla war against Rome.

In 67 CE Emperor Vespatian entered Galilee with his army. By 70 CE his son Titus had overcome Jerusalem and razed its temple. By 73 CE Massada, the final stronghold of revolt, fell to Rome and the whole area was under Roman control. Tens of thousands had been killed, tens of thousands taken captive and tens of thousands had been resettled. Rome administered this area in the same way it did all of its imperial provinces and, for the next 60 years tranquillity reigned.

However, revolts against Rome again broke out in 132 to 135 CE when Emperor Hadrian decided to rebuild Jerusalem as Aelia Capitolina, to erect a temple to Jupiter there and to institute anti-mutilation laws forbiding circumcision. After rebels captured Jerusalem and destroyed a complete Roman legion, Rome decimated 50 fortresses, 985 villages and killed 580,000 men, to end Judea's era as a centre of Jewish population.

It may well be that the first humiliating punishment and destruction referred to in the Qur'an alludes to the year 597 BCE when the Temple in Jerusalem was completely destroyed by Nebuchadnezzar, and the second to the decimation by Rome in 135 CE, but none should forget Ayat 8, 'It may be that your Lord will show you mercy, but when you return to disobedience His chastisement will follow. In the afterlife, Hell will confine all those who reject faith'.

Contemporary Arrogance

In his book *Nothing Sacred: The Truth About Judaism* (ISBN 0-609-61094-5, Crown, New York, 2003) Douglas Rushkoff, Professor of Communications at New York University, writes that the disparaging notion of a 'Jewish race', made in the Bible by Pharaoh and later articulated by the Spanish Inquisition and the Third Reich, has for years been assiduously promoted by the Zionist propaganda machine. Zionists understood that the more dire their depiction of the affairs of the 'Jewish race' in Palestine, the more generous the donations from Jews in the Diaspora would become.

Their success was so great that by the 1970s, American Reform Jewish Schools and synagogues, of the type that Douglas Rushkoff had attended, concentrated on Zionism and the benefits of marrying within the faith, rather than on Jewish religious education. He is, thus, not surprised that Jewish culture is currently expressed through support for and donations to Zionist causes, rather than by any quest for spiritual nourishment and fulfilment.

He says that arid, politically centred education has led many Jews to eschew religion completely or, if seeking connection to something greater than the self, to turn to other religions. This situation apparently was confirmed in November 2002 when the annual conference of the United Jewish Communities, an umbrella group of Jewish federations and communities, warned that as Judaism in America is now so imperilled by ageing population, rampant intermarriage, low birth rates and declining synagogue membership, they would not publish the findings of their current ten-year survey.

It would appear that a by-product of the Zionist hatred of Arabs, expressed through unashamed humiliation and attempts to destroy the Palestinian peoples, has resulted in a decrease in the number of practising Jews. Is this a Divine warning and a reminder?

From the letter below, it is clear that Britain adopted the Zionist project and supported the establishment of a national home for Jewish people in Palestine. However, it betrayed its promise of freedom and independence to the Arabs under the leadership of Sharif Husayn, by dividing the areas of influence in Sham and Iraq between itself and France. Britain gained control of Palestine according to the San Remo Agreement (April 1920) and managed to include 'The Balfour Declaration' in the mandate for Palestine granted by the League of Nations in July 1922.

The text of the letter below, from Arthur James Balfour, 1st Earl of Balfour, British Foreign Secretary (1916–19), to Lionel Walter Rothschild, 2nd Baron Rothschild, a leader of British Jewry, is referred to as 'The Balfour Declaration':

> Foreign Office
>
> November 2nd, 1917
>
> Dear Lord Rothschild,
>
> I have much pleasure in conveying to you, on behalf of His Majesty's Government, the following declaration of sympathy with Jewish Zionist aspirations which has been submitted to, and approved by, the Cabinet.
>
> "His Majesty's Government view with favour the establishment in Palestine of a national home for the Jewish people, and will use their best endeavours to facilitate the achievement of this objective, it being clearly understood that nothing

shall be done which may prejudice the civil and religious rights of existing non-Jewish communities in Palestine, or the rights and political status enjoyed by Jews in any other country."

I should be grateful if you would bring this declaration to the knowledge of the Zionist Federation.

Yours truly,

Balfour

A sequence of events linked to Jerusalem

3000–2500 BCE	Canaanites migrate to Palestine
1900–1850 BCE	The Prophet Ibrahim ﷺ migrates from Ur to Palestine
1720 BCE	The Children of Yaqub (Jacob) migrate to Egypt from Palestine
1304–1237 BCE	The reign of the Pharaoh Ramses II of Egypt in whose time the Children of Isra'il left Egypt under the leadership of the Prophet Mūsa ﷺ
1010–791 BCE	The reign of Dawud ﷺ as king over the Children of Isra'il
597 BCE	Nebuchadnezzar (also known as Nebuchadrezzar II and Nabuchodonosor) conquers the kingdom of Judah and, in 597, 587 and 583 BCE, deports the 'Children of Isra'il'
539 BCE	The Persian Emperor Creusus conquers Babylon in Iraq and permits the Jews to return to Jerusalem to rebuild their temple
165 BCE	Jews in Palestine are forced to desert Judaism for Greek gods
70 BCE–476 CE	The period of the Roman Empire
63 BCE	The Roman leader Pompey conquers Jerusalem and places Palestine under the Syrian Governor
66 CE	The Jews rebel against the Romans
70 CE	Romans conquer Jerusalem and disperse its population
135 CE	Emperor Hadrian totally destroys Jerusalem to build a new city, which he names 'Aelia Capitolina'
313 CE	Emperor Constantine permits Christian worship throughout his empire
323 CE	The Assembly of Nicea
324–638 CE	The Byzantine era
326 CE	Queen Helena visits Jerusalem and builds the Church of The Holy Sepulchre

527–565 CE	Emperor Justinian builds the famous 'Golden Gate', which remains known by that name to this day, and a Church on the site of the 'Farthest Mosque'
614 CE	The Persian Emperor Parvees conquers Syria and Palestine and demolishes many churches including Constantine's Church of the Resurrection
628 CE	Emperor Hercules' victory over the Persians and re-conquest of Syria and Palestine
638–1099 CE	The Muslim period: this commences after the Caliph Umar enters Jerusalem
1099–1187 CE	The Crusader Kingdom of Jerusalem
1187 CE	Salah al-Din defeats the Crusaders and recaptures Jerusalem
1517 – 1917 CE	The Ottoman Empire controls Jerusalem
1917 CE	The Balfour Declaration, followed by General Allenby's entry into Jerusalem, results in British occupation
1948 CE	End of British Mandate: the State of Isra'il is proclaimed
December 13, 1949	The City of Jerusalem declared capital of the Isra'ili state
June, 1967	Six Day War – Isra'il occupies the West Bank
July 21, 1967	Isra'ilis burn part of the Al-Aqsa Mosque
November 15, 1988	The Proclamation of the State of Palestine by the 'Palestinian Liberation Organisation' (PLO)
October 18, 1990	The massacre of worshippers within Al-Aqsa Mosque
2003	Genocide of the Arab population which continues unabated

3 Comprehensive guidance of the Qur'an

9. This Qur'an guides human beings towards ethical and principled behaviour and confirms that those who believe and do good will receive generous rewards.

10. And it warns of the painful torment that awaits those who deny the 'hereafter'.

The Holy Qur'an is a comprehensive book of guidance which offers inexhaustible illumination for the hearts of humanity to reflect, like myriad mirrors, the Might and Beauty of the Almighty. The Holy Qur'an is the only Divine revelation to provide a truly comprehensive range of sophisticated methodologies by which to ensure success and prosperity in the life to come.

Allah provides guidance at every level, from the basic needs of insects to the highest aspirations of humanity. When Pharaoh asked Mūsa ﷺ and his brother Harūn ﷺ, 'Who is your Lord, O Mūsa?' Mūsa replied, 'Our Lord is He who has created everything, and guided it aright'. (*See* Qur'an 20:50) While for insects the most fundamental guidance is sufficient to achieve the peak of their success (*See* Qur'an 16:68–9), it is only through continuous awareness and striving that human beings may attain their highest level, namely meeting their Lord. (*See* Qur'an 84:6)

Imam ʿAli ﷺ describes the comprehensive guidance in the Qur'an as follows,

> The Qur'an is an advisor who never deceives, a leader who never misleads and a narrator who never lies. No one reads the Qur'an without achieving an addition or dimunition. Addition in respect of guidance or diminution in respect of spiritual blindness. You should also know that no one needs anything after being guided by the Qur'an and that no one is free from want before they are guided by the Qur'an. Therefore, seek from it the cure for your ailments and its assistance in your distress. There is nothing like it to turn people toward Allah the Sublime.
>
> It is an intercessor whose intercession will be accepted. On the Day of Judgement the announcement will be made, 'Beware, every sower of a crop is in distress other than those who have sown the teachings of the Qur'an in their hearts; it is they alone who will draw benefit'.

Nahj al-Balagha, Sermon 176

11. Human beings frequently pray for things that are bad for them, in the mistaken belief that they are asking for something good. They are often hasty [in their judgements].

Many people seek only immediate gratification or advantage and do not consider possible consequences of their actions. When overwhelmed by their egos' desires, like spoilt children who crave the things that parents wisely withhold from them, they readily pray for that which might harm them or be forbidden. Any subsequent dismay is manifest by outbursts of angry emotion.

According to many 'ahadith', hasty decisions are to be avoided whenever possible. Some even describe hasty decisions or actions as the work of Satan – Shaytan.

12. Night and day are but signs of Our Omnipotence. The night cloaked in darkness [so that you can rest], the day illuminated [so that you can] seek the bounty of your Lord and calculate the passage of time. All is made clear [for you].

The reference to night and day, immediately after the previous ayah's reference to the disadvantages of being hasty, may be explained in the following two ways:

1) Those who are inclined to make impetuous decisions illustrate a degree of immaturity, instability, or inability to reflect. On the other hand, those who consider their opinions and the consequences of their actions, show themselves as being reliable and trustworthy. However, circumstances do frequently change, as is illustrated by the sequence of day and night.

and

2) As previous ayat elaborate on Allah's ultimate guidance in the Qur'an, this example – by drawing attention to the complexity in the creation of the world, the solar system, and the effect that the sequence of day and night have – serves to exemplify both His Omnipotence and the advantages in considering the consequences of actions.

13. We have tied the destiny of human beings around their own necks and will, on the 'Day of Resurrection', produce an open record for them.

On the Day of Judgement He will take into account the way in which you yourself choose to assess the auspiciousness of forthcoming events. There is no compulsion or determinism in Islam. Everyone is held to be fully responsible for their own actions. These are recorded 'in a book', from which each person will have their own deeds presented to them on the Day of Reckoning.

We have translated the word 'ṭair' in the above ayah as 'Destiny', despite it being the word for 'bird' in the Arabic language. The link between bird and destiny in this Ayah came about as the result of pre-Islamic beliefs that the examination of bird entrails could indicate proposed actions to be propitious or not. The Arab peoples in particular made such predictions by observing the movement of birds.

14. [And will tell them] 'Read, and let your soul be its own judge'.

The commentary on this ayah is to be found under heading number eight, 'The Restoration of Life' (*see* p. 90).

4 Benefits of Divine guidance

15. Those who seek Allah's guidance benefit their souls. Those who go astray suffer the consequences themselves. Each has its own burden to bear. But We do not punish those to whom We have not sent a Messenger [with warnings].

This ayah clarifies three important concepts:

1) Those who go astray suffer as the result. One of Allah's Most Beautiful Names is The Self-Sufficient – Al-Ghanī. This underlines that no benefit or harm reflect on Him as the result of the obedience and worship of human beings, nor can the results of their disobedience affect Him. The Messengers of Allah called upon people to come to the 'Right Path'; those who do not listen and are determined to go their own way must themselves suffer the results of their choice.
2) Everyone must bear his/her own burden. This is only just as none can be expected to be accountable for the actions of another.
3) Allah always sends timely warnings, so none can claim to have acted in ignorance. This is what is meant by 'No chastisement before raising a messenger'.

Thus, in principles of jurisprudence, when a jurist – 'faqih' – is faced with a subject not mentioned in either the Qur'an or the ahadith, when permissibility and non-permissibility may be equally valid, most jurists tend to conclude that the subject is permissible.

Jurists hold the view that any injunction which overrules basic presumptions of permissability must be decisive in both meaning and transmission. It follows that unless an authentic text conveys a decisive prohibition, the act is permissable. Allah Almighty has clearly explained His prohibitions and there is no need for jurists to add to these by personal deduction. Thus, unless Allah or His Messenger ﷺ have decreed something forbidden, it is correct to conclude that they are not forbidden. This principle of permissability applies to both acts of worship and to transactions.

Allah tells us in the Qur'an:

> It is He who created for you all that is on the earth.
>
> Qur'an 2:29

> We have created for your benefit all that is in the heavens and earth.
>
> Qur'an 45:13

> Allah has provided detailed clarification of all that He has forbidden [which is binding upon you] except in the most dire of circumstances.
>
> Qur'an 6:119

Why were earlier peoples destroyed?

> **16. [When this has been done], if communities reject guidance and lose themselves in immoderate behaviour, We warn them to return to obedience before [if they decline to desist] We determine to destroy them completely.**
>
> **17. And We have destroyed many generations since Nūh's time! Only your Lord sees and fully comprehends His creatures' sins.**
>
> **18. Some seek only to indulge in the instant pleasures of this fleeting life. And We readily grant as much of those to whichever of them We please, but in the end, they are consigned to endure the suffering and disgrace of Hell.**
>
> **19. However, true believers – those who strive for [the good of] the life to come – will find favour with their Lord.**

The Holy Qur'an frequently links incidences with conditional phraseology, *viz.*, when A happens, B will follow. This underlines the consequences of not following what is specified in the Qur'an and, in other circumstances, to not anticipate results that cannot be rationally expected. Here are some examples from the Qur'an:

> Truly Allah does not change the condition of people until they change themselves.
>
> Qur'an, 13:11

1) Unless people themselves change their attitudes and ways, Allah will not improve their situations. Thus, if society determines to improve anything it must strive to actually do that, and not just state that desire, do nothing and hope for miracles.

   If they remain steadfastly on the Right Path, We will certainly provide them with water [sustenance] in abundance.

   Qur'an 72:16

2) The wealth of a society is related to social justice. That is, if a society desires A, it must observe B, namely promote the means to achieve A and pay the political dues necessary to effect that change.

   They indulged themselves extravagantly and persisted in heinous sins claiming, 'What, when we die and become dust and bones, will we then be raised again?'

   Qur'an 56:44–47

3) Surat al-Waqi'ah – Qur'an 56 – provides a clear link between '. . . those on the left hand and their suffering' because of their deeds and actions.

The method used in the Qur'an is to indicate that if people are not happy with the consequences of actions they should avoid them. That is what Allah has decreed for His creation and clarified in Ayat 16 and 17 of this Surah. When people leave His path of guidance and indulge in immoral behaviour, they cannot claim not to have been made aware of the warning in these ayat.

5 Everyone benefits from Allah's unrestricted generosity

20. But it is possible for the former, as well as the latter [hedonists as well as believers], to draw benefit from Divine Generosity without constraint.

21. Observe how [on earth], some receive more and achieve higher status than others – but positions in the hereafter will be superior and levels of excellence incomparably greater.

Allah, the Ultimate Provider, does not reserve His grace and bounty exclusively for those who believe in Him and obey Him. His unrestricted generosity covers all of humanity. This is what is meant by 'true' generosity.

Allah permits everyone to act with free will, to do good or bad. He has given us the ability to think and to use our physical and mental abilities as we wish. Therefore, responsibility for the consequences of our actions is ours and ours alone. Allah does not prevent anyone from fulfilling their unlimited worldly desires, but advises us to be mindful of the consequences of pursuing such a course. On the other hand, those who desire and strive for the hereafter will attain their objective and benefit from the reward of their Lord. In this ayah, two elements are essential: a) to be a believer; and b) to strive for Allah's everlasting reward.

Allah has no associates

22. Worship no Divinity other than Allah so that you are not reproved and forsaken.

In the Days of Ignorance – 'Jahiliyyah' – people worshipped idols in the belief that they would derive some benefit from them. A visit to Roman or Greek archaeological sites will indicate the assortment of 'gods' to whom appeals were made in various circumstances. Despite clear Divine indications about the harm and falseness of such beliefs, vestiges continue to exist, for example, in the concept of 'Trinity'. It is not always clear in the New Testament who is being referred to – The Father, the Son or the Holy Ghost or a combination of the three. Yet in other places there is clarity, e.g., in the Son praying to the Father.

Islam makes it clear that God begets not nor is He begotten. To associate anyone with Allah is considered the greatest sin, the only sin for which no forgiveness is granted. Creation is the act of Allah alone. He is the Bestower of Life and the Ordainer of Death. He is the

Sustainer and Provider. It is He who cures all ailments, be that through the medium of a physician. Reliance on Him is the ultimate means for our salvation. Those who concentrate on 'natural causes' do not comprehend that nature has been created by Him and that 'natural causes' merely reflect His authority and will.

(Further commentary is found under heading number seven, 'Allah's Oneness': *see* p.82.)

6 Socio-ethical ordinances

6.1 Parental rights

> **23. For your Lord has ordered you not to worship any except Him. He also commanded you to be good to your parents. Should either or both of them reach old age and need care, do not behave irritably or reproach and reject them but always respond to them gently.**
>
> **24. Treat them with humility and tenderness praying, 'Lord be merciful to them, as they were to me when I was little'.**
>
> **25. Your Lord is aware of what is in your heart and how you behave [towards His Creation]. He is All-Forgiving to those who repent.**

Here, as well as in Ayah 151 of Surah 6, Allah Almighty links His order not to worship any other than Him with His command to treat parents well.

> Come, I will clarify what Allah really prohibits: do not associate anyone or anything with Him; and be good to your parents . . .
>
> Qur'an 6:151

Linking these commands clearly emphasises the significance of parental rights. The assertion 'Allah is Divine' separates atheist from Muslim, as does obedience to heavenly injunctions, such as being good to parents.

A sound society is based upon parents remaining responsible for the education and nurture of their offspring. This is balanced by the reciprocal responsibility of children being good to their parents.

The Qur'anic expression – 'lower the wing of humility' – implies compliance and acceptance of the will of another. The analogy of a bird lowering its wings to conceal and protect its offspring is used to illustrate tender, caring treatment, the tenor of behaviour which parents who are old most need. When we respond with gentleness, we ensure we do not express any irritation which might upset our ageing parents, no matter how they themselves may behave in their dotage.

Many ahadith emphasise the need for patience and kindness towards parents, beautifully expressed by Imam ʿAli ibn Hussayn ﷺ in the du'a:

> O Allah, fill me with an awe of my parents like the awe with which people hold tyrannical sovereigns; let me be devoted to them with the devotion of a compassionate mother!
>
> Make my obedience and commitment to them more pleasing to me than sleep to the drowsy, more refreshing than drink to the thirsty; so that I prefer their inclination over mine.
>
> O Allah, thank them for my upbringing, reward them for their kindness, and protect them as they protected me in my infancy.

The Psalms of Islam, Prayer number 24

In considering the degree of parental duty to mature children, jurists have debated if a father's responsibility extends to making decisions regarding his son's property. Some conclude that no limit exists to a father's complete authority over his offspring. They base their conclusion on the hadith, 'You and your property belong to your father'. However, we understand this to relate to ethical values and not any civil laws concerning ownership.

During the daily formal prayers – 'ṣalat' – we are recommended, standing in submission to Allah – Qunut – to request: 'O Lord, be merciful to my parents as they were to me in infancy'. It is highly recommended that gratitude towards parents continues to be expressed even after they have died. After that time Muslims should beg Allah to shower their parents' souls with His mercy. We take comfort in the belief that prayers, which Allah has specifically ordered us to offer, will indeed be accepted by Him.

6.2 Charity

> **26. Give close relatives what they are entitled to, and be generous to travellers in need and the poor; however, do not fritter your wealth away.**
>
> **27. Those who squander resources are, like Satan, ungrateful to the Lord [for what He has provided].**

The generic term 'charity' – generosity (as opposed to miserliness) and spending in the way of Allah (aid to those in need) – are mentioned in the Qur'an in a variety of places. One of these encourages charitable acts by telling us that Allah considers them to be 'loans from us for which He Himself has applied' this, despite emphasis in Islamic theology that Allah is beyond need and indeed has none. He is self-subsistent, His creatures depend on Him, and that the whole of humanity needs His succour. This encourages everyone, but especially the self-centred, to purify themselves and their wealth through acts of giving.

In the Holy Qur'an, Allah provides a beautiful illustration of the recompense for 'spending in the way of Allah'. He tells us that the reward for giving is 700 times greater than that which was given (Qur'an 2:261). Those not willing to give freely are encouraged to provide interest-free loans. However, He reminds us in the Qur'an that He will increase our charity and destroy any loans based upon interest (Qur'an 2:276). An authentic hadith relates that, 'At the entrance of paradise the reward for giving charitably is recorded as being ten units, while the reward for interest-free loans is eighteen units'. When Imam Sadiq ﵇ was asked to explain this difference, he responded by saying that while alms might be received by those in need, loans are only sought by those whose situation is truly dire. The greater reward emphasises the virtue of helping the desperate.

The following ahadith are only a few of the references to confirm the significance of being of assistance to others:

> The Prophet ﷺ said, 'Generosity is a tree of Paradise whose branches extend into this life. Those who are generous are holding a branch which leads to Paradise'.
>
> Bihar al Anwar, Vol. 8, p. 171
>
> Kanz ul-Uma'al, Tradition, number 15926

> The Prophet ﷺ said to Adii, son of Hatam al-Tai, [a non-Muslim from the Jahiliyyah who was renowned for his generosity], 'The severest punishment was removed from your father because of his generosity'.
>
> Bihar al Anwar, Vol. 71, p. 354

> The Prophet ﷺ said, 'A young, generous, good-natured person is more loved by Allah than a mean, bad-tempered, elderly worshipper'.
>
> Kanz ul-Uma'al, Tradition, number 16061

> The Prophet ﷺ said, 'Food offered by the generous is a remedy, but food offered by those who are mean generates discomfort'.
>
> Bihar al Anwar, Vol. 71, p. 357

> The Prophet ﷺ said, 'Ignore the faults of the generous because whenever they fall Allah picks them up'.
>
> Kanz ul-Uma'al, Tradition, number 16213

Imam 'Ali and Imam Ṣadiq ﷺ say the same thing in two different ahadith, 'Generosity is evidenced when nothing is requested, the yield from begging evidences embarrassment, not generosity'.

Bihar al Anwar, Vol. 71, p. 357

Commentary on Nahj al-Balaghah, Vol. 18, p. 184

Imam 'Ali ﷺ said, 'The most worthy people in this life are those who are generous; in the life to come, it will be those who were pious'.

Ghorar al-Hikam

Imam Ṣadiq ﷺ said, 'The best amongst you are those who are generous, the worst, those who are mean'.

Bihar al Anwar, Vol. 71, p. 350

Imam Ṣadiq ﷺ said, 'Generosity, the habit of prophets, is a pillar of faith. Those who truly believe are generous'.

Bihar al Anwar, Vol. 73, p. 169

Subsequent to the wonderous occasion of the Prophet's ascension towards the Sublime, he told what he saw once the curtains of materialism had been drawn from before his eyes,

> . . . I saw two angels speaking loudly to the heavens. One said, 'O Allah, give in abundance to those who give', the other said, 'O Allah, bring ruin upon the miserly'.

Jami' Al-S'aadat, Vol. 2, p. 113

28. But if [your current situation is such that you are not able to assist people], because you yourself are in need of your Lord's support, decline their request with kind words and compassion.

29. Do not be miserly and worthy of reproach, nor be so generous that you become destitute.

30. Your Lord sees and is aware of His servants' needs. He showers some with abundance, yet limits the resources of others as He wills.

In the Ayat 26 to 30 of this Surah, Allah orders Muslims to give charity to their relatives, the needy and the traveller. He forbids immoderate spending, considering squanderers to be 'brothers of Satan' because, like him, they place little value on that which is provided. However, those in need who are unable to assist others, should themselves seek Allah's mercy and decline requests for charity with kindness and compassion. Moderation in all things is both recommended and approved.

6.3 Infanticide

> **31. Do not let fear of poverty induce you to murder your children, for We will provide for both you and for them. It is wicked to kill them.**

When the mainly pastoral pre-Islamic Arabs, who frequently suffered droughts and food shortage, anticipated a dry year, they were inclined to kill new-born children rather than to let them suffer. Some historians refer to the burial of girls, mentioned in Surah al-Nahl,

> When news was brought to one of them that a female had been born, his face would darken and fill with grief and shame. Should he retain that contemptuous package or bury it in the dust.

Qur'an 16:59

Infanticide, categorised as murder, will be covered later to underscore just how wicked a sin it is! Allah Almighty tells those who fear poverty that He will provide for them and for their dependants. (This is covered under heading number five: 'Everyone benefits from Allah's unrestricted generosity': *see* p. 60.)

6.4 Adultery

> **32. Do not have sexual relationships outside marriage because that is improper and withholds honour.**

The Almighty Creator provided human beings with specialised organs to reproduce and perpetuate life on earth. The desire to procreate belongs as much to parental love and preoccupation as to Allah's plan to secure life. Sex is a natural need of both men and women. However, Allah prohibits all sexual relationships outside marriage, describing them as improper, indecent and an evil way to gratify sexual urges.

All civilised societies have encouraged the legal sanction of marriage and condemned unfettered expressions of sexuality. Despite contemporary acceptance of both heterosexual and homosexual promiscuity, concern is still expressed over steeply rising rates of childhood pregnancy, births out of wedlock and venereal diseases such as HIV Aids.

The international conference in Beijing in the 1990s unfortunately tended to ignore family ties and the morality of sexual relationships, with attendees appearing rather to encourage unrestricted sexual relations between people. Despite this, the time will come when exceedingly high rates of divorce, rape and abortion will endanger society as we know it. Divine religions once shared a common reaction to adultery; both the old and the new testaments prohibited it. In Islam it is still regarded a major sin, liable to severe punishments.

6.5 Murder

> **33. Do not take life [which Allah has decreed sacred], other than in the legitimate pursuit of justice. The heirs of those who have been unjustly slain are authorised to extract lawful retribution, but not more than that.**

The first murder on earth recorded in the Qur'an was of Adam's son Abel – Hābil, killed by his brother Cain – Kabil. The younger Hābil is described as innocent and righteous. The elder Kabil as having been driven to murder by his jealous and arrogant nature. At the end of the story Allah tells us, 'On that occasion We told the Children of Isra'il that the slaying of another is tantamount to slaying all of humanity unless that is done in retribution or to halt anarchy and treason' – 'the spread of mischief in the land'. The issue of retaliation is discussed in *Al-Mizan*, Vol. 2, p. 327–33.

However, life is a gift of the Creator to His creatures and none are permitted to take it.

6.6 Orphans

> **34. Safeguard the property of orphans until they have attained maturity. ...**

Allah tells us in the Qur'an that those who unjustly swallow the property of orphans are indeed ingesting the fire that will soon envelop them. (A reference to Qur'an 4:10)

This is one of the ayat that prove 'the embodiment of deeds' – Tajassum al-'Amal. It indicates that all human activity is ultimately destined to be transformed into appropriate physical forms. Our generosity, forgiveness, justice and fairness towards others on earth will, in our graves, be manifested by flowers, beautiful scenery and pleasant scents. However, jealousy, backbiting and ill will towards others will be manifested by snakes and scorpions, which will accompany us. In one hadith it is related that, 'All remembrance of Allah, recitation of His Most Beautiful Names and sincere and devoted glorification of Him, will be evidenced by bricks of gold and silver, the material from which angels will build castles in paradise for us'. (*Al-Mizan,* Vol. 7, p. 379). With good deeds balanced against bad, we are led to understand that jealousy consumes good deeds in the same way that fire consumes wood. Thus, usurping the property of an orphan is described as feeding on fire rather than on food.

A lady came to the Prophet ﷺ saying, 'O Messenger of Allah, my husband died leaving me and his daughter, but we did not inherit a thing'. The deceased's brother said, 'O Messenger of Allah, how can she expect to inherit from him when she neither rides a horse, attacks her enemies, nor earns. What she needs, others have to give her?' It was in response to this that the above ayah was revealed. (The Ideal Muslimah p. 249)

Islamic jurisprudence comprehensively covers the guardianship of minors, including orphans. Guardians are obliged to continue to support orphans in their care until they reach physical and spiritual maturity and become competent to deal with their own property .

6.7 Promises

34. (Cont'd). . . . Remain true to your word for you are accountable.

The fulfilment of promises is a sign of maturity, honour and self-respect. In Islamic theology people are accountable for being true to their word. Those not able to fulfil promises should refrain from making them, particularly in dealing with their offspring. Parents who do not fulfil their promises deny their children good exemplars and this has a lasting and detrimental effect on their spiritual and moral development. Pledges made to both Allah and human beings are considered to be legally binding.

6.8 Honesty in measurement

35. [Be just!] Always give full measure and weigh with accurate scales, for to do so is better for you in the long run.

Islam orders honesty in every aspect of life. Allah's final Messenger ﷺ was renowned for being trustworthy and truthful, even prior to receiving Revelation. All Muslims should adhere to their limits and not take that which does not belong to them. This ayah emphasises the need for honesty.

6.9 Blind following

36. Remembering that you are [ultimately] accountable [for your actions], use [your faculties] of sight, hearing and intellect to appraise [the value of] advice before you follow it.

Allah gave us means to analyse and distinguish between good and bad. In matters relating to belief, we should arrive at our own conclusion and seek our own proofs. The Holy Qur'an condemns those who, when asked about their beliefs, answer, 'We are following what our ancestors did'. It is important for Muslims to remain aware of what they do for We all are to be held accountable for every decision made during life.

6.10 Arrogance

37. Do not strut the earth in triumph and arrogance. You can neither tear it apart nor match the grandeur of its mountains.

38. Avoid these evils for the wickedness of such things is odious in the sight of your Lord.

Arrogance leads to enmity. People need to express mutual respect for one another as everyone is created equal, regardless of social standing and wealth. This ayah warns the arrogant that whatever they might think about their superiority, they are still restricted by the laws of nature and the laws of man, in addition to Divine ruling. Arrogance is derived from egotism and a false understanding of superiority. It was arrogance that caused Iblis, a highly designated being, to be banished from Allah's Mercy.

Realisation that life starts with an insignificant spermatazoa and ends as sustenance for worms should be a sufficient reminder to prick anyone's pomposity.

7 Allah's 'Oneness'

39. These are but examples of the wisdom your Lord revealed to you, but [even more importantly] worship Allah only or face being cast, guilty and rejected, into Hell.

40. Has your Lord given you sons but created daughters in the form of angels for Himself? This is certainly a monstrous claim you make!

41. Despite Our repeated explanation of its various aspects, this Qur'an has not increased any awareness in them other than their own aversion to it.

42. Say [O Muḥammad], 'If there are other divinities, as they assert, they would have been able to manifest the [nature] of the Lord of the Throne'.

After the forbidden acts He mentioned in previous ayat, Allah emphasises that they are all disliked 'in the view of your Lord' by stating that this is indeed the wisdom He has revealed to His Messenger. Therefore, do not associate divinity with anything other than Allah or you will be reproached and banished.

In Ayah 40, Allah tells the Makkan idolaters who conjectured that angels were Allah's daughters that theirs is certainly a monstrous claim. The ayat go on to stress that there is only one true Divinity. If any of the gods of polytheism were endowed with power, would they not have tried to contend for Lordship of the Throne and have their own wills executed?

In Islamic theology, when believers set out in the direction of the Absolute Existent, they leave dependent finite existence. When they utter the formula of 'tawhid', turn from Contingent Existence to behold Necessary Existence, they liberate themselves of every aspect of associating partners with Allah – 'shirk'. For with the affirmation of the Oneness of Allah, they become beings of spiritual realisation with both inward and outward aspects purified.

Allah tells us in the Holy Qur'an that shirk is not forgivable,

> Surely Allah does not forgive those who associate any being with Him. Other than that, He forgives whomever He pleases . . .
>
> Qur'an 4:48

Many scholars such as Sayyid Haidar Amuli, in his book, *Inner Secrets of the Path*, present varying levels of awareness of Divine Unity – 'tawḥid'.

The First Level of Tawḥid

At its simplest, tawḥid is the rejection of many deities for the affirmation of one Divinity. Expressed in other words, the rejection of finite deities for the affirmation of One Absolute and Infinite Divinity. This level of tawḥid has two aspects: one associated with people who follow those who are more learned than themselves in matters of religion, the other, associated with people of perception and the facility of intellectual reasoning.

The former's way is to believe that God is One, that there is no associate to His Divinity; none to rival Him or equal Him in existence; none like the One Who hears, the One Who sees. They strongly hold to this belief, conscious that Allah tells them in the Qur'an:

> If there are other divinities as they assert, these would have been able to manifest the [nature] of the Lord of the Throne.
>
> Qur'an 17:42

and

> Say! Allah is One. Allah is He on Whom all depend. He begets not, nor is He begotten. And there is none like Him.
>
> Qur'an 112:1–4

They believe He is Omnipresent, Omniscient, Omnipotent, the One who hears, sees and wills, the One who is the Possessor of Speech. They believe that,

> Not the weight of an atom escapes His knowledge in the heavens or on the earth.
>
> Qur'an 34:3

They believe that those claimed to be gods other than Him, are merely idols who,

> . . . do not in themselves cause harm or profit nor do they control death or life.
>
> Qur'an 25:3

They believe that they are obliged not to associate with those who do not believe, for Allah Himself says:

> O you who believe! If they prefer unbelief over belief, do not take fathers and brothers for guardians, for those who accept these as guardians are unjust.
>
> Qur'an 9:23

> You will not find people who believe in Allah and the last day who maintain relations with those who oppose Allah and His Messenger, even if they are their [own] fathers, sons, brothers, or kinsfolk.
>
> Qur'an 58:22

Those who believe live within the protection of Islam, secure their wealth and honour in this world and safeguard themselves from their ego's desires. In the next world they will be rewarded with the generosity and mercy of Allah, for He is truly the Possessor of vast bounty.

The latter – the tawḥid of reasoning – establishes the Oneness of God by intellectual proofs to show that acceptance of the existence of more than one god is not logical. For if there were two independent gods, each would be distinct in essence from the other while sharing common attributes; each would, therefore, be compounded of one part which separates and distinguishes them, and a common part, shared with the other 'independent god'. However, every compound is contingent because it is dependent on something else. Only Necessary Existence is not Contingent Existence. It would be true to say that people at this level are only partially aware of the truth. They will be saved from the Fire and will, on the Day of Resurrection, enter the Garden, as Allah has promised believers. This is referred to as the tawḥid of action because it demonstrates the existence of the Creator via action. This level of understanding is meant by the following ayah,

> They only know the appearances of this world's life, but of the hereafter, they know absolutely nothing.
>
> Qur'an 30:7

For a deeper understanding of tawḥid one may bear witness with the eye of inner vision that Allah is One and that there is none other than Him in existence. The whole of creation is an act and manifestation of His alone. Those with such understanding cease to look to natural causes or chains of events which arise from those causes and rely on Him alone with true reliance. They hand over their affairs to Him entirely and are pleased and content with what comes to them from Him. Hence Allah says,

> Allah is well pleased with them and they are well pleased with Allah.
>
> Qur'an 5:119

As stated in the Qur'an, that is how they attain the various stations of reliance, submission, contentment, etc.,

> And Allah is sufficient for those who put their trust in Him. Surely Allah accomplishes His will, He has indeed appointed measures for everything.
>
> Qur'an 65:3

Once one has moved from the Tawḥid of Unity of Action to the level of the Unification of Attributes which follows the Unification of Actions, the highest rank of tawḥid is attained:

> But, best of all [of the bounties of paradise] is Allah's goodly pleasure.
>
> Qur'an 9:72

> The Prophet ﷺ told us that 'Contentment is the greatest of Allah's doors.
>
> Al Mizan, Vol. 9, p. 348

Contented people are able to witness the supremacy of the reality of His Power and Knowledge; they are able to bear witness to His placing all things in their rightful place; His connection to these things; their longing for Him despite of His invisibility. This level of tawḥid leads to the Inner Knowledge of Causes and the abandonment of the phenomenal world.

The difference between this level of tawḥid and the more basic understanding of the other levels of tawḥid, is that the former depend on the factual knowledge of ordinary people, while the latter depend on levels of understanding which need to be intellectually conceived. The first allows one to rid oneself of manifest shirk, the second, of the greater and more difficult hidden shirk.

The Second Level of Tawḥid

Finally, there is a level of tawḥid only attainable by the most devoted and sincere. This is based on total and utter annihilation and extinction of the self. From that level one is able to pass beyond all stations, levels and manifestations of the contingent phenomenal world. At this stage, tawḥid is the abandonment of everything extraneous to His Sole Existence. What a difference between this level of tawḥid and the others! What a difference between those who continue by themselves and those who are annihilated in their Lord,

> This is the grace of Allah, which He bestows on whom He pleases and Allah is the Lord of abounding Grace.
>
> Qur'an 57:21

All creatures glorify Allah

42. Say [O Muḥammad], 'If there are other divinities as they assert, they would have been able to manifest the [nature] of the Lord of the Throne'.

43. All praise is due to Him for He is immeasurably exalted, beyond their comprehension.

44. All creatures in the seven heavens and the earth below, extol their Lord. All glorify Him even if we are unable to understand their praises. He is Most-Tolerant, Most-Forgiving.

Many ayat in the Qur'an refer to all creatures glorifying and praising Allah Almighty. The clearest are those which teach that everything in the heavens and the earth, all animal and plant life, from the tiniest atom to large heavenly bodies and even space itself, praise and glorify the Creator. The Holy Qur'an teaches that the entire universe praises the Lord and that each distinct part glorifies Him in its own way. Although the ignorant remain unaware of this, those illumined with the light of faith in their hearts are able to discern it.

Scholars and theologians hold various viewpoints regarding the reality of such praise and glorification:

1) One clarification is that everything in the universe has its own level of awareness, comprehension and ability to glorify. For example, Allah tells us in Qur'an 2:74 that some rocks 'sink for fear of Allah' and in Qur'an 41:11 that Allah addressed the heavens and the earth, 'Come you together willingly or unwillingly'; they said, "We come together in willing obedience." ' Thus, according to Qur'anic terminology, rock, earth and heavens all have the ability to communicate.
2) Another clarification interprets praises referred to above as 'body language'. One may see friends desperate, angry or confused and ask them, 'What is the matter?' Even though they might not utter a single word, it can be read from their demeanour that something is amiss. Imam ʿAli ﷺ is recorded as having said,

> 'When people conceal something in their heart it is likely to manifest itself through unplanned words of their tongue and the expressions of their face.'
>
> Nahj al-Balaghah, Maxim number 26

Praise and glorification of all things may be communicated without words – for example, in the way a painting is a witness to the painter's intention.

This opinion seems more acceptable in the way that all Divine Attributes can be summarised by Allah being the Perfect, Pure and Absolute Existent. Because perfection is His alone, all else requires His grace, guidance and light. Hence, every single leaf, flower and pebble glorifies Him, even though we may not be able to understand their praises.

3) A third clarification tends to combine the two previous opinions to conclude that praise and glorification are practised via utterances as well as 'body language'. We, however, prefer the second opinion.

The error-free Imams from the progeny of the Holy Messenger ﷺ refer to the glorification of creation in the following ahadith. Imam Muḥammad al Baqir ؑ said,

> The Messenger of Allah forbade beating or branding the faces of animals on the ground that they glorify their Lord.
>
> Tafsīr Nur al-Thaqalain, Vol. 3, p. 168

Imam Muḥammad al-Baqir ؑ heard a pigeon cooing and said,

> A pigeon glorifying and asking the Lord for its daily provisions.
>
> Allamah Tabatabai in Tafsīr al-Mizan

When the Prophet ﷺ asked Aysha to clean his robe and she responded saying that she had already done that the previous day, the Prophet ﷺ said,

> Did you not know that clothes glorify Allah when they are clean but cease to do so when they are dirty.
>
> Allamah Tabatabai in Tafsīr al-Mizan

This last hadith emphasises the significance of cleanliness and indicates that all things in nature strive to maintain their purity.

The Hidden Barrier

> **45. When [O Muḥammad] you recite the Qur'an, We insert invisible barriers between you and those who do not believe in the life to come.**
>
> **46. We lay veils over their hearts to prevent them understanding, and heaviness over their ears to prevent their hearing. For, when you refer to there being no divinity other than Allah, they turn away in dislike.**
>
> **47. When they listen to you, We know very well what they listen for and that behind your back they say, 'If you follow him, you will be led by one possessed'.**
>
> **48. Observe [O Prophet] what they identify you with, they are so far astray they will never find their way [to truth].**

The above ayat refer to the disturbances and obstacles contrived by those who worshipped idols and disbelieved in the One True God. They interrupted the Prophet ﷺ when he recited the Qur'an or prayed at the Ka'bah. Occasionally, they even threw stones to discourage others from joining him.

Al-Fakhr al-Razi refers to this recurrent behaviour, saying,

> Whenever the Prophet ﷺ recited Qur'an one of the descendants of Qusay would stand at his right side, another at his left, clap hands, whistle and confuse his recitation with readings of poetry.

Al-Tafsīr al-Kabeer, Vol. 20, p. 220

> According to Tabrisi, the Invisible Veil with which Allah Almighty separates disbelievers and the Prophet ﷺ, is the terror and fear He instills in their hearts.

Majma al-Bayan, Vol. 3, p. 418

It would seem that stubbornness and adamant rejection of faith are the biggest barriers to understanding. Allah Almighty describes those reluctant to hear Qur'anic recitation as turning away in dislike. This is expressed in stronger language in the following ayah,

> What is the matter with them that they turn away from admonition as if they were frightened asses fleeing a lion?

Qur'an 74:49–51

According to the above ayat, there are three obstacles to the discernment of Truth and the Right Path:

1) The veil and barrier between believers and non-believers is in reality nothing other than jealousy, hatred and enmity. Such psychological barriers restrain non-believers from communicating with believers or understanding what they say to the extent that even good words appear bad in their eyes.
2) Ignorance and blind imitation of tribal practices prevent listening or agreement to what is logical.
3) Their senses and abilities are so jaded that they do not hear as though they are deaf; or unable to see facts as though they are blind. This attests to the fact that inner feelings and emotions may sometimes impact upon our senses to the extent that they are rendered useless.

The result of such obstacles was that those who did not believe never listened to Allah's Messenger ﷺ and tried to justify their rejection by accusations of his being a magician, poet or even a mad person. They employed the word 'possessed' to indicate that they thought he had no understanding or responsibility for his words. A few commentators explain that by 'possessed' they meant that he had the ability to bewitch others. If this was so, it acknowledges the profound impact his words had on the hearts of others.

But why were unbelievers so terrified of the call to the Divine Unity? The answer is that everything of their society's social and commercial life was based on idols and idol worship. If those who did not believe had accepted Divine Unity, it would have destroyed their previous beliefs and entirely shattered their commercial, cultural, political and social establishment. On the other hand, people free from the beliefs that underpinned their society would see no reason not to reject the existing authorities.

8 The Restoration of Life

49. They ask, 'When we [have perished and] are bones reduced to dust, shall we really be raised up and given a new existence?'

50. Tell them, 'Even if you have turned into stone or iron'.

51. 'Or any other substance which you cannot even conceive of being brought to life, even then you will be restored to life.' And if they ask, 'Who can bring us to life?' Tell them, 'The One who first created you'. Then, when they shake their heads and ask, 'And when will that be?' Tell them, 'It may well be soon'.

52. On the day that He summons you, you will respond with His praises and will think that you have only been [in your grave] a short while.

All religions recognise that accountability on the Day of Judgement can have an important effect on peoples' behaviour. Those who deny resurrection focus their attention entirely on this world. They imagine that the gains and losses of this life are the only yardstick of human success. For them, winning or losing is based solely on the criteria of this world. Now, while it is exceedingly difficult to find reference to the Hereafter in the Torah, both the Injil and Holy Qur'an discuss it in detail. The Islamic creed is based on two pillars: a) belief in the Oneness of Allah who created the universe; and b) belief that everyone is accountable on the Day of Judgement. These two principles fashion the Muslim personality and inform it of how to behave. Indeed, these are the principle elements that restrain people from sin and encourage their responsible behaviour.

The journey towards perfection, like a marathon or any other endeavour, has both a starting and a finishing point. Our start on this journey is faith in Allah – tawḥid – and our finish is final judgement – ma'ad. The above Ayat were revealed in response to three key questions put to the Prophet ﷺ by those who denied resurrection:

> Q. 1) When we [have perished and] are bones reduced to dust, shall we really be raised up and given a new existence?'

This thought questions whether decayed bones reduced to dust and widely scattered are ever able to be restored to their former state. It is clear from this ayah that the Prophet ﷺ taught that both body and soul are to return after death. If only the soul were to return, there would not have been any reason for those who denied resurrection to question him about the restoration of disintegrated bones. Allah points out in the Holy Qur'an, that restoration is not a particularly difficult task for The One who created everything in the heavens and the earth: ‘Even if you have turned into stone, iron or any other substance which you could not ever conceive as being brought to life.’

The interesting aspect of this comparison lies in its clarity. The reduction of bone or anything else to dust is simply a stage in the process by which elements – the building blocks of all matter – are returned to the earth. All matter is composed of different combinations of any of more than 100 fundamental metallic and non-metallic substances which consist of atoms of only one kind. Such chemical elements, listed in what is known as the Periodic Table, are referred to as the ‘building blocks’ from which all life is constructed. Earth is the medium from which vegetation draws its nutriment to flourish. In turn it is vegetation that directly or indirectly feeds and nourishes all other life forms. There is no possibility of commonly known vegetables flourishing on a medium of solid iron, but traces of iron and the plethora of other metals vital to life are obtained from the earth. If creation is possible, resurrection should not be considered impossible.

Q. 2) ‘Who can bring us to life?’ The answer provided is, ‘The One who first created you’. Those who have doubts might consider why The One who created human life from earth cannot again bring them to life from the same medium. Q. 3) ‘And when will that be?’ This assumes that even if resurrection were possible for The One who created us, it would not occur. What is the point of resurrection taking place in a million or more years’ time? Surely our concerns should be with the present, not the far distant future? The answer Allah provides is, ‘It may well be soon’. No matter how long a human being’s life on earth is, that period is insignificant in relation to eternity.

Qur'anic Ayat in Support of Resurrection

1) His Divine power

> Is not He who created the heavens and the earth able to create the like of them? Indeed He is the All-Knowing Supreme Creator:
>
> Truly, when He intends a thing, He commands it ‘Be’ and it is.
>
> Qur'an 36:81–2

> Have they not seen that Allah, who was not wearied by the creation of the heavens and the earth, has the power to give life to the dead? Indeed, He has power over all things.
>
> Qur'an 46:33

> They do not regard Allah with the esteem due to Him. The whole earth will remain in the grip of His Divine power on the Day of Judgement and He will roll the heavens up in His right hand. Glory be to Him, High is He above what they associate to Him.
>
> Qur'an 39:67

2) His earlier creation

In the Qur'an Allah Almighty points out that the One who is able to create something has little difficulty in resurrecting it:

> He it is who originates creation, then turns it back. This is easy for Him. His attributes are the most exalted in the heavens and the earth and He is All-Mighty, All-Wise.
>
> Qur'an 30:27

> He [who] questions us about resurrection has forgotten his own origin [when] he says, 'who will put life back into bones that have decayed?' Say [O Muḥammad], 'He who created them will give them life. He has the absolute knowledge of all creation'.
>
> Qur'an 36:78–9

> On the Day of Judgement We will roll up the heavens as though they were written scrolls. As We began the first creature, so shall We return it. This is a promise binding upon us. Truly We will do it.
>
> Qur'an 21:104

3) The growth of vegetation

> You see the earth all withered, but when We send rain, it bestirs itself, swells up and brings forth every kind of attractive herbage. This is because Allah is the true Reality, and He gives life to that which is dead.
>
> Qur'an 22:5–6

> We send down water as a blessing from the heavens, grow gardens with it from which grain is harvested and tall palm trees with fruit-stalks layer upon layer, to provide sustenance for our servants. With it We give new life to land that was dead. That is what resurrection will be like.
>
> Qur'an 50:9–11

> Allah is He who sends the winds that raise clouds. Then We drive them towards the land which is dead and We give life therewith to the earth after its death. That is what resurrection will be like.

Qur'an 35:9

4) The supra-natural incidents of earlier times
   a) The four birds and the Prophet Ibrahim ﷺ

> Ibrahim said, 'My Lord, let me see how you give life to the dead?' He asked, 'What! Do you not believe?' Ibrahim replied, 'I do, but so that my heart may be at ease'. Allah replied, 'Take four birds and train them to follow you, then kill them and cut them into pieces and place the various pieces on different mountains. When you call them, the birds will come flying to you'.

Qur'an: 2:260

   b) The People of the Cave

> You might have seen the sun rise and move to the right of the cave and turn back to the left . . . you would have thought them awake while they slept . . .
>
> They remained in the cave for three hundred and nine years.

Qur'an 18:17, 18, 25

   c) Ezra – ʿUzair

Allah Almighty tells us in the Qur'an about the Prophet Ezra – ʿUzair – who, when passing a derelict township exclaimed, 'How shall Allah give life to this place now that it has died?' (In certain historical references the following incident is said to have occurred to Jeremiah rather than to ʿUzair).

> Do you not see the like of him who, when he passed a completely ruined town, questioned, 'How shall Allah give this place life now that it is dead?' So Allah caused him to die and lie for 100 years before again raising him to life. He then asked him, 'How long have you tarried here?' He responded, 'Perhaps a day or a part thereof'. Allah said, 'No, you have lain there for 100 years, look at how your food and drink have remained fresh and look at the skeleton of your donkey. Truly We will make you a sign for humanity. Observe how We set the bones together again and clothe them in flesh'. When these events became clear to him, he said, 'I now comprehend Allah's power over all things'.

Qur'an 2:259

Resurrection – a necessity

1) Without resurrection, creation would have been mere vanity. There would be no need or purpose whatever in human beings undergoing the tests and trials of this life, if there was no final accountability.
2) Without resurrection, one would have to question Allah's justice for He tells us in the Holy Qur'an that the establishment of justice was the principal reason behind His sending 124,000 Messengers and Warners to the nations and tribes of this earth.

> Truly We sent Our Messengers with clear proofs, and sent with them the book and the scale so that humankind may stand forth in justice.
>
> Qur'an 57:25

If the pious and the criminal, the people who submitted to His Will as well as those who disobeyed Him were treated alike, without having one day to account for their actions, could we believe in the justice of Allah? In the Qur'an Allah Almighty asks,

> Shall we treat those who believe and do good deeds [in the same way] as those who make mischief in the land, or shall We treat those who safeguard themselves against evil [in the same way] as those who turn away from truth?
>
> Qur'an 38:28

3) The whole of creation progresses towards perfection and purification and is elevated to return to Him. While the spiritual journey begins at maturity with the start of awareness, it also has an end. Indeed, it terminates at the boundary of material life and the hereafter. This is confirmed in the following ayat:

> Truly, We are Allah's and to Him shall We return.
>
> Qur'an 2:156

> With your Lord, that day will be the place where you will settle.
>
> Qur'an 75:12

> To your Lord that day will you be driven.
>
> Qur'an 75:30

> And to your Lord is the final goal.
>
> Qur'an 53:42

> All shall return to Us.
>
> Qur'an 21:93

Dialogue with those who do not believe

53. And tell My servants to conduct themselves with circumspection, for Satan is ever ready to provoke discord. He is the declared enemy of humanity.

54. Your Lord has perfect awareness [of what you deserve and do not deserve] and grants mercy or punishment as He pleases. Therefore [O Muḥammad], We have not made you responsible for their actions.

55. Moreover, your Lord has perfect awareness of all who are in the heavens and on the earth; We endowed certain Prophets more highly than others and gave the Zabūr [Psalms] to Dawūd [David].

56. Tell them, 'Call on those other than Him whom you imagine to be divine; they have neither the power to alleviate your distress nor to remove it'.

57. Those they call upon seek to approach their Lord themselves. Even those who are nearest, long for His mercy and dread His punishment. The Lord's chastisement is truly to be feared.

The above ayat explain how discussion and dialogue are to be conducted when faced with those who do not believe. Because the concepts and ideas introduced by Islam are logical and profound, they need to be communicated in a manner to encourage consideration and comprehension. The first ayah in this section, 'And tell My servants to conduct themselves with circumspection', instructs us to do just that. But why does Allah recommend it even when we are confronted by denial of His existence and the Day of Judgement?

He warns that if His servants are harsh in dealing with others, 'Satan is ever ready to provoke discord'; thus, His servants must remain conscious that, 'Satan is the declared enemy of humanity'.

Commentators differ over what is meant by the term 'Servants of Allah'

There are people whom, even though they do not believe and have gone astray, Allah still refers to as servants, still cautions to protect themselves against the seductive attractions of Satan, and continues to invite to what is best – by which is meant belief in tawḥid and rejection of idol worship. Therefore, there are commentators for whom 'Servants of Allah' is understood to be a clever phrase by which to win the hearts of those who disbelieve.

Other comentators, however, understand that 'Servants of Allah' refer exclusively to those who do believe. According to them, Allah knows that when His Holy Messenger is accused of being a magician, a madman or a poet, believers find it difficult to withstand those insults. When outraged, many will lose self-control and rush to counterattack. To avoid such confrontation Allah advises believers to retain their composure, to behave with circumspection and to leave no opportunity for Satan to sow discord.

The context and psychological considerations of these ayat lead us to favour this second opinion. However, the next ayah, 'Your Lord has perfect awareness [of what you do and do not deserve] and grants mercy or punishment as He pleases . . .' covers both possibilities:

1) It is either addressed to disbelievers to inform them that Allah can be either merciful or severe in chastisement, that He is perfectly aware of what people do and what they do not deserve, and that it is always prudent to seek guidance and mercy from Him.
2) Alternately, it is addressed to believers, to inform them that they should never imagine that they alone will prosper. All is as Allah wishes: He punishes disobedience, or when He wishes, forgives and grants mercy.

The ayah ends with the statement, 'Therefore [O Muḥammad], We have not made you responsible for their actions'. You have accomplished your mission with your continuous call to follow the truth, so do not be disturbed by their denials or rejections. And this salutary advice is applicable to all believers.

Dawūd [David] and the Zabūr [Psalms]

> **55. Moreover, your Lord has perfect awareness of all who are in the heavens and on the earth; We endowed certain Prophets more highly than others and gave the Zabūr [Psalms] to Dawūd [David].**

This is an indirect response to a question which preoccupied the minds of disbelievers. What puzzled them was Allah bestowing prophethood on an insignificant orphan, specifically the Final Prophet, whom He sent to end the line of prophets forever. In response to their preoccupation, Allah informed them that He had endowed certain prophets more highly than others. One was given the honour of receiving the Psalms – Zabūr – (David – Dawūd عليه السلام), another to speak directly to Allah (Moses – Mūsa عليه السلام), yet another to be the 'Spirit of Allah' (Jesus – 'Isa عليه السلام) and one was 'chosen above all others' (Muḥammad ﷺ).

So, what is the significance of the Zabūr being mentioned here?

1) The Zabūr are supplications which promote the concept of dialogue and circumspection,

> Let integrity and uprightness preserve me; for I wait on thee. Rest in the Lord, and wait patiently for him: fret not thyself because of him who prospereth in his way, . . . Cease from anger, and forsake wrath: fret not thyself in any wise to do evil.
>
> Psalms 25:21 and 37:7, 8

2) They announce good news for the deprived and oppressed, which equates with Prophet Muḥammad's call to the deprived and dispossessed, e.g.:

> For evildoers shall be cut off: but those that wait upon the Lord, they shall inherit the earth. For yet a little while, and the wicked shall not be . . . But the meek shall inherit the earth; and shall delight themselves in the abundance of peace.
>
> Psalm 37:9–11

> The wicked have drawn out the sword, and have bent their bow, to cast down the poor and needy, . . . Their sword shall enter into their own heart, and their bow shall be broken. A little that a righteous man hath is better than the riches of many wicked.
>
> Psalm 37:14–16

It is, therefore, not at all surprising that Allah should refer to the Psalms in this ayah, for He also tells us in the Qur'an,

> We wrote in the Psalms, after the message given to Mūsa, My servants, the righteous, shall inherit the earth.
>
> Qur'an 21:105

3) The Prophet Dawūd ﷺ held sovereignty over a large and important kingdom, to the extent that Jews today still dream of it and employ the star of David as a symbol of their government. Notwithstanding this, Dawūd ﷺ himself never grew arrogant with power. Rather, he related to his Psalms, as if to demonstrate and clarify that greatness has nothing at all to do with power and might and everything to do with unconditional submission to the Lord of Creation.

4) Certain Jews claimed that no divine scripture could possibly follow the revelation of the Torah – Tawrāt. This ayah refutes their argument because it makes it impossible to rule out of hand, that Allah also sent other revelations, including the revelation of the Qur'an.

What is 'Wasilah'?

In translating the Arabic of Ayah 57, 'Those they call upon, seek themselves to approach their Lord', the word 'Wasilah' has been rendered into English as 'approach'. Wasilah is mentioned twice in the Qur'an, here and in Qur'an 5:35 – 'O you who believe, observe piety and seek means to approach Him'. Means of approach signify acts which draw one closer to Allah Almighty, idols of course having no ability to contribute to this end. However, all acts of worship and all charitable deeds are suitable means by which to 'approach' or 'draw closer to Him'.

In the words of Imam ʿAli ﷷ,

> The best approach for those who seek nearness to Allah, the Glorified, the Exalted, is to believe in Him and His Prophet, to fight in His cause . . . to establish prayer, to pay zakah, to fast for the month of Ramadan, to go on Hajj and Umrah, to maintain ties of kinship, to give alms in secret and to extend benefit to people, with the intention of drawing nearer to Him and to prosper.

Nahj al-Balagha, Sermon 110

The acceptability of intercession by prophets and Imams is another way in which to achieve this end. However, their intercession does not imply that they have any capacity other than as intercessors, or that one can rely on their intercession without making any efforts of one's own.

9 The Accursed Tree

58. There is not a population whom We will not severely punish or who will not perish before the Day of Resurrection. This is documented in the Book of Records.

59. Nothing stood in the way of Our sending Ayat [signs], even though former generations treated them with contempt. When We sent the she camel as a clear sign to the Thamūd people, they mistreated her. But We never send signs other than as warnings.

60. We informed you [O Prophet] that the Lord encompasses humankind [within His Knowledge and Omnipotence]. We did not institute the vision We showed you in your dream, nor the accursed tree in the Qur'an, other than as a trial for people. Yet despite Our instilling fear in them, their transgressions increase.

These ayat constitute argument and dialogue with unbelievers regarding resurrection, the existence of Allah, and an admonishment which clarifies that life on earth is not eternal, as all things here perish. Their purpose is to encourage non-believers to reconsider their behaviour and attitudes in the full knowledge that they, too, will one day have to face the consequences of their deeds. The tyrant and the unjust are to be severely punished; everyone is to simply follow in the pattern of life and death. 'This is documented in the Book of Records', which is a reference to Allah Almighty's endless and limitless knowledge and irrevocable Divine injunctions.

To the response of the non-believers, that they would not object to belief in Allah and the Day of Resurrection, provided His Messenger brought about supra-natural occurrences of their choosing, Allah responds, 'Nothing stood in the way of Our sending signs despite the contempt expressed for them by former generations. When We sent the she camel as a clear sign to the Thamūd people they mistreated her. But We never send signs other than to warn people'. This ayah emphasises that even if requests for miracles were to be fulfilled, denials of previous nations attest to the fact that, even then, they would still not believe.

Allah Almighty assures His final Messenger that he is not the only Messenger to have been rejected. Even though most may reject guidance, many pure-hearted souls will believe and accept it.

What is the Accursed Tree?

In his well-known commentary on the Qur'an, Al-Fakhr al-Razi quotes Ibn Abbas, the renowned companion of the Prophet Muḥammad ﷺ, now regarded as the 'father of tafsir', who understood that the Accursed Tree referred to the Bani Umayyah. That opinion was also expressed by Ayesha (a wife of the Messenger) in a conversation with Marwan, the head of the Bani Umayyah, when she told him,

> Allah cursed your father while you were in his loins and you are included in that curse.
>
> Tafsīr Qortubi, Vol. 6, p. 3902 and Tafsīr Al-Fakhr al-Razi, Vol. 20, p. 237

It is reported that the Prophet ﷺ was distressed when he dreamed of apes playing on his minbar. According to Ahl al-Bayt, that dream referred to the antics of Bani Umayyah who, after his death, set out to destroy the spirit of Islam – a time of real trial for true believers. The dream of the Holy Prophet ﷺ resonates the curses of Dawūd ﷺ and 'Isa ﷺ:

> Cursed by Dawūd and 'Isa, son of Maryam, were those amongst the Children of Isra'il who did not believe, that is because they disobeyed and exceeded the limit. They did not prevent one another from committing evil actions.
>
> Qur'an 5:78–9

The New Testament refers to:

> *Ye* serpents, *ye* generation of vipers, how can ye escape the damnation of hell? Wherefore, behold, I send unto you prophets, and wise men, and scribes: and *some* of them ye shall kill and crucify; and *some* of them ye shall scourge in your synagogues, and persecute *them* from city to city: That upon you may come all the righteous blood shed upon earth, from the blood of the righteous Abel unto the blood of Zacharias son of Barachias, whom ye slew between the temple and the altar.
>
> Matthew 23:33–5

It is clear that Bani Umayyah manifested what Allah refers to in Qur'an 14:26 as 'the evil tree'. Indeed, authentic ahadith confirm that the Accursed Tree refers to Bani Umayyah and not to the tree of Zaqqūm which is mentioned in the following ayat:

> Is this a better dwelling, or the tree of Zaqqūm We made as a trial for those who are unjust? – a tree which grows at the very lowest part of hell.
>
> Qur'an 37: 62–4

> The tree of Zaqqūm shall be food for the sinful and will boil in their bellies as though it were molten brass.
>
> Qur'an 44:43–6

The Zaqqūm is a tree with a knotted stem and small, dust-coloured, bitter-tasting, stinging leaves. It signifies the contrast between hell and the beautiful gardens of paradise with their delicious fruit. When those who dwell in hell eat the Zaqqūm, they are compelled, as further punishment, to drink boiling water.

Zaqqūm is clearly not an Accursed Tree, because hell and all its contents are not accursed but merely means by which Allah punishes those who have been wicked. No authentic ahadith exist to support any other opinion. This ayah is thus a clear warning to those who do not pay heed, but choose instead to transgress.

10 Satan's enmity towards humankind

61. When We ordered the angels to bow down in respect to Adam, all prostrated themselves. But [the Jinn] Iblis retorted, 'Is it appropriate that I prostrate myself before a creature You created out of clay?'

62. Iblis then added, 'Grant me Your authority until the Day of Resurrection and I will surely reduce to subjection almost all the offspring of that creature which You have honoured above me'.

63. Allah then ordered, 'Go with those who follow you to reap the rewards of Gehennam [Hell]. An ample recompense for all of you'.

64. Proposition and entice as much as you like. Attack people [with all the forces at your disposal] on horse or on foot, conspire with them to procure wealth and children, and make promises to them [as you will]. Satan's promises are deceptive!

65. But you will not hold sway over My servants for your Lord will protect them.

Similar references to Allah creating Adam ﷷ – and Satan declining to prostrate himself before him – occur in Qur'an 2:30–38; 7:11–18 and 15:28–42.

When the Angels heard Allah announce that He would create a vicegerent on earth, they comprehended that He intended His vicegerent to manifest inherent qualities of the earth. As they had already seen that the earth is a place of unceasing change and deterioration, a place of constant struggle and confrontation for finite resources, the Angels knew that to survive on earth, Allah's new vicegerent would need the support and co-operation of a host of similar creatures – a whole new species. And that they, for their mutual survival, would have to support and protect each other. In other words, they would have to try to establish a just, well-regulated society, in which individual desires and angers remained checked and under control.

The question that occurred to the Angels was, 'How could earthly creatures, with the inherent defects, deficiencies, desires and anger manifested by other creatures of the earth, be able to represent the majesty, splendour and perfection of Allah?, Allah whose sublime perfection would be way beyond their comprehension. How could lowly mischievous creatures mirror His Divine Majesty and Splendour?' That was the question that occurred to them: a question, not a protest, and not an objection. They affirmed their belief that Allah is All-Knowing, All-Wise, and did not express any doubt whatever that what was about to occur would be grounded on His Knowledge and Wisdom. Nonetheless, they could not understand how the presence of such a vicegerent would celebrate Allah's praises and glorify His Holiness. And if the main purpose of vicegerency is the praise and glorification of Allah's Holiness, they, the Angels, already did that. And if they were already *de facto* vicegerents, what need then to create another creature to fulfil this role? Allah replied with a sentence, 'Surely I know what you do not know' and an action, 'He taught Adam ﷺ all the names'. This also appears in the following surah,

> And when the Lord said to the Angels, 'Truly, I am going to make in the earth a vicegerent', they said, 'will you make in it such as will make mischief and shed blood in it, while we celebrate Your praises and extol Your Holiness?' He said, 'Surely I know what you do not'. And He taught Adam the names, all of them, then presented them to the Angels and said, 'Tell me names of those if you are right'. They said, 'Glory be to You! We have no knowledge but that which You have taught us; surely You alone are All-Knowing, All-Wise.' He said: 'O Adam, inform them of their names.' And when he had, Allah said, 'Did I not tell you that I certainly know the unseen [what is concealed or secret] from the heavens and the earth and [that] I know what you display and what you hide?'
>
> Qur'an 2:30–33

It is apparent from Allah's response that He was going to 'make in the earth' an entirely new creature whom He would appoint as His vicegerent, and that He would not appoint His vicegerent from any of the creatures which had preceded Adamﷺ.

When Allah tells us in the Qur'an that, 'He taught Adam the names, all of them, then presented them to the Angels', the Arabic word He uses for 'them' – 'hum' – is a pronoun that is only ever used to describe things that are alive and rational. The Arabic word for 'them', used when inanimate objects are referred to, is 'ha'. It is evident that Allah used that particular form of 'them', because He was referring to specific and particular beings. It is also evident that the word 'knowledge' does not designate anything which would have enabled the Angels to claim to be as knowledgeable as Adam ﷺ the moment he had 'informed them of their names'. The knowledge that the Angels gleaned from Adam ﷺ was clearly of a lower order to that which Allah had taught Adam ﷺ. They instantly knew that only a being who was superior to them could comprehend that which they could not, which is why they declared, 'Glory be to you. We have no knowledge but what you have taught us'.

Let us consider this analogy: being taught all the 'Names' listed by Lloyds of London benefits one little; for in order to comprehend the framework of the insurance industry, one has to understand that it is the wealth, pledged by 'Lloyd's Names' which, over the years, has enabled Lloyds to guarantee settlement of insurance claims. One must also realise that, in order to be able to make such pledges, the personal wealth of 'Lloyd's Names' must be of such an order as to let them carry substantial losses without facing bankruptcy. Another example might be 'knowing' the name of the present Chancellor of the Exchequer. That in itself is of less importance than understanding that the person who holds that post is in charge of the mechanisms which determine the financial structure of the nation. We are thus led to understand that Adam ﷺ comprehended the reality and substantial existence of those to whom the names referred.

The names – al-Asma' – in the sentence, 'And He taught Adam the names' is a plural preceded by the definite article 'al'. This denotes the comprehensiveness emphasised by the statement, 'all of them'. It, thus, becomes clear that Adam ﷺ was taught, without restriction or limitation, the names and qualities of all the living and knowledgeable beings who were as yet unseen and unknown by the heavens or the earth – in other words, beings which existed beyond the sphere of the universe. This concept matches perfectly the following ayah,

> And there is not a living thing in existence of which We are not the source and which We have not sent down in a well-defined measure.
>
> Qur'an15:21

The named ones, presented before the Angels, were therefore sublime unseen beings who, until then, had remained concealed and protected by Allah. Having created the souls of all those in heaven and on earth from their light and splendour, He sent them, with their legacy and blessings, to the universe. Although on earth they manifested numerous identities, all of them were created from the same light and splendour.

The acquisition and accumulation of knowledge is a never-ending process which, as time passes, yields ever greater dividends. That knowledge passes from one generation to the next, evidences that it is the nation of Adam ﷺ – and not Adam ﷺ alone – who was appointed vicegerent. The word is used here to denote those appointed to fulfil a function on behalf of Allah; to exercise His authority in religious matters; and to be His deputy.

The same Arabic word, in the following ayat, is rendered into English as 'successor':

> And remember [O people of Ād] when He made you successors of Nūh's people. . .
>
> Qur'an7:69

> When We made you successors in the land after them.
>
> Qur'an 10:14

> . . . and He makes you successors in the earth.
>
> Qur'an27:62

The main ayat under this heading refer to Satan's deception and seduction and its effect upon human beings. In referring to Satan's refusal to prostrate before Adam ﷺ, Allah Almighty shows those who do not believe, that it is in their being obdurate and inflexible that they resemble Satan. Satan symbolises arrogance and disbelief in the superiority or power of human beings. To recognise the stupidity of nonsensical pride is to realise how ridiculous it is to follow such a path.

'When We ordered the Angels to bow down in respect to Adam, all prostrated themselves other than Iblis.' Although it might appear from this wording that Iblis is one of the Angels, other ayat in the Qur'an clarify that he is one of the jinn who had been elevated to a high position due to his long history of worship. However, he became so egotistical and preoccupied with himself that he questioned the wisdom of his Creator. Assuming that clay and earth – the source of all vegetation and nutrition – is inferior and less important to fire with its hugely destructive powers, he asked, 'Is it appropriate that I [created from fire] prostrate myself before the creature You created out of clay?'

Even after being forever expelled from the world of Sublime Beings, he remained stubborn and arrogantly demanded, 'Grant me Your authority until the Day of Resurrection and I will surely reduce to subjection almost all the offspring of that creature You have honoured above me'.

Why does Allah permit Satan to continue to tempt humankind? It is clear that trial and testing are essential in teaching humanity to distinguish truth from falsehood. In this they perceive their own innate characteristics and personalities, and consequently the need to purify their souls. Islam proscribes active practice, not merely verbalisations of faith. There can be no salvation for any individual without the discipline to heed Allah Almighty's guidance. He tells us in the Qur'an,

> Do people think that they can get away with saying 'We believe?' without ever being tested and tried? Truly We have tried those who came before them, thus Allah clearly knows the truthful from the liar.
>
> Qur'an 29:2–3

Imam 'Ali ﷺ said 'Allah knows' and that means that Allah tests and examines believers in order to separate the righteous from the wicked.

Satan's Means to deceive

> **64. Proposition and entice as much as you like. Attack people [with all the forces at your disposal] on horse or on foot, conspire with them to procure wealth and children, and make promises to them [as you will]. Satan's promises are deceptive!**

Throughout recorded history incessant violations and warfare show that Satan's efforts have not been without success. Indeed, contemporary media coverage reveals that Satanic attacks determine the world we live in. For, when commercial or national interests conflict with moral and ecological issues, governments and corporations find 'sound' reasons for ignoring them.

The objective of this section is to show the extent and ingenuity of contemporary assaults on human values and the environment. In our preparation we have been truly fortunate in receiving daily e-mails of world news and comment linked to in-depth articles on the Internet.

Burke [more probably Macaulay] said that 'There are Three Estates in Parliament [the Lords Spiritual, the Lords Temporal and the Commons]; but in the Reporters' Gallery yonder, there sat a Fourth Estate more important far, than they all.'

Carlyle, *Heroes and Hero-Worship: The Hero as Man of Letters*, 1839

No government ought to be without censors; and where the press is free none ever will.

Thomas Jefferson, *Writings*, Vol. viii, p. 406

Contemporary reports in reputable English-language newspapers, which signpost the variety and ingenuity of contemporary assaults, illustrate the validity of the above statements.

While the imbalance in our examples, to some extent, reflects press coverage, evidence of the extent of 'Satan's Means to Deceive' referred to in this section of the Qur'an, is openly available in the democratic heartland of the white Anglo-Saxon world. This has the advantage of 'un-packing', for the English-speaking reader, the extent of deception better than any number of reports from countries suspected of having lesser standards. This is in no way to infer that the inhabitants of Muslim majority countries behave any differently to those of other places, as may be seen from the reports of organisations such as Amnesty International and Islamic Human Relief. However, the range of examples listed below is not readily available from territory controlled by notoriously secretive and despotic rulers. That despotic regimes are not appreciated, may be evidenced by the numbers who seek to migrate to places that espouse liberty, freedom, noble ideals and appreciation of what is right and wrong, *viz.*, places in which the press is given free reign to report the facts it uncovers and its opinions.

That there is a preponderance of references from the USA attests to the openness of American society, compared to other countries, even the British and, in particular, to the quality and ease of access of the resources of the *New York Times*. The Uniform Resource Locators (URLs) or Internet addresses, that consist of the access protocol (http), the domain name (www.nytimes.com), and the path to the file residing on their server, are included below to lead readers to freely accessable abstracts of reports in the *New York Times*, from which the original and complete articles may be easily acquired. These are invaluable and well worth the very small fee charged to download them.

Our cursory investigation has been somewhat inadequately expanded in an attempt to provide breadth and variety in our categories.

Lastly, we applaud and acknowledge our indebtedness to the press.

Allah's permission to Satan to attack humankind 'by every means' is most strikingly presented in a contemporary listing of wide-scale assault.

I ATTACK BY EVERY MEANS

1) Military Initiatives

a) International Terrorism.
b) Developing Weapons of Mass Destruction.
c) War Crimes.
d) Genocide.

2) Diplomatic Initiatives

a) Arrogant and Dishonourable Manoeuvres.
b) Consort With and Support of Dictatorships.
c) Double Standards.
d) Economic Interference.
e) Foreign Interference.
f) Disregard of International Agreements.

3) Governmental Malfeasance/Failure to Protect Citizens

a) Authorise Assassinations.
b) Failure to Protect Citizens from Injustice.
c) 'Spin'.
d) Deception, Secrecy and Stifling the Press.
e) Disadvantage Political Opposition.
f) Favour Political Supporters.
g) Hijacking Democracy.
h) Infringements of Human Rights.
i) Ignore Citizens' Needs.
j) Ignore Due Process of Law.
k) Constructive Deception.

4) Malfeasance by the Public

a) Mindless Terrorist Activity.
b) Racism.

II PURSUIT OF WEALTH

a) Commercial and Financial Institutions.
b) Procure Wealth and Children.

III MAKING PROMISES

a) The Advertising Industry.

IV DECEPTIVENESS OF SATANIC PROMISES

I ATTACK BY EVERY MEANS

1) MILITARY INITIATIVES

a) INTERNATIONAL TERRORISM

According to the *Encyclopaedia Brittanica* – http://www.britannica.com/eb/article?eu=34493 – in the United States the standard definition used by the Federal Bureau of Investigation describes terrorism as 'the unlawful use of force and violence against persons or property to intimidate or coerce a government, the civilian population, or any segment thereof, in furtherance of political or social objectives'.

http://www.sfgate.com/cgi-bin/article.cgi?file=/chronicle/archive/2002/03/18/MN105584.DTL

San Francisco Chronicle, March 18, 2002, Monday

Chomsky to speak in Bay Area, MIT linguist critiques U.S. foreign policy

JONATHAN CURIEL, *Chronicle* Staff Writer

'Chomsky says the United States itself was practicing terrorism when it bombed Afghanistan and forced the Taliban from power. And it was terrorism, Chomsky says, when President Bush – without publicly providing conclusive proof, and without going to an international court of law – decided he wanted Osama bin Laden "dead or alive".'

http://query.nytimes.com/gst/abstract.html?res=F10D1EFF3A580C758CDDAC0894DB404482

New York Times Editorial Desk, May 6, 2003, Tuesday

Missing In Action: Truth

By NICHOLAS D. KRISTOF (NYT) 777 words

Late Edition – Final, Section A, Page 31, Column 1

'There are indications that the U.S. government manipulated intelligence, exaggerating the Iraqi threat to win support for the war.'

http://query.nytimes.com/gst/abstract.html?res=F30615F73F550C7B8DDDAA0894DB404482

New York Times Foreign Desk, March 18, 2003, Tuesday

Threats and Responses: News Analysis; A New Doctrine for War

By DAVID E. SANGER (NYT) 1290 words

Late Edition – Final, Section A, Page 1, Column 1

'In an age of unseen enemies, the president said, waiting for America's foes to attack "is suicide".'

b) DEVELOPING WEAPONS OF MASS DESTRUCTION

If WPM are rightly decried, on what basis do the most vociferous nations justify their own development and maintenance of such weaponry?

http://query.nytimes.com/gst/abstract.html?res=F20F16F635550C7A8EDDAC0894DB404482

New York Times National Desk, May 29, 2003, Thursday

Cold War Long Over, Bush Administration Examines Steps to a Revamped Arsenal

By CARL HULSE and JAMES DAO (NYT) 1511 words

Late Edition – Final, Section A, Page 23, Column 1

'Backed by Congressional sentiment favoring a new approach to nuclear weapons, the administration is looking at ways to update the nation's cold-war-era atomic arsenal.'

http://query.nytimes.com/gst/abstract.html?res=F60D11F734540C738DDDAA0894DA404482
New York Times Foreign Desk, March 10, 2002, Sunday
U.S. Nuclear Plan sees New Targets and New Weapons
By MICHAEL R. GORDON (NYT) 2145 words
Late Edition – Final, Section 1, Page 1, Column 5
'In a major shift in strategy, a secret Pentagon report calls for developing nuclear weapons that would be better suited for striking potential enemies.'

http://query.nytimes.com/gst/abstract.html?res=FB0E15F8345D0C758DDDAA0894DA404482
New York Times Foreign Desk, March 16, 2002, Saturday
Europe's Military Gap
By STEVEN ERLANGER (NYT) Military Analysis, 1647 words
Late Edition – Final, Section A, Page 1, Column 3
'Europe's unwillingness to spend more for defense may have undermined its credibility with the United States and damaged NATO as a military alliance.'

http://www.washingtonpost.com/ac2/wp-dyn?pagename=article&node=&contentId=A16892-2002Mar25&notFound=true
Washington Post, March 26, 2002, Tuesday
Afghan War Is a Lab for U.S. Innovation; New Technologies Are Tested in Battle
By VERNON LOEB *Washington Post* Staff Writer
Section A, Page 16
'Thirty new technologies, from armed aerial drones to dosimeters that measure exposure to toxic chemicals, have been rushed into use at home and abroad.'

c) WAR CRIMES

In refering to the US's newly developed 'Big Blue Two' thermobaric bomb, whose blast sucks up oxygen, collapses lungs, breaks eardrums and pulls out eyes, a Greenpeace disarmament spokesman said, 'They are inhumane and should not be used in a conventional war context.'

http://www.nytimes.com/2003/06/17/international/asia/17PRIS.html?th
New York Times Foreign Desk, June 17, 2003, Tuesday
Tales of Despair From Guantánamo
By CARLOTTA GALL with NEIL A. LEWIS (NYT) 1878 words
Late Edition – Final, Section A, Page 1, Column 1
'Afghans and Pakistanis who were held by the U.S. military say conditions were so bad that some captives attempted suicide.'

http://query.nytimes.com/gst/abstract.html?res=F40B1FF9345C0C748EDDAE0894DA404482

New York Times Editorial Desk, July 27, 2002, Saturday

Costs of Targeting Civilians

By CALEB CARR (NYT) 678 words

Late Edition – Final, Section A, Page 11, Column 6

'In an age when global public opinion is of dramatically increased importance, killing civilians only undermines a nation's force in both the field and the international arena.'

http://www.nytimes.com/2003/06/11/international/middleeast/11DIPL.html?th

New York Times Foreign Desk, June 11, 2003, Wednesday

Bush Rebukes Israel for Attack in Gaza

By STEVEN R. WEISMAN (NYT) 1165 words

Late Edition – Final, Section A, Page 1, Column 6

'The president asserted that Israel's attempt to kill a Palestinian militant leader undermined recent Mideast peace efforts.'

http://query.nytimes.com/gst/abstract.html?res=F60B10FB395C0C778EDDAE0894DA404482

New York Times Foreign Desk, July 24, 2002, Wednesday

Bush Denounces Israeli Airstrike as 'Heavy Handed'

By DAVID E. SANGER (NYT) 1176 words

Late Edition – Final, Section A, Page 1, Column 6

ABSTRACT – 'President Bush in a sharp change of tone, the Bush administration today condemned the Israeli bombing that killed a Hamas leader and 14 civilians . . .'

http://query.nytimes.com/gst/abstract.html?res=FA0E1FFA3E580C768DDDAD0894DA404482

New York Times Editorial Desk, April 15, 2002, Monday

Why Deterrence Failed in the West Bank

By DAVID K. SHIPLER (NYT) 811 words

Late Edition – Final, Section A, Page 23 , Column 1

'The first step toward relative peace in the Middle East has to be a standoff that implies an equal power relationship.'

http://www.washingtonpost.com/ac2/wp-dyn?pagename=article&node=&contentId=A64269-2002Nov3&notFound=true

Washington Post Foreign Service, November 4, 2002, Monday

Israel Committed War Crimes in West Bank, Rights Group Says

By JOHN WARD ANDERSON

Section A, Page 13

'There is "clear evidence" that Israeli soldiers and their commanders committed unlawful killings and torture in the West Bank, Amnesty International says in a report to be released today.'

http://www.nytimes.com/2002/07/23/international/middleeast/23GAZA.html?ex=1055563200&en=5dd2f66f6fca4b80&ei=5070

New York Times Foreign Desk, July 23, 2002, Tuesday

Israeli Strike in Gaza Kills a Hamas Leader and 14 Others

By JAMES BENNET (NYT) 1012 words

Late Edition – Final, Section A, Page 1, Column 6

'An Israeli missile today killed Sheik Salah Shehada, one of Israel's most wanted men, and at least 11 others, including several children.'

d) GENOCIDE

Webster's Third New International Dictionary describes genocide as: 'the use of deliberate systematic measures (as killing, bodily or mental injury, unlivable conditions, prevention of births) calculated to bring about the extermination of a racial, political, or cultural group or to destroy the language, religion, or culture of a group.'

The broader thinking behind Israel's military escalation was unveiled by Mr Sharon when he said that Israel must kill ever larger numbers of Palestinians until they submit.

http://query.nytimes.com/gst/abstract.html?res=F00917FE395C0C728EDDAC0894DA404482

New York Times Editorial Desk, May 21, 2002, Tuesday

How the Settler Suburbs Grew

By DAVID NEWMAN (NYT) Op-Ed 1373 words

Late Edition – Final, Section A, Page 21, Column 2

'200,000 Israelis live on captured land. They can't all stay.'

http://query.nytimes.com/gst/abstract.html?res=F20E11F8355D0C738EDDAE0894DA404482

New York Times Foreign Desk, July 20, 2002, Saturday

Israel Threatens to Deport Relatives of 2 Fugitive Militants

By JOHN KIFNER (NYT) 1090 words

Late Edition – Final, Section A, Page 3, Column 1

'In a change of tactics, the Israeli Army on Friday rounded up 21 male relatives of two fugitive Palestinian militants whom it blamed for attacks this week.'

2 DIPLOMATIC INITIATIVES

a) ARROGANT AND DISHONOURABLE MANOEUVRES

Financial Times Published: April 24, 2002 19:23/ Last Updated: April 24, 2002 19:27

Israeli fears drive effort to stall UN Jenin team

By HARVEY MORRIS in Jerusalem

'Fears of an internationally imposed solution to the Middle East crisis are prompting Israel's growing resistance to the United Nations fact-finding team due to investigate events in the war-devastated Jenin refugee camp.'

http://query.nytimes.com/gst/abstract.html?res=F00C15FD3F550C7B8DDDAA0894DB404482

New York Times Editorial Desk, March 18, 2003, Tuesday

Things to Come

By PAUL KRUGMAN (NYT) Op-Ed 802 words

Late Edition – Final, Section A, Page 33, Column 5

'Victory in Iraq won't end the world's distrust of the United States, because the Bush administration has made it clear that it doesn't play by the rules.'

http://query.nytimes.com/gst/abstract.html?res=F30C15F83B5A0C708EDDAB0894DA404482

New York Times Foreign Desk, February 23, 2002, Saturday

A Nation Challenged: The Allies; Europe Seethes as the U.S. Flies Solo in World Affairs

By STEVEN ERLANGER (NYT) 1512 words

Late Edition – Final, Section A, Page 8, column 5

'Europe's solidarity with the Bush administration, declared so quickly after Sept 11, has faded almost as suddenly.'

http://query.nytimes.com/gst/abstract.html?res=F30815FE3D5D0C738DDDAA0894DA404482

New York Times Foreign Desk, March 10, 2002, Sunday

A Nation Challenged: Washington; 6 Months after Sept. 11, Bush to Give Strategy for Intensified War on Terror

By DAVID E. SANGER (NYT) 922 words

Late Edition – Final, Section 1, Page 26, Column 1

'President Bush will describe his strategy for the war on terrorism on Monday, suggesting that he may pursue Al Qaeda inside countries that do not ask for an American presence.'

b) CONSORT WITH AND SUPPORT OF DICTATORSHIPS

http://query.nytimes.com/gst/abstract.html?res=F70614FD3C540C768CDDAA0894DA404482

New York Times Foreign Desk, March 5, 2002, Tuesday

U.S. Rights Report Criticizes Allies in Antiterror Campaign

By TODD S. PURDUM (NYT) 887 words

Late Edition – Final, Section A, Page 14, Column 1

'Many of the Bush administration's strategic allies in the war on terror abused human rights in their own countries last year.'

http://query.nytimes.com/gst/abstract.html?res=FB0B14F93E5F0C778CDDA10894DA404482

New York Times Editorial Desk, August 4, 2002, Sunday

Bush's Shame

By THOMAS L. FRIEDMAN (NYT) 788 words

Late Edition – Final, Section 4, Page 13, Column 1

'The response to Egypt's decision to imprison a democracy advocate leaves one wondering whether the Bush foreign policy team isn't just a bunch of phonies.'

http://query.nytimes.com/gst/abstract.html?res=F00E16F73F550C768EDDAC0894DB404482

New York Times Editorial Desk, May 25, 2003, Sunday

Hummers Here, Hummers There

By THOMAS L. FRIEDMAN (NYT) 807 Words

Late Edition – Final, Section 4, Page 9, Column 1

'We never talk straight to Saudi Arabia because we are addicted to its oil. Addicts never tell the truth to their pushers.'

c) DOUBLE STANDARDS

http://query.nytimes.com/gst/abstract.html?res=F1061FF939550C718DDDA00894DA404482

New York Times A Nation Challenged, September 12, 2002, Thursday

VIGILANCE AND MEMORY: UNITED NATIONS; Departing Rights Commissioner Faults U.S.

By JULIA PRESTON (NYT) 590 words

Late Edition – Final, Section B, Page 22, Column 2

'UNITED NATIONS, Sept. 11 – In the final days of her five years in office, Mary Robinson, the United Nations' high commissioner for human rights, has sharply criticized the United States for eroding civil liberties at home and human rights standards around the world since the Sept. 11 terrorist attacks.'

http://query.nytimes.com/gst/abstract.html?res=F30A15FC3D5C0C748DDDAA0894DA404482

New York Times Editorial Desk, March 17, 2002, Sunday

Better Late Than . . .

By THOMAS L. FRIEDMAN (NYT) Op-Ed 821 words

Late Edition – Final, Section 4, Page 15, Column 1

'President Bush's speech on Thursday announcing a big increase in foreign aid for poor countries is a breakthrough for this administration.'

http://query.nytimes.com/gst/abstract.html?res=F20911FA38590C7B8DDDA10894DA404482

New York Times Foreign Desk, August 18, 2002, Sunday

Officers Say U.S. Aided Iraq in War Despite Use of Gas

By PATRICK E. TYLER (NYT) 1463 words

Late Edition – Final, Section 1, Page 1, Column 6

'A covert American program during the Reagan administration provided Iraq with critical battle-planning assistance at a time when American intelligence agencies knew that Iraqis would use chemical weapons.'

d) ECONOMIC INTERFERENCE

http://query.nytimes.com/gst/abstract.html?res=F10714FC3B550C768CDDAE0894DA404482

New York Times Editorial Desk, July 5, 2002, Friday

Farm Subsidies that Kill

By NICHOLAS KRISTOF (NYT) 756 words

Late Edition – Final, Section A, Page 19, Column 1

'By inflating farm subsidies, Congress and the Bush administration are impoverishing and killing Africans whom they claim to help.'

e) FOREIGN INTERFERENCE

http://query.nytimes.com/gst/abstract.html?res=F00715F635540C728EDDA00894DA404482

New York Times Arts & Ideas/Cultural Desk, September 21, 2002, Saturday

Belgium Confronts Its Heart of Darkness

By ALAN RIDING (NYT) 1569 words

Late Edition – Final, Section B, Page 9, Column 4

'Belgium's pride in its colonial past in the Congo has always been shadowed by a darker history, one marked by two decades of perhaps the cruelest rule ever inflicted on a colonized people.'

http://query.nytimes.com/gst/abstract.html?res=F60914F93C540C768CDDAA0894DA404482

New York Times Editorial Desk, March 5, 2002, Tuesday

Our Own Terrorist

By NICHOLAS D. KRISTOF (NYT) 774 words

Late Edition – Final, Section A, Page 23, Column 1

'If we want to fathom how countries like Saudi Arabia or Pakistan could possibly support terrorists, we might peek into a mirror.'

http://query.nytimes.com/gst/abstract.html?res=F50811F83C5E0C728FDDAA0894DA404482

*New York Time*s Foreign Desk, March 31, 2002, Sunday

From Old Files, a New Story of U.S. Role in Angolan War

By HOWARD W. FRENCH (NYT) 757 words

Late Edition – Final, Section 1, Page 4, Column 1

'Historians and former diplomats who have studied documents say they show conclusively that the United States intervened in Angola weeks before the arrival of any Cubans, not afterward as Washington claimed.'

f) DISREGARD OF INTERNATIONAL AGREEMENTS

http://query.nytimes.com/gst/abstract.html?res=F30D10F7385C0C768EDDAE0894DA404482

New York Times Foreign Desk, July 25, 2002, Thursday

U.S. Fails in Effort to Block Vote on U.N. Convention on Torture

By BARBARA CROSSETTE (NYT) 501 words

Late Edition – Final, Section A, Page 7, Column 5

'The United States lost a bid on Wednesday to rewrite a United Nations' plan intended to reinforce the 1989 convention against torture.'

http://query.nytimes.com/gst/abstract.html?res=F30E10FB3C5D0C728EDDA80994DA404482

New York Times Editorial Desk, November 21, 2002, Thursday

How War Left the Law Behind

By MICHAEL J. GLENNON (NYT) 765 words

Late Edition Final, Section A, Page 37, Column 2

'In a breakdown of international rules governing the use of force, the Security Council's decisions are binding for Iraq, but not the United States.'

http://query.nytimes.com/gst/abstract.html?res=FA0615F73F5C0C768CDDAD0894DB404482

New York Times National Desk, April 5, 2003, Saturday

A Nation at War: Weapons; U.S. Use of Tear Gas Could Violate Treaty, Critics Say

By NICHOLAS WADE with ERIC SCHMITT (NYT) 861 words

Late Edition – Final, Section B, Page 13, Column 3

'President Bush has authorized American military forces to use tear gas in Iraq, a development that could be seen as a breach of the Chemical Weapons Convention.'

3) GOVERNMENTAL MALFEASANCE / FAILURE TO PROTECT CITIZENS

a) AUTHORISE ASSASSINATIONS

http://query.nytimes.com/gst/abstract.html?res=FB0916FE3D590C768DDDAB0994DA404482

New York Times Foreign Desk, December 15, 2002, Sunday

Threats and responses: Hunt for Al Qaeda; Bush Has Widened Authority of C.I.A. to Kill Terrorists

By JAMES RISEN and DAVID JOHNSTON (NYT) 1336 words

Late edition – Final, Section 1, Page 1, Column 6

'The Bush administration has prepared a list of about two dozen terrorist leaders that the C.I.A. is authorized to kill.'

b) FAILURE TO PROTECT CITIZENS FROM INJUSTICE

http://query.nytimes.com/gst/abstract.html?res=F00810F8355D0C718EDDAE0894DA404482

New York Times Editorial Desk, July 22, 2002, Monday

Remember Our Slaves

PROF ERIC FONER Letter to the Editor (NYT) 203 words

Late Edition – Final, Section A, Page 16, Column 4

'The opening in Battery Park City of a memorial to victims of the Irish famine of 1845–52, near the Living Memorial to the Holocaust, suggests that Americans are more comfortable remembering others' violations of human rights than our own.'

c) 'SPIN'

http://query.nytimes.com/gst/abstract.html?res=F10615FD3C5A0C738EDDAB0894DA404482

New York Times Editorial Desk, February 20, 2002, Wednesday

Office of Strategic Mendacity

By MAUREEN DOWD (NYT) 696 words

Late Edition – Final, Section A, Page 21, Column 1

'People at the Defense Department and elsewhere are cringing at the news that the Pentagon's shadowy new Office of Strategic Influence is plotting to plant deliberately false stories in the foreign press.'

http://query.nytimes.com/gst/abstract.html?res=FA0B10FB3A5A0C778EDDAB0894DA404482

New York Times Editorial Desk, February 24, 2002, Sunday

Coyote Rummy

By MAUREEN DOWD (NYT) Op-Ed 753 words

Late Edition – Final, Section 4, Page 13, Column 5

'I want the secretary of defense to tell the Pentagon to kick its addiction to fiction.'

http://query.nytimes.com/gst/abstract.html?res=F40810FC39540C768EDDAA0894DB404482

New York Times Editorial Desk, March 25, 2003, Tuesday

Channels of Influence

By PAUL KRUGMAN (NYT) 732 words

Late Edition – Final, Section A, Page 17, Column 6

'Pro-war rallies are being promoted by key players in the radio industry with close links to the Bush administration.'

http://query.nytimes.com/gst/abstract.html?res=F20A12FC345F0C7A8EDDAA0894DA404482
New York Times Editorial Desk, March 29, 2002, Friday
The Smoke Machine
By PAUL KRUGMAN (NYT) 810 words
Late Edition – Final, Section A, Page 29, Column 1
'The "vast right-wing conspiracy" is not an overheated metaphor but a straightforward reality, and it works a lot like a special-interest lobby.'

http://query.nytimes.com/gst/abstract.html?res=F30C1EFF3A580C758CDDAC0894DB404482
New York Times Editorial Desk, May 6, 2003, Tuesday
Man on Horseback
By PAUL KRUGMAN (NYT) 787 words
Late Edition – Final, Section A, Page 31, Column 6
'There was a time when patriotic Americans would have denounced any president who tried to take political advantage of his role as commander in chief.'

http://query.nytimes.com/gst/abstract.html?res=F10612FB3E540C768EDDAA0894DB404482
New York Times Editorial Desk, March 25, 2003, Tuesday
In this war, News Is A Weapon
By LUCIAN K. TRUSCOTT IV (NYT) 800 words
Late Edition – Final, Section A, Page 17, Column 2
'The Pentagon may have been dragged kicking and screaming into its current embrace of the news media. But it is making the most of it.'

http://www.nytimes.com/2003/08/05/opinion/05KRUG.html?th=&pagewanted=print&position=
New York Times Editorial Desk, August 5, 2003, Tuesday
Everything Is Political
By PAUL KRUGMAN (NYT) Op-Ed 775 words
Late Edition – Final, Section A, Page 15, Column 6
'The erosion of the Treasury's intellectual integrity is exemplified by its denial and deception on the subject of tax cuts.'

d) DECEPTION, SECRECY AND STIFLING THE PRESS

http://query.nytimes.com/gst/abstract.html?res=F10E13F734540C7B8EDDAA0894DB404482
New York Times Editorial Desk, March 28, 2003, Friday
Delusions of Power
By PAUL KRUGMAN (NYT) 712 words
Late Edition – Final, Section A, Page 17, Column 1
'In the last two years Dick Cheney and other top officials have gotten it wrong on energy, on the economy – and their mistakes keep getting bigger.'

http://query.nytimes.com/gst/abstract.html?res=F30C17FE3B5C0C7B8CDDAD0894DB404482
New York Times Editorial Desk, April 8, 2003, Tuesday
The Last Refuge
By PAUL KRUGMAN (NYT) Op-Ed 757 words
Late Edition – Final, Section A, Page 23, Column 6
'Self-styled patriots are trying to impose constraints on political speech, accusing anyone who criticizes the president of undermining the war effort.'

http://query.nytimes.com/gst/abstract.html?res=F20913FB38550C728CDDAA0894DA404482
New York Times Editorial Desk, March 1, 2002, Friday
Two Thousand Acres
By PAUL KRUGMAN (NYT) 764 words
Late Edition – Final, Section A, Page 23, Column 1
'Deceptive advertising pervades the administration's effort to sell the nation on its energy strategy.'

http://query.nytimes.com/gst/abstract.html?res=F30813FB3A550C718CDDAA0894DA404482
New York Times Editorial Desk, March 2, 2002, Saturday
Freedom From the Press
By FRANK RICH (NYT) 1513 words
Late Edition – Final, Section A, Page 15, Column 1
'There is still scant evidence to suggest that George W. Bush condones the idea of a free press.'

http://query.nytimes.com/gst/abstract.html?res=F10D14FD3B5F0C748EDDAA0894DA404482

New York Times National Desk, March 27, 2002, Wednesday

Bush Energy Paper Followed Industry Push

By DON VAN NATTA Jr. and NEELA BANERJEE (NYT) 1783 words

Late Edition – Final, Section A, Page 20, Column 1

'The energy secretary did not meet with environmental organisations or consumer groups as he helped the Bush administration write its national energy report last year.'

e) DISADVANTAGE POLITICAL OPPOSITION

http://query.nytimes.com/gst/abstract.html?res=FA0C1FF9345C0C748EDDAE0894DA404482

New York Times Editorial Desk, July 27, 2002, Saturday

A Growing Gap in American Democracy

By SASHA ABRAMSKY (NYT) 716 words

Late Edition – Final, Section A, Page 11, Column 1

'Felony disenfranchisement, coupled with very high incarceration rates, has become a major challenge to our democratic values.'

http://query.nytimes.com/gst/abstract.html?res=F00D1FFA3F5C0C768CDDAD0894DB404482

New York Times Editorial Desk, April 5, 2003, Saturday

The World's Other Tyrants, Still at Work

By ARYEH NEIER (NYT) 787 words

Late Edition – Final, Section A, Page 13, Column 1

'With international attention focused on Iraq, despots are seizing the opportunity to get rid of their opposition – real or imagined.'

http://www.nytimes.com/2003/06/29/politics/campaigns/29CAMP.html?th=&pagewanted=print&position=#top

New York Times National Desk, June 29, 2003, Sunday

Bush Plays It Fast, With Hard Money

By DAVID E. ROSENBAUM (NYT) 1305 words

Late Edition – Final, Section 1, Page 20, Column 4

'President Bush's re-election campaign is raising massive amounts of money with which to paint an unfavorable picture of the candidate Democrats nominate for president.'

f) FAVOUR POLITICAL SUPPORTERS

http://www.nytimes.com/2003/06/30/opinion/30HERB.html?th=&pagewanted=print&position=

New York Times Editorial Desk, June 30, 2003, Monday

Oblivious in D.C.

By BOB HERBERT (NYT) 685 words

Late Edition – Final, Section A, Page 21, Column 1

'The president, buoyed by the bountiful patronage of the upper classes, seems indifferent to the harsh struggles of the working classes and the poor.'

http://www.nytimes.com/2003/06/23/opinion/23HERB.html?th

New York Times Editorial Desk, June 23, 2003, Monday

The Money Magnet

By BOB HERBERT (NYT) 750 words

Late Edition – Final, Section A, Page 21, Column 1

'While these may be the best of times for George W. Bush, this is not such a great moment for America.'

g) HIGHJACKING DEMOCRACY

http://query.nytimes.com/gst/abstract.html?res=F70B1FF7355C0C718EDDAA0894DA404482

New York Times Editorial Desk, March 22, 2002, Friday

Free the Hatemongers!

By NICHOLAS KRISTOF (NYT) 717 words

Late Edition – Final, Section A, Page 25, Column 5

'We should not allow the war on terror to erode the freedom even of those Islamists whom we despise.'

http://query.nytimes.com/gst/abstract.html?res=F30914FF3A5A0C708EDDAB0894DA404482

New York Times Business Desk, February 23, 2002, Saturday

Agency files suit for Cheney papers on energy policy

By DON VAN NATTA Jr. (NYT) 1323 words

Late Edition – Final, Section A, Page 1, Column 6

'The General Accounting Office sued Vice President Dick Cheney on Friday for failing to provide access to records of meetings of the national energy task force.'

http://query.nytimes.com/gst/abstract.html?res=F20E11FA3D550C718CDDAE0894DA404482
New York Times Foreign Desk, July 2, 2002, Tuesday
Study Warns of Stagnation in Arab Societies
By BARBARA CROSSETTE (NYT) 1163 words
Late Edition – Final, Section A, Page 11, Column 1
'A lack of political freedom, the repression of women and an isolation from the world of ideas are crippling Arab societies, a new report says.'

http://query.nytimes.com/gst/abstract.html?res=F30A13FD3B5D0C728CDDAD0894DB404482
New York Times Editorial Desk, April 1, 2003, Tuesday
A Red-Blue Terror Alert
By PAUL KRUGMAN (NYT) 758 words
Late Edition – Final, Section A, Page 19, Column 5
'Driven by its hostility to government spending and its exaltation of the "heartland" over urban states, the Bush administration has neglected homeland security.'

http://query.nytimes.com/gst/abstract.html?res=FA0F13FC3B550C728CDDAA0894DA404482
New York Times Editorial Desk, March 1, 2002, Friday
Putting Us to the Test
By NICHOLAS D. KRISTOF (NYT) 823 words
Late Edition – Final, Section A, Page 23, Column 5
'A university, even a country, becomes sterile when people are too intimidated to say things out of the mainstream.'

http://query.nytimes.com/gst/abstract.html?res=FA0A1FF6395F0C778CDDA10894DA404482
New York Times Editorial Desk, August 4, 2002, Sunday
Broken Promises and Political Deception
By AL GORE (NYT) 1056 words
Late Edition – Final, Section 4, Page 13, Column 1
'How do we make sure that political power is used for the benefit of the many, rather than the few?'

http://query.nytimes.com/gst/abstract.html?res=F30D17F73A540C7A8CDDAA0894DA404482
New York Times Editorial Desk, March 9, 2002, Saturday
Taking Our Liberties
By ANTHONY LEWIS (NYT) 738 words
Late Edition – Final, Section A, Page 15, Column 6
'War without end is likely to have, indeed is already having profound consequences for the American constitutional system.'

http://query.nytimes.com/gst/abstract.html?res=F60E10FC35550C708CDDAA0894DA404482
New Your Times Editorial Desk, March 3, 2002, Sunday
60 Feet Under
By MAUREEN DOWD (NYT) 685 words
Late Edition – Final, Section 4, Page 15, Column 5
'The shadow government suits this administration to a T-ball, reflecting its twin obsessions with secrecy and self-perpetuation.'

http://www.nytimes.com/2003/06/24/opinion/24MART.html?th
New York Times Editorial Desk, June 24, 2003, Tuesday
Let Judges Do Their Jobs
By JOHN S. MARTIN Jr. (NYT) 696 words
Late Edition – Final, Section A, Page 31, Column 2
'For a judge to be deprived of the ability to formulate a just sentence is completely at odds with the American system of justice.'

http://query.nytimes.com/gst/abstract.html?res=F40617FE355A0C728EDDAC0894DB404482
New York Times National Desk, May 21,. 2003 Wednesday
Justice Dept. Lists Use of New Power to Fight Terror
By ERIC LICHTBLAU (NYT) 1178 words
Late Edition – Final, Section A, Page 1, Column 1
'Federal agents have conducted hundreds of bugging and surveillance operations and visited numerous libraries and mosques using new law-enforcement tools.'

http://www.nytimes.com/2003/05/27/opinion/27KRUG.html?ex=1058414400&en=935bc873c97ea50f&ei=5070

New York Times Editorial Desk, May 27, 2003, Tuesday

Stating the Obvious

By PAUL KRUGMAN (NYT) 784 words

Late Edition – Final, Section A, Page 25, Volumn 6

'The Bush administration is setting the country up for a fiscal crisis in which popular social programs can be sharply cut.'

h) INFRINGEMENTS OF HUMAN RIGHTS

The repression and violence of those who are determined to grasp or maintain their political, financial, or military advantage, blight the lives of millions. Many suffer the effects of genocide, other atrocities, or are abused because of their race, religion, or gender, and many of those who flee to the safety of other countries, meet with obstacles and hostility.

Organisations that oppose crimes against humanity, such as Amnesty International and the Islamic Human Rights Commission, chronicle crimes under headings such as abuse of the mentally ill, arbitrary arrests, beatings, cruel judicial punishments, cruel, inhumane, or degrading prison conditions, curtailment of freedom of expression and association, executions, extrajudicial killings and 'disappearances', genocide, hostage taking, ill-treatment of indigenous peoples in land rights disputes, incarceration of prisoners of conscience, indefinite detention without charge or trial, infliction of psychological damage, lack of medical care, mistreatment, mutilations, rape, secret, summary and unfair trials, subjugation of people or groups of people, torture and war crimes.

Human rights violations and abuses are more frequent and widespread than many imagine and occur everyday in one part of the world or another. Amnesty International reports and lists these abuses country by country.

http://www.nytimes.com/2003/06/19/national/19IMMI.html?tntemail1

New York Times National Desk, June 19, 2003, Thursday

Study Says Government Improperly Detained Foreign Children

By RACHEL L. SWARNS (NYT) 789 words

Late Edition – Final, Section A, Page 15, Column 6

'Foreign children fleeing violence and persecution in their home countries are often kept for months in bleak detention centers in the United States, the study said.'

http://query.nytimes.com/gst/abstract.html?res=F0061EF635550C7A8EDDAC0894DB404482

New York Times Foreign Desk, May 29, 2003, Thursday

Amnesty Calls World Less Safe

By SARAH LYALL (NYT) 277 words

Late Edition – Final, Section A, Page 13, Column 1

'The world has become more dangerous, and governments more repressive, the human rights group Amnesty International said.'

http://query.nytimes.com/gst/abstract.html?res=F30B13FD385C0C748CDDAD0894DB404482

New York Times Editorial Desk, April 7, 2003, Monday

A Global Catalog of Wrongs

Editorial (NYT) 410 words

Late Edition – Final, Section A, Page 18, Column 1

'The State Department's annual report of human rights' violations around the world looks at friend and foe alike with candid scrutiny.'

http://query.nytimes.com/gst/abstract.html?res=F3081EFB3A5E0C778DDDAB0994DA404482

New York Times Editorial Desk, December 14, 2002, Saturday

The Selective Conscience

By BILL KELLER (NYT) 1506 words

Late Edition – Final, Section A, Page 29, Column 1

'The Bush administration's enthusiasm for human rights would be more believable if it were less selectively applied.'

http://query.nytimes.com/gst/abstract.html?res=F30612FE3F550C7B8DDDAA0894DB404482

New York Times Foreign Desk, March 18, 2003, Tuesday

U.S. Could Come Under Scrutiny of the U.N. Rights Commission

By ALISON LANGLEY (NYT) 576 words

Late Edition – Final, Section A, Page 13, Column 1

'The U.N. Commission on Human Rights, with Libya's ambassador as its chairman, is likely to focus on the U.S. record and recent actions.'

http://query.nytimes.com/gst/abstract.html?res=F10810FA3F5C0C768CDDAD0894DB404482
New York Times Foreign Desk, April 5, 2003, Saturday
Israel Stems Suicide Bombings, but at a Cost
By GREG MYRE (NYT) 1509 words
Late Edition – Final, Section A, Page 3, Column 1
'The relentless and uncompromising approach taken by Israel has raised questions about what is a legitimate response to suicide bombings.'

i) IGNORE CITIZENS' NEEDS

http://www.nytimes.com/2003/06/17/opinion/17KRUG.html?th
New York Times Editorial Desk, June 17, 2003, Tuesday
Dereliction of Duty
By PAUL KRUGMAN (NYT) 797 words
Late Edition – Final, Section A, Page 27, Column 6
'Behind the rhetoric of the Bush administration's "war on terror" lies a pattern of refusing to take crucial actions to protect us from terrorists.'

http://query.nytimes.com/gst/abstract.html?res=F60B13FC3A5C0C728EDDAA0894DA404482
New York Times National Desk, March 21, 2002, Thursday
Minorities Get Inferior Care, Even if Insured, Study Finds
By SHERYL GAY STOLBERG (NYT) 954 words
Late Edition – Final, Section A, Page 1, Column 1
'Racial and ethnic minorities in the U.S. receive lower quality health care than whites, even when their insurance and income are the same.'

http://query.nytimes.com/gst/abstract.html?res=F10810FF3F5E0C7A8CDDA10894DA404482
New York Times National Desk, August 9, 2002, Friday
Neediest Schools Receive Less Money, Report Finds
By DIANA JEAN SCHEMO (NYT) 903 words
Late Edition – Final, Section A, Page 10, Column 5
'A report shows that in most states, school districts teaching the neediest students receive far less money from state and local sources than schools with the fewest children in poverty.'

http://query.nytimes.com/gst/abstract.html?res=F10912F93A540C748EDDAA0894DB404482

New York Times Editorial Desk, March 27, 2003, Thursday

Casualties at Home

By BOB HERBERT (NYT) 778 words

Late Edition – Final, Section A, Page 23, Column 5

'The administration is actually fighting two wars, one against Iraq and another against the idea of a humane and responsive government here at home.'

http://www.nytimes.com/2003/07/03/opinion/03HERB.html?th=&pagewanted=print&position=

New York Times Editorial Desk, July 3, 2003, Thursday

Picking Workers' Pockets

By BOB HERBERT (NYT) 763 words

Late Edition – Final, Section A, Page 23, Column 6

'I wonder how many Americans agree with the Bush administration that working longer hours for less money is a good thing.'

j) IGNORE DUE PROCESS OF LAW

http://www.nytimes.com/2003/06/03/opinion/03TUE1.html?th

New York Times Editorial Desk, June 3, 2003, Tuesday

The Abusive Detentions of Sept. 11

Editorial (NYT) 534 words

Late Edition – Final, Section A, Page 30, Column 1

'A blistering report by the inspector general of the Justice Department criticizes the round-up of terrorist suspects after Sept. 11.'

http://query.nytimes.com/gst/abstract.html?res=F50917F8395F0C778CDDA10894DA404482

New York Times National Desk, August 4, 2002, Sunday

After Sept. 11, a Legal Battle On the Limits of Civil Liberty

This article was reported and written by ADAM LIPTAK, NEIL A. LEWIS and BENJAMIN WEISER (NYT) 4115 words

Late Edition – Final, Section 1, Page 1, Column 1

'A battle over the detention of more than 1,200 people is redefining the balance between individual liberties and national security.'

http://query.nytimes.com/gst/abstract.html?res=F40D16F93E5F0C708CDDA10894DA404482
New York Times National Desk, August 3, 2002, Saturday
Judge Orders U.S. to Release Names of 9/11 Detainees
By NEIL A. LEWIS (NYT) 1142 words
Late Edition – Final, Section A, Page 1, Column 6
'A federal judge ordered the Bush administration to release the names of most the people arrested within 15 days.'

k) CONSTRUCTIVE DECEPTION

http://query.nytimes.com/gst/abstract.html?res=F50D10F83B5C0C738FDDAE0894DA404482
New York Times Editorial Desk, July 30, 2002, Tuesday
Our Banana Republics
By PAUL KRUGMAN (NYT) 785 words
Late Edition – Final, Section A, Page 19, Column 5
'In recent years many states have been run like banana republics: responsibility gave way to political opportunism, and in some cases to mob rule.'

http://www.nytimes.com/2003/07/15/opinion/15KRIS.html?th
New York Times Editorial Desk, July 15, 2003, Tuesday
16 Words, and Counting
By NICHOLAS D. KRISTOF (NYT) 759 words
Late Edition – Final, Section A, Page 21, Column 1
'The Niger uranium hoax is only part of the picture. The bigger the picture gets, the more it looks like a pattern of dishonesty.'

http://www.nytimes.com/2003/07/15/international/worldspecial/15ASSE.html?th=&pagewanted=print&position=
New York Times Foreign Desk, July 15, 2003, Tuesday
After the War: The Speech; A Shifting Spotlight on Uranium Sales
By DAVID E. SANGER (NYT) 1138 words
Late Edition – Final, Section A, Page 11, Column 4
'Some in the intelligence world say that the evidence did not change – but the political environment around it did.'

http://www.nytimes.com/2003/06/19/politics/19CLIM.html?th

New York Times Washington Desk, June 19, 2003, Thursday

Report by the E.P.A. Leaves Out Data on Climate Change

By ANDREW C. REVKIN with KATHARINE Q. SEELYE (NYT) 1119 words

Late Edition – Final, Section A, Page 1, Column 1

'After editing by the White House, a section describing risks from rising global temperatures has been whittled to a few noncommittal paragraphs.'

http://www.nytimes.com/2003/06/24/opinion/24KRUG.html?th

New York Times Editorial Desk, June 24, 2003, Tuesday

Denial and Deception

By PAUL KRUGMAN (NYT) 748 words

Late Edition – Final, Section A, Page 31, Column 6

'There is no longer any doubt that we were deceived into war. The key question now is why so many influential people are unwilling to admit the obvious.'

http://query.nytimes.com/gst/abstract.html?res=F70913FF35590C738FDDAD0894DB404482

New York Times Editorial Desk, April 30, 2003, Wednesday

Hypocrisy & Apple Pie

By MAUREEN DOWD (NYT) 736 words

Late Edition – Final, Section A, Page 27, Column 2

'America is a furtive empire, afraid to raise its flag or linger too long or even call things by their real names.'

http://www.nytimes.com/2003/05/16/politics/16IMAG.html?ex=1058414400&en=e113fc64d9e548dd&ei=5070

New York Times National Desk May 16, 2003, Friday

Keepers of Bush Image Lift Stagecraft to New Heights

By ELISABETH BUMILLER (NYT) 1757 words

Late Edition – Final, Section A, Page 1, Column 1

'The White House is using the powers of television and technology to promote President Bush's presidency in ways that have not been seen before.'

http://www.nytimes.com/2003/07/15/opinion/15KRUG.html?th

New York Times Editorial Desk, July 15, 2003, Tuesday

Pattern of Corruption

By PAUL KRUGMAN (NYT) 752 words

Late Edition – Final, Section A, Page 21, Column 6

'The case of the bogus uranium purchases was part of a broad pattern of politicized, corrupted intelligence.'

http://query.nytimes.com/gst/abstract.html?res=FB0F17FB38540C708CDDAF0894DB404482

*New York Time*s Editorial Desk, June 3, 2003, Tuesday

Standard Operating Procedure

By PAUL KRUGMAN (NYT) 788 words

Late Edition – Final, Section A, Page 31, Column 6

'Misleading the public has been a consistent strategy for the Bush team on issues from tax policy to the war in Iraq.'

http://www.nytimes.com/2003/06/10/opinion/10KRUG.html?th=&pagewanted=print&position=

New York Times Editorial Desk, June 10, 2003, Tuesday

Who's Accountable?

By PAUL KRUGMAN (NYT) 745 words

Late Edition – Final, Section A, Page 29, Column 5

'It's outrageous that nobody is being held accountable for misleading the nation into war.'

4) MALFEASANCE BY THE PUBLIC

Society collaborates in the erosion of boundaries – between child and adult, innocence and experience, youth and maturity, morality and indulgence. The fashion, toy, music and film industries target under-eights to seamlessly transform the innocent into sex objects. Schools expropriate the parental role, not to teach morality, but to set boundaries for sexual behaviour and advise young schoolgirls on the availability of contraception and abortifacient pills. Television programmes dismantle the norms of morality with programmes on a seemingly infinite range of sexual misbehaviour. Adult responsibilities are postponed and marriages delayed by desires to indulge in commitment-free hedonistic behaviour.

While most children are loved and cared for, many are abused by parents, by paedophiles and assaulted, stabbed, or shot by other children. Unsuspecting women become victim to illegal drugs which render them unable to resist sexual assault and rape.

Ethnic minorities, the elderly and the vulnerable are easy targets for attack and robbery. And every household and personal effect has now to be securely protected and insured.

a) MINDLESS TERRORIST ACTIVITY

Although it would be appropriate to include mass murder of innocent people in the category 'Human Rights and Abuses' or 'Outrageous Military Force', the scale, the world-wide incredulity and shock engendered by the heinous attacks of 11 September, 2001 have highlighted the necessity to include a specific category to cover politically motivated atrocities by demented, deranged and depraved people.

b) RACISM

Some entice support by proclaiming that their 'race is, or is in danger of being usurped by people who are different and supposedly inferior'. Their power is based on promises of land, or of work and property redistribution. Thus, Serbs displace Bosnians and Kosovans, Hutus kill Tutsis, Dayaks kill Madurese, Shona attack Matabele. Every possible means to kill, maim and exterminate is used in nefarious attacks to terrorise and massacre victims. The perpetrators then demand recognition as a legal government, on the grounds that they control populations, mineral wealth, land and armaments. Adolph Hitler justified the necessity of the Holocaust's ethnic cleansing by claiming a 'Jewish Problem' – today, Zionists justify equally disgusting ethnic cleansing and persecution with claims of an equally elusive 'Palestinian Problem'.

II PURSUIT OF WEALTH

a) Commercial and Financial Institutions

http://query.nytimes.com/gst/abstract.html?res=F10817F734540C7B8EDDAA0894DB404482

New York Times Business/Financial Desk, March 28, 2003, Friday

HealthSouth Inquiry Expands to Medicare

By KURT EICHENWALD (NYT) 1354 words

Late Edition – Final, Section C, Page 1, Column 2

'Federal officials are investigating whether HealthSouth used an illegal accounting scheme to cheat Medicare out of millions.'

http://query.nytimes.com/gst/abstract.html?res=FB0711FF35540C748EDDAA0894DB404482

New York Times National Desk, March 27, 2003, Thursday

Panel Finds Manipulation By Energy Companies

By RICHARD A. OPPEL Jr. (NYT) 1139 words

Late Edition – Final, Section A, Page 14, Column 5

'During the 2000–2001 energy crisis in California, electricity and natural gas prices were driven higher because of widespread manipulation by over 30 energy companies.'

http://www.nytimes.com/2003/07/03/business/03TAX.html?th

New York Times Business/Financial Desk, July 3, 2003, Thursday

Ernst & Young to Pay U.S. $15 Million in Tax Case

By DAVID CAY JOHNSTON (NYT) 780 words

Late Edition – Final, Section C, Page 1, Column 5

'The accounting firm will make the payment because it did not properly register tax shelters and similar transactions or properly maintain lists of people who bought them.'

http://query.nytimes.com/gst/abstract.html?res=F30F12F7355F0C718CDDA10894DA404482

New York Times Business/Financial Desk, August 2, 2002, Friday

E-Mail Gaps May Mean Fines for Big Firms

By PATRICK McGEEHAN (NYT) 638 words

Late Edition – Final, Section C, Page 4, Column 1

'Securities regulators have told six investment banks that they may have to pay as much as $10 million in penalties for not keeping e-mail messages as required.'

http://query.nytimes.com/gst/abstract.html?res=FB0A1FFF3F5E0C758EDDA80894DA404482

New York Times Editorial Desk, January 26, 2002, Saturday

Enron for Dummies

By BILL KELLER (NYT) 1593 words

Late Edition – Final, Section A, Page 15, Column 1

'Column explaining questionable business dealings that eventually led to collapse of Enron Corp.'

http://query.nytimes.com/gst/abstract.html?res=FB0716FA3D550C718CDDAE0894DA404482
New York Times Editorial Desk, July 2, 2002, Tuesday
Everyone Is Outraged
By PAUL KRUGMAN (NYT) 738 words
Late Edition – Final, Section A, Page 21, Column 6
'Might government outrage have something to do with public dismay over crooked corporations?'

http://query.nytimes.com/gst/abstract.html?res=F60813FC355C0C728FDDAE0894DA404482
New York Times Business/Financial Desk, July 31, 2002, Wednesday
Corporate Conduct: Wall Street; Senator Says Merrill Lynch Helped Enron Cook Books
By RICHARD A. OPPEL Jr. (NYT) 1282 words
Late Edition – Final, Section C, Page 1, Column 5
'Lawmakers on a Senate panel argued that Merrill Lynch repeatedly cut corners and compromised its business practices to win more investment-banking fees from Enron.'

b) Procure Wealth and Children

Investigative journalists report stories of international gangs smuggling narcotics, girls for prostitution, economic migrants and child slaves – all carried out with total disregard for human suffering. The highest incomes are earned by those who offer success, wealth, or oblivion, i.e. trade in weapons, drugs, sex and cosmetics.

Doctors buy body organs from the poor in under-developed countries to sell at huge profit in wealthy countries. Fortunes are charged to fertilise women, well past child-bearing age, with 'bought-in' eggs and sperm. Scientists encourage hopes for eternal youth for those who can afford to fund 'research into the ageing process'; others grow rich with assurances that they will soon be able to clone human beings, through which process the gullible imagine they can achieve eternal life.

A plethora of self-help and self-improvement courses promise virtually everything to psychologically needy souls. It is claimed that money will ensure material and spiritual success, health and fitness, beautiful bodies to attract other equally beautiful bodies, physical and/or mental health, happiness, plus every other dreamed up 'opportunity' to make people rich, happy and famous.

Other people sell their own children or grow fat on illegally claimed 'benefits' which governments pledge for the support of the utterly helpless.

III MAKING PROMISES

a) The Advertising Industry

A plethora of advertisements promote specious financial, social, physical and sexual advantage via the purchase of one or other product or service. Although some claim these to be 'just a bit of fun', their costs to the nation can be huge. While the drinks industry in Britain spends £200 million on advertising each year, there are associated social costs. For example, according to the *Evening Standard* newspaper of the 21 December, 2001, around 40% of 13- and 14-year-olds were 'drunk or stoned' when they first had sexual intercourse and, in a recent survey of 14-to 20-year olds, alcohol was identified as the main reason for the first sexual experiences of 20% of young men and 13% of young women. Cirrhosis of the liver currently kills 1,600 women a year. The link between alcohol and violence is also inescapable, with the Home Office acknowledging that alcohol is a factor in 40% of violent crimes, 78% of assaults and 88% of criminal damage cases.

Social norms and moral standards, public dissatisfaction and societal cohesiveness are influenced and endangered by a wide variety of propositions in otherwise respectable British newspapers:

> By people being encouraged to 'be a devil', 'spoil yourself', 'look after number one', 'flaunt it if you've got it' or 'be the envy of your friends'.
>
> By holiday advertisements such as 'A great holiday in some refreshingly stimulating company. That's guaranteed! The chances are 90% you'll get much more!'
>
> By advertisements for gay and lesbian intros to find '. . . genuine' friends or 1-to-1 partners.'
>
> Advertisements by women who seek men 'Tropical Treat . . . for fun time's, 'Wanted! . . . uncomplicated relationship', 'Seeking sensuality?'
>
> Advertisements by men who seek women. 'Fancy a pint? . . . a few drinks, laughs & snogs!', 'City Slicker . . . for passion and romance.'

Negative public reaction is most vocal when propositions and justifications blatantly endanger young people. For example, in 1999, a former British Chief Inspector of Schools, in response to reports that he had had an 'affair' with a pupil he had taught, claimed that relationships between teachers and pupils can be 'experiential and educative'. The law had to be changed to clarify that it is not only indecent, but illegal for a teacher to have sexual relationships with a pupil, regardless of the pupil's age.

IV DECEPTIVENESS OF SATANIC PROMISES

While there is a rich mine of examples, the following illustrates well what can happen when promises and deceptions interact.

Secure in their belief that science was sufficiently advanced to provide all the answers, Europe elected to develop a Common Agricultural Policy. It was promised that intensive and scientifically controlled production would provide a plenitude of cheap food, that nature could be controlled and soil improved by scientifically developed fertilisers and improved seed varieties. Farmers would have a central authority for up-to-the-minute technical advice. Such authorities would administer the Agricultural Policy and dispense subsidy rewards and favours to those who improved or intensified production.

However, what was never mentioned were the detrimental effects that the realisation of this plan would have:

- For the viability of bulk food processing depends on large amounts of uniform quality produce being available at specific times. Animals must be shipped to slaughter houses, an average of a 100- (and not unusually, 200-) or 400-mile (160-650-km) journey. To do this economically they are cramped together in cruel conditions, making the containment of serious disease almost impossible. Intensive production necessitates the use of synthetic chemicals that put at risk those who eat the antibiotic-laden flesh. Such farming produces 98% of the United Kingdom's 750 million broiler chickens. These spend the last weeks of their lives in spaces no larger than an A4 sheet of paper, being fed more antibiotics than is used by the entire medical profession, including the UK National Health Service.

  Approximately 100,000 farmed salmon are kept in spaces the size of a bathtub where they frequently attack and damage each other.
- According to a California-based agricultural think-tank, multinational corporate farmers dominate and manipulate world trade in foodstuffs. Ten companies, involved in seeds, fertilisers, pesticides, processing and shipments, control more than 60% of the international food chain. One – Cargill – controls 80% of the world's grain supplies, four companies control 87% of the beef in the US, and five account for 65% of the global pesticide market. Such companies are powerful enough to manipulate prices by withholding supplies and buy at almost give-away prices to dominate markets. In addition, they can afford the cost of 'modernising' farms to intensify production and qualify for agricultural incentives and export subsidies. In a report in *The Independent on Sunday* on 25 March, 2001, Dr Caroline Lucas claimed that the UK exports 33,100 tons of poultry meat to the Netherlands at the same time as it imports 61,400 tons of poultry meat from the Netherlands; it exports 195,000 tons of pork and 102,000 tons of lamb to the EU at the

same time as it imports 240,000 tons of pork and 125,000 tons of lamb from the EU. This cross-exchange of produce makes money for multinational corporations, hauliers, petroleum producers and the governments which derive taxation. All profits are paid for by the consumer.

- Rules of the Common Agricultural Policy (CAP) are similar to those of other countries. In many, farmers are obliged to choose crop seed from a list of 'permissible seeds' produced for their governments by the multinational purveyors of expensive, genetically modified (GM) and other seed, who chose to deal only in specified strains of grain.

  Such contrived circumstances have allowed multinational corporate farmers and dealers to capture and increase their share of the markets around the world. This has contributed to smaller farmers being driven out of business; in the US, 235,000 farms and 60,000 rural companies were put out of business in the 1980s. In Europe, 200,000 farmers left agriculture in 1999. Several hundred million Chinese had to abandon the countryside as the result of agricultural modernisation.
- The hidden costs of intensive farming include the costs of cleaning up and clearing the mess after tragedies such as BSE (£607 million), and Foot and Mouth (yet to be determined but some estimate to be £9 billion). In addition, environmental bodies claim that kerosene, creosote and red diesel used to ignite pyres to destroy rotting carcasses, pumped lethal dioxins into the air. The National Environmental Technology Centre reported evidence of dangerous levels of dioxins entering the atmosphere within a half-mile (3-km) radius of such pyres. Minute concentrations in the air can cause cancer, changes in the body's genetic make-up, fertility problems, genital malformation and learning difficulties. These concentrations may be difficult to detect and impossible to remedy.
- The true costs of the 'cheap food' policy must, therefore, also include: the costs involved in diseases being easily and rapidly spread from one area to another; the disregard of animal suffering; the value of the public's subsidies; the costs of social upheaval; the effects of greenhouse gas emissions from trade-related transport (one of its fastest growing sources); the long-term effect on life on earth; the cost to the nation's health budget from increasing incidences of food poisoning and other effects; the legal cost of detecting and dealing with fraud; and the cost of unemployment.
- Policies that encourage and support farming in the 'developed' world have a catastrophic effect on un-subsidised farming in the developing world. In many countries it is almost impossible for farmers to survive on earnings from staple crops that must compete with subsidised produce flooding into their countries, as the result of the 'free-trade' agreements that have been imposed upon their governments by international gerrymandering.

To conclude

The comprehensive manner by which Satan achieves his ends, covered in this one ayah of the Holy Qur'an, have led to all manner of social and ethical problems which once were recognised as the unsuitable manipulation of wealth, power and immorality.

Despite all of the above, Allah tells us that no matter what Satan attempts to pervert, true believers retain the protection of their Lord and their behaviour and deeds will remain immune from infection. Allah clarifies this in the ayah, 'But, you will not hold sway over My servants for your Lord will protect them'.

11 Arguments regarding the existence of God

66. It is your Lord who powers ships across the seas for you so that you may obtain His Bounty. He is always Merciful to you.

67. And whenever danger threatens you at sea, all those to whom you appeal, abandon you other than Him: but as soon as He returns you safely to shore, you ignore Him. Human beings are truly thankless creatures.

68. Can you rest assured that He will not cause you to be buried under a landslide or caught in a sandstorm? Then you would have no one to protect you.

69. Can you be certain that your ingratitude will not result in His sending you back to sea, to perish in a raging tempest? Who would you then find to support you other than Us?

The above ayat reiterate the need to avoid associating anything with Allah – shirk – and promote the concept of Divine Unity – Tawḥid.

The rational argument regarding the existence of God, 'It is your Lord who powers ships across the seas for you', constitutes what is known as the Teleological Argument concerning Divine Existence. This 'Argument' belongs to a list of four theological arguments concerning Divine Existence:

1) The Cosmological Argument posits the existence of an 'unmoved mover', and 'uncaused cause' as the principle of the universe.
2) The Ontological Argument is based on the definition of 'existence' and of differentiation between what is inherent and what is acquired. It concludes that whatever is acquired must firstly be rooted in the 'source of existence' (that which is).
3) The Teleological Argument is based on the concept that the whole of creation is moving towards a specific goal.
4) The Argument from Experience is based upon the concept of 'certainty', satisfying an inner comprehension regarding the whole universe and its Creator.

Going back to Ayah 66, 'It is your Lord who powers ships across the seas for you', ships are the largest means of transportation to have been devised by man, sometimes even being described as floating cities. A plethora of elements need to be co-ordinated for shipping to operate successfully. Everything that floats, displaces its own weight of water and requires the motive power of wind, steam, or oil to move, and most importantly, precise navigation. In the past, people relied on the stars and basic maps; nowadays, there are sophisticated satellite navigation systems which make navigation comparatively easy. Transportation enables us to 'obtain His Bounty' and conduct trade, another sign of Allah's Mercy.

'And whenever danger threatens you at sea, all those to whom you appeal, other than Him, abandon you: but as soon as He returns you safely to shore, you ignore Him. Human beings are truly thankless creatures.' When the ocean is turbulent and death is imminent, everyone readily begs the Almighty for assistance and conveniently ceases to remember their previous disbelief in the existence of the Creator and their antagonism towards religion. At times of ease many hold the belief that natural causes are responsible for everything. However, once materialistic values are perceived to be worthless and without function, hearts are attracted to the light of guidance, the source of mercy, the Omnipotent provider of succour. Just as the lights of the city conceal the illumination of the stars and moon, if they are switched off, the true source of light is clearly apparent. Hardship is an excellent psychological tool for spiritual awakening.

However, 'as soon as He returns you safely to shore, you ignore Him. Human beings are truly thankless creatures'.

The same picture is illustrated in other words,

> When waves cover them like awnings, they call upon Allah with exclusive faith in Him, but after He has safely brought them to land, there are among them those who hover between right and wrong.

Qur'an 31:32

Humanity is neither safe on land nor at sea, other than by the grace and mercy of Allah. After judgement has been passed on the Day of Resurrection, His Grace and Mercy will not shelter the wicked. Disbelievers will not escape his wrath. Even if He saves them from the oceans, there are other calamities to be faced, as described in the following ayat:

> Can you rest assured that He will not cause you to be buried under a landslide or caught in a sandstorm? Then you would have no one to protect you.
>
> Can you be certain that your ingratitude will not result in Him sending you back to sea to perish in a raging tempest? Who would you then find to support you other than Us?

These ayat inform us that true believers find little difference between times of hardship and calamity, and times of comfort and ease, for they willingly submit to their Lord at all times. Neither ailment nor good health, poverty or wealth, prison or freedom, power or helplessness affect their supplication and reliance on Allah. Imam ʿAli ﷺ was the same person when head of state and as an ordinary citizen forced to remain at home. Islam is not an occasional or seasonal faith which changes with circumstances, but rather a faith which accompanies believers at all times.

The above ayat conclude that none can escape Allah's governance. A simple earthquake may demolish an entire city, the tiniest clot of blood may bring about brain death or a stroke. In Ayah 37 we read, 'Do not strut the earth in triumph and arrogance. You can neither tear it apart nor match the grandeur of its mountains'. All these are admonishments to be heeded.

12 The Dignity of humankind

70. We truly honoured the Children of Adam, carried them over land and sea, sustained them with wholesome things and preferred them to most of Our other creation.

71. On the Day in which all human beings are summoned by their Imams, those given records in their right hand will read them [joyously] without suffering the slightest discomfort.

72. However, those who were blind in this life, will be raised blind in the Hereafter, even further astray from the Path [of Truth].

The above Ayat show the high status and dignity with which Allah regards human beings so that people may become acquainted and familiar with their status and not undervalue themselves. 'We truly honoured the Children of Adam.'

There are three aspects to the dignity mentioned here. First, He 'carried them over land and sea'. Second, 'He sustained them with wholesome things'. Third, He 'preferred them to most of our other creation'.

Commentators' opinions differ regarding the phrase, 'We truly honoured the Children of Adam'. Some say it is because of our power of reason, logic and free will; others think it relates to humans' ability to stand upright – the only creature to do so; yet others think it related to our manual dexterity and ability to write, paint, or undertake other precise and exacting tasks. Still others think that the honour given to humanity refers to the authority given them over the universe. Few relate it to the ability to recognise the Lord and obey Him.

Nonetheless, all of these factors may be considered in the above issue. There is no controversy over them or over which may be selected as right. Human beings have been granted many instincts and abilities, each greater than the others in one way or another. In addition to those already mentioned, there is the human soul's aspiration towards perfection.

So what is the reason behind humankind being preferred above most, but not ALL, of Allah's other creation? Some commentators think that Angels have higher status than human beings. However, this is not supportable because Allah Almighty told Adam ﷺ to teach the Angels, not the Angels to teach Adam ﷺ. Ṭabrisi, in his tafsīr, *Majma al-Bayan,* says that in Arabic literature it is a common practice to use 'most' to refer to 'all'. For example, in Qur'an 26:223, Allah tells us that devils descend to every wicked liar because most devils are themselves liars. It is obvious that all devils are liars, but in this ayah of the Qur'an 'most' has been used to refer to 'all'.

In Islamic belief, the whole of creation consists of three groups of creatures:

1) Those who have reason without ill-desire are manifested as Angels.
2) Those who have desires without reason are manifested as animals.
3) Those who have both reason and desire are manifested as human beings.

Imam ʿAli ﷺ was quoted by his grandson Imam Sadiq ﷺ, when Abdullah ibn Sinan asked him, if Angels or humans were superior,

> If humans control their desires with the power of their reason, they are superior to Angels. However, if they fail to do this and permit their wisdom and reason to be dictated to by their desires, they sink lower than animals.
>
> Tafsir Nur al-Thaqalain, Vol. 3, p. 188

A question often asked is, 'Are the unjust and corrupt also superior to Angels in spite of being the worst of people?' The answer must be that they, as all human beings, 'have the ability' to attain superior rank if they employ the faculties they have been provided with. Those who misuse that gift and do not value themselves as Allah has guided them to, ruin their opportunity to attain that status.

According to Qur'anic teaching, human beings migrate in either of two directions during their lives – one direction, when they aspire toward 'the best form'; the other, when they behave badly and sink to the lowest. This is spelled out in the following Surah:

> By the fig and the olive
>
> By Mount Sinai
>
> By this inviolate city [Makkah]
>
> We indeed created humankind in the best form
>
> Then reduced them to the lowest of the low
>
> All except those who believe and do good deeds, for whom there is never-ending reward.
>
> Qur'an 95:1–6

There is no fault in Allah's creation, no stigma of original sin. Allah has endowed humanity with intelligence, free-will and faculties to observe, judge and act. As His chosen representatives, humans are exalted above the Angels. However, those who rebel against their Lord, misuse their freedom of choice and violate His laws, are abased to the lowest possible position.

Leadership – Wilayah

Having told us how He preferred and honoured human beings, Allah now tells us about leadership and its significance to human society, 'On the Day in which all human beings are summoned by their Imams, those given records in their right hand will read them [joyously] without suffering the slightest discomfort'.

Leadership is the most essential pillar of faith. Imam Muḥammad al-Baqir ﷺ is reported to have said,

> Islam has been established on five pillars; prayer, zakah, fasting, pilgrimage and leadership and that no pillar is given the same degree of significance as the pillar of leadership.'

Usul al-Kafi, Vol. 2, p. 15

Wassail al-Shi'ah, Vol. 1

Prayer represents the relationship between Creator and creation; fasting epitomises the restraint of desire; zakah secures the financial needs of Muslim society; and pilgrimage provides the most beautiful presentation of the unity of the Muslim nation. Yet the significance of the fifth pillar is far greater than those of the other four.

Allah informs us in the Qur'an that, after the Prophet Ibrahim ﷺ had successfully passed several tests, Allah appointed him leader – Imam. Ibrahim ﷺ anticipated that that rank would be inherited by his progeny, but Allah told him that the requisite characteristics needed to be manifest before that could occur. Ibrahim ﷺ was given the Imamah when Allah told him,

> I am going to make you an Imam for humankind.

Qur'an 2:124

Imam Sadiq ﷺ clarified this,

> Allah accepted Ibrahim as a servant before making him a prophet and made him a prophet before appointing him messenger. He appointed him as a messenger before He took him as a friend, but took him as his friend before making him an Imam. Once He had combined for him all the above positions, He said, 'I am going to make you an Imam for humankind'. Imam Sadiq ﷺ continued; it was because of the significance of Imamah in the eyes of Ibrahim that he said, 'And of my offspring?' Allah responded, 'My covenant will not include the unjust'.

Al-Mizan, Vol. 2, p. 86

It is essential for an Imam to be a man of absolute certainty, a man able to see the world of the Divine Kingdom – Malakut – which is based upon the 'word' of Allah. That kingdom is 'the command' of Allah, the esoteric aspect of the universe. We compare this ayah with others such as,

> We made them leaders to guide people by Our command, and We revealed to them the necessity of doing good deeds, of establishing prayer – ṣalah – and of giving their welfare due – zakah – and they then worshipped Us.
>
> Qur'an 21:73

We have to conclude that whatever the subject of guidance – i.e., 'the heart or the deed' – the Imam knows its inner reality. It is the Imam who remains in constant contact with all aspects of 'the command', which are never hidden from him. There cannot be even a single moment in which there is no need for an Imam because Allah tells us in the Qur'an, 'On the Day in which all human beings are summoned by their Imams' which clearly indicates that all human beings need Divine leadership.

The Imamate is such a sublime and exalted position that it cannot be given to any other than the exceedingly virtuous. If someone's soul is polluted by any injustice or sin, even to the minutest degree, they are in need of another to guide them. As Allah asks us,

> Is he who guides to truth more worthy to be followed, or he who is unable to find the right path without being guided?
>
> Qur'an 10:35

The characteristics of an Imam:

1) Imamah is a Divinely appointed rank.
2) The earth cannot continue to exist without a rightful Imam while a single human being continues to exist upon it.
3) No Imam can be effective without Divine support.
4) The Imam must be free from making errors.
5) The Imam must be the most knowledgeable of human beings, effectively able to answer all of humanity's questions regarding this life and the life to come.
6) No deed is hidden from the Imam's vision.
7) It is not possible for any to surpass the Imam in virtue.

Although some commentators interpret 'leader' in the above ayah as Messenger, Divine Scripture, or even scholar, it is evident that the general concept of leadership is meant here to be understood as it is expressed in the ayah above.

The second part of the ayah refers to the way in which people react towards leadership, 'those given records in their right hand will read them [joyously] without suffering the slightest discomfort'. 'However, those who were blind in this life, will be raised blind in the Hereafter, even further astray from the Path [of Truth]'. In other words, those who follow the right path will be successful, and those who decline to follow it are those who will be resurrected blind, as they have been to their opportunities on this earth.

In another Surah blindness of the heart is clearly illustrated,

> Whoever turns away from My admonition will have their means of livelihood restricted, and on the Day of Judgement We will raise them blind. They shall say, 'O my Lord, why have you raised me blind, whereas I was previously able to see?' Allah will respond, 'it must be because Our signs came to you yet you ignored them, so it is that you are ignored now'. Thus We shall recompense those who transgress and do not believe in the signs of their Lord and, truly, the torment of the hereafter will be far more severe and longer lasting,
>
> Qur'an 20:124–127

The life to come is a precise reflection of our thoughts, feelings and deeds in the present life. It is obvious that ignoring Allah's admonishments and warnings will result in a lack of vision in the hereafter.

Makkan's suggestions rejected

> **73. They strove hard to beguile you away from what We revealed to you, and to get you to fabricate something quite different in Our name. They would then certainly have accepted you in friendship.**
>
> **74. And had We not entrenched you in faith, you might well have inclined to them a little.**
>
> **75. In which case, We would have made you bear a double [punishment] in life and a double [chastisement] after death, with no one to support you against Us.**

The above ayat are amongst those which have been misinterpreted. Ṭabrisi in *Majma al-Bayan* reports five different opinions related by various exegetes regarding these specific ayat:

1) The Makkans said to the Prophet ﷺ, 'We do not permit you to touch the Black Stone in the corner of the Ka'bah unless you also pay respect to our other idols'. The Prophet ﷺ

felt that as he had abandoned them in his heart there would be no harm in looking at them to please the Makkans and gain permission to touch the Black Stone. At that moment the above ayat were revealed to alter the Prophet's train of thought.

2) The Makkans urged the Prophet ﷺ to stop degrading their idols, and criticising their judgements as irrational and to expel the slaves and lower echlons of society whom they regarded as unclean and malodorous. In return they – the Makkans – would themselves attend his circle of lectures. The Prophet ﷺ welcomed this in order to win their hearts until the above ayat were revealed, saying that he should not.
3) When the Prophet ﷺ demolished the idols within the Ka'bah and its sacred precincts the Makkans suggested he leave one idol on the Mount of Marwa. At first the Prophet ﷺ was inclined to agree in order to win their hearts, but ordered it to be demolished once the above ayat were revealed.
4) A group from the Bani Thaqīf stipulated three conditions before they would offer the Prophet ﷺ their allegiance: a) They would not be required to bow or prostrate during the prayer; b) They would not themselves demolish their idols, insisting that he himself did it on their behalf; c) They requested permission to keep for one year a particular idol whom they referred to as Lāt.

   The Prophet ﷺ responded that there was no point in a religion without humbleness and prostration and that if they wished themselves to demolish the idols they could; if not, the Muslims would do it for them. However, he rejected the third suggestion out of hand. Umar stood up to address the Bani Thaqīf, saying that they had hurt the Prophet ﷺ who would not permit any idols to remain within the Arabian peninsula. Representatives of the Bani Thaqīf insisted on their demands being met and at this time the above ayat were revealed to prevent this from happening.
5) The delegates of Bani Thaqīf requested that the Prophet ﷺ permit them to receive the donations dedicated to the idols for one year prior to their destruction. The Prophet ﷺ intended to comply, but at that time the above ayat were revealed to prevent that from occurring.

The simplest step in analysing and evaluating the truth of the above five interpretations leads us to reject all on the ground that every one of them was only reported after the conquest of Makkah in year eight of the Hijra. The incontrovertible evidence is that these ayat were revealed prior to the Prophet's migration from Makkah to Madinah.

However, if we focus attention on the ayah, '. . . had We not entrenched you in faith . . . ,' we realise that this clearly indicates that the Prophet ﷺ was, and indeed needed to be safeguarded from commiting errors, if he was to accurately and faithfully deliver what had been revealed to him. There was, of course, a dual aspect of Allah's final Messenger ﷺ –

human being as well as Final Messenger – sent to guide the whole of humanity. While there is always a possibility of emotions rising from within a person, Allah's Messenger, directed to deliver revelation on behalf of the Creator and Law-Giver, had to have been 'entrenched in faith', to be thoroughly cleansed and protected from error – 'Ismah'.

So why does Allah mention, 'We would have made you bear a double [punishment] in life and a double [chastisement] after death, with no one to support you against Us'? All societies attempt to match punishment with the severity of the crime. Whereas all who are liable are held accountable, those who are most learned, who are comprehensively equipped to comprehend the consequences of their deeds and actions, are levied the most severe punishments. A mistake of a doctor undergoing training might be tolerated while the same mistake made by a highly qualified consultant may be regarded as irresponsibility and not forgiven. We find support for this in the following hadith,

> Seventy sins of one who is ignorant will be forgiven before a single sin of a scholar is even considered.
>
> Usul al-Kafi, Vol. 1, p. 37

This is the reason why Allah warned the wives of the Prophet ﷺ that their sins would receive twice the normal punishment. On the other hand, they could also expect double the reward,

> O wives of the Prophet, whichever of you commit manifest indecency, will receive double punishment, and this is simple for Allah. But whichever of you is obedient to Allah and His Messenger will be twice recompensed . . .
>
> Qur'an 33:30–31

Islamic sources inform us that when the above ayat were revealed to the Prophet ﷺ he raised his hands and prayed, 'O Allah, don't leave me alone even for the blink of an eye'. Humanity is in ever continuous need of Allah's support and protection without which they might at any time go astray.

A Plot to Expel

> **76. Then they tried to banish you and drive you off the land. Had that succeeded they would not have remained there [safely] for long.**

By the 13th year of the Prophet's mission, the position, status and supremacy of the Makkan establishment was being increasingly undermined by Divine authority. Fearing for their future they called a meeting to discuss what they should do about Muḥammad ﷺ and his preaching. When they learned that the willing support of the Bani Aws and Bani Khazraj clans had enabled a Muslim community to develop and flourish at Yathrib, all agreed he had to be silenced whatever the cost:

> They considered appointing a 'champion warrior' to challenge and kill him, and the 'blood money' they might need to pay in order to stifle protestations from his Bani Hashim clan. An unidentified elder, referred to simply as 'Najdi', pointed out that the Bani Hashim would not spare the life of anyone whom they regarded as a murderer, regardless of offers of 'blood money'. No one would undertake a task with that predictable consequence.
>
> Someone thought that if Muḥammad ﷺ was held in solitary confinement and fed via a small 'feeding hatch', his religious ideas could no longer be disseminated. The 'Najdi' warned that a combined Bani Hashim force would certainly be raised to free him. Another suggested Muḥammad ﷺ be tied to an unruly camel, to be enraged before being driven off, but the 'Najdi' thought that foolish.
>
> Abu-Jahl finally pointed out that if a combined group, comprising a representative from every one of the tribes, were to join together to murder Muḥammad ﷺ, it would not be feasible for the Bani Hashim clan to launch revenge attacks on them all. His proposal was unanimously accepted, would-be assassins selected and instructions given for the mission to be undertaken at nightfall.

Tabaqatul Kubra, Vol. 1, p. 227

Sirah of Ibn Hisham, Vol. 1, p. 480

However, Jibra'il revealed their plan and advised the Prophet ﷺ to migrate to Yathrib immediately.

Ayah 76 in this Surah and Ayah 30 of Surah 8 refer to these events,

> Remember how the disbelievers plotted against you. They sought to take you captive, kill you, or banish you. They devised their plan but Allah planned too, and He is the best of planners.

Qur'an 8:30

The Practice of Allah

> **77. This was Our practice when We sent Messengers before you, and you will observe that Our practice has not altered.**

The word 'Sunnah' is applied to Allah as well as to His final Messenger, Muḥammad ﷺ. In the case of the latter, it refers to the Prophet's sayings and way of life. In its Divine context, it is used in the Qur'an to convey the Divine ways in which Allah deals with nations. Some have translated it as 'the practice of Allah'.

Allah is the ultimate source of guidance, for it is He who guides His creatures to the fulfilment of their potential. When Fir'awn asked Mūsa ﷺ about his Lord, he replied, 'Our Lord has created and guided everything'. This is what Allah does; it is his practice or way.

One aspect of this practice is the sending of Messengers and Warners, another is the punishment of those who dare to disregard or mistreat them, for punishment is another aspect of His guidance.

In the above ayah, having narrated the plot of the Quraish to destroy His final Messenger ﷺ, Allah confirms that His Sunnah does not alter.

13 Daily Prayer

78. Establish prayer when the sun begins to descend from its summit [at noon], and at the darkening of the night, and the recitation of the Qur'an at dawn. For the [recital] at dawn is witnessed.

79. And forsake sleep for [part] of the night in order to offer additional prayers, for your Lord may well raise you to an honourable position.

80. And pray, 'Lord, make me worthy to carry out everything I undertake and worthy of everything I complete, and grant me Your support'.

81. And say, 'Truth has flourished and overcome falsehood, for all falsehood must ultimately be defeated'.

The above ayat refer to the times of the daily obligatory prayers and the recommended midnight prayer. The first ayah mentions only three times – noon, the darkening of the night and dawn. Four prayers are due from the time when the sun begins to decline from its meridian up until the darkest moment of the night. One is in the early morning at dawn:

1) Dhuḥr, immediately after the sun begins its decline until . . .
2) ʿAṣr, in the late afternoon
3) Maghrib, immediately after sunset
4) Isha, after the glow of sunset has disappeared and full darkness has set
5) Fajr, dawn.

Ayah 79 refers to the midnight or Tahajjud prayer. This is a recommended act of worship closest to the obligatory prayers. Performing it was obligatory for the Prophet Muḥammad ﷺ and was one means by which he ﷺ achieved his honourable position – al-Maqam al-Mahmoud – which, according to all commentators, is his authority to intercede and to receive the standard or banner of praise and glory – Liwa al-Hamd – under which all Prophets, believers and Angels will one day gather.

The significance of the midnight prayer is that in the day, the mind is usually preoccupied with all manner of worldly affairs. The hustle and bustle of commerce and everyday existence leave the heart and soul of the believer little peace and tranquillity. However, after midnight, when most of the world sleeps and the cacophony of the materialist world is reduced to its minimum, the possibility for peace, concentration and self-awareness exists. Most spiritual training programmes in Islam are based on the significance of Tahajjud and emphasise that particular time as the best opportunity we have to purify our soul and elevate our status. The following ahadith underline this:

> The Prophet ﷺ said, 'The best of you is the one who speaks well and offers food and prayers at night while others sleep'.
>
> The Prophet ﷺ said, 'The faces of those who pray at midnight will radiate brightness throughout the day'.

Bihar al-Anwar, Vol. 83, p. 126

> Imam 'Ali ؑ said, 'Night prayers secure health, please the Lord, entitle one to His mercy and enable one to adopt the behaviour of the prophets'.

Ghurar al-Hikam

> Imam Sadiq ؑ once advised a pupil, 'Do not ignore midnight prayer because those who deprived themselves of it will surely fail'.

Bihar al-Anwar, Vol. 83, p. 127

The Qur'an is a Remedy and Cure

> **82. Our revelations of the Qur'an are sources of healing and mercy for those who believe, but sources of pain and loss for those who are unjust.**

This ayah refers to the significance of the Holy Qur'an and its constructive role in the life of Muslims. 'Our revelations of Qur'an are sources of healing and mercy for those who believe'; however, for those who are unjust and harm or humiliate others, they constitute a source of pain and loss.

With regard to the Qur'an, the difference between its healing aspect and its aspect of mercy, is the awareness that its prime purpose is to cleanse and purify people of all ideological and ethical diseases. Once this is achieved, the Qur'an's mercy lies in its provision and establishment of moral values and spiritual disciplines. In any refurbishment we need first to demolish and remove dirt and pollution before we can begin to paint and re-decorate.

Spiritual and ethical diseases are similar to physical ones in that they pose great potential danger. Both need prevention and cure, the possibility of the disease spreading is applicable to both. Unfortunately, most people concern themselves with physical ailments only and entirely neglect spiritual ones. We know that some diseases are curable and that others are not; however, the Qur'an provides an effective cure for all spiritual diseases, even though this might be both painful and a source of loss for the unjust. A well-balanced and healthy meal may provide a scholar with the nourishment and energy to pursue scientific and/or academic work, but, the same meal may also be the nourishment a tyrant needs to effectively oppress others.

The Holy Qur'an and its teachings are good prescriptions for those who wish to counter ignorance, arrogance, jealousy, greed and hypocrisy. It is a healing for humiliation, fear, disunity and cowardice. The Holy Qur'an cures love for worldly things and extinguishes the flames of war in every corner of the globe. Those dominated by superior power and heavy artillery require the Qur'an as a healing remedy.

Allah tells us in the Qur'an:

> O humankind, truly an exhortation comes to you from your Lord, a cure for that which is in your breast, a guidance and mercy for believers.
>
> Qur'an 10:57

Also:

> For those who believe, it is both guidance and cure.
>
> Qur'an 41:44

The healing role of the Qur'an has been emphasised by Imam ʿAli ﷺ in various sermons:

> Therefore, seek your cure from the Qur'an for your ailments and seek its assistance in your distress. It contains a cure for the greatest disease, namely disbelief, hypocrisy, revolt and misguidance.
>
> Nahj al-Balaghah, Sermon 176

> Know that the Qur'an contains knowledge of what is to come, history of the past, cures for all your ills and regulations for all that you might face.
>
> Nahj al-Balaghah, Sermon 158

> You should adhere to the Book of Allah because it is a strong rope, a clear light, a benefiting cure, a source to quench thirst, a protection for the adherent . . . whoever speaks according to it speaks the truth and whoever acts by it is ahead in being guided.
>
> Nahj al-Balaghah, Sermon 156

The above quotations do not exaggerate the Qur'an being the remedy for all spiritual and ethical disease. Ready evidence may be found by comparing the status of the Arabs prior to the revelation of the Qur'an and what they achieved immediately after its revelation.

Allah tells us that, 'For every people there is a guide' (Qur'an 13:7). In his tafsīr, Al-'Ayyashi reports the following discussion with Imam Baqir ﷺ who said , 'Ali is the guide, and the guide is always one of us'. I said, 'Then you are now the guide'. 'You are right', said the Imam ﷺ. 'The Qur'an lives and will not die. If an ayah were to die with the death of those to whom it was revealed, the Qur'an would certainly have died. However, all ayat continue to apply to those now alive, just as they did for those who have already died.'

The brilliant oration of Imam 'Ali ﷺ regarding the Qur'an illustrates many key points such as the Qur'an being 'a lamp whose flame will not die' by which Imam 'Ali ﷺ indicates that the Qur'an is a book whose significance will never be exhausted. It will remain fresh and new until the Day of Resurrection.

By saying a path which shall not lead astray, the Imam means that the Qur'an's guidance is a road upon which a person does not loose his/her way. This is because the Almighty Creator guards those who follow it.

Whoever desires eternal bliss in addition to religious and worldly success should heed the Book of Allah day and night, memorise its ayat and blend them with their thoughts. The merits of reciting the Qur'an are mentioned in numerous ahadith:

> Imam Sadiq ﷺ said, 'The Qur'an is Allah's covenant for His creation. Thus, it is necessary for every Muslim to examine their covenants and read daily fifty of its ayat'.
>
> Wasa'il al-Shi'ah, Vol. 2, p. 849

> He also said, 'What prevents a merchant who has been busy in the market from returning home and not being able to sleep until he has recited a Surah of the Qur'an? For every ayah he recites, ten good deeds will be recorded for him and ten bad deeds erased'.
>
> Wasa'il al-Shi'ah, Vol. 2, p. 851

> In another hadith the Imam ﷺ said, 'It is your duty to recite Qur'an, because your position in paradise will equate to the number of ayat you recite. On the Day of Resurrection those who recited the Qur'an will be told, "Recite and ascend". And for every ayah they recite they shall be elevated a station'.
>
> Wasa'il al-Shi'ah, Vol. 2, p. 840

Human Attitudes to Allah's Bounties

> **83. When Our favours make lives agreeable, human beings frequently turn away in disdain; yet when ill-fortune afflicts them they frequently despair.**
>
> **84. Say [O Muḥammad], 'Everyone's behaviour accords with their own beliefs, but the Lord knows best whose path is true'.**

The first of these ayat refers to the attitudes of those without faith who completely disregard Allah's bounties and doubt His very existence. For example, while humble folk often find support in their faith, many arrogant people reject it. However, Allah tries people both in prosperity and in distress. While the selfish pride of those who prosper hinders their remaining humble and kind, in times of distress, the false value of worldly possessions makes them resentful and miserable rather than patient and reliant on their Lord. For those without proper education, wealth and prosperity may lead to arrogance. Even though the human ability to acquire knowledge and develop faculties are the gift of Allah, those who are vain mistakenly consider everything their own personal achievement.

14 The Spirit

85. When they ask you [O Muḥammad] about the spirit, tell them, 'The spirit is at the command of my Lord and He has revealed only a little knowledge of it'.

Spirit – 'Rūh' – has been used in Qur'anic terminology in various ways:

1) The life which was breathed into Adam ﷺ
2) The life in every conscious creature
3) The Prophet 'Isa ﷺ being the 'Spirit of Allah'
4) The spirit which comes down with the Angels on the night of Qadr
5) The Holy Ghost – Rūh al-Qūds
6) The spirit sent to Maryam ﷺ which appeared to her as a man.

Muslim philosophers differentiate between soul, spirit and heart, giving each one a role in the existence of humanity. However, four elements are mentioned in the ahadith which present non-materialistic aspects of humanity. These are soul, spirit, heart and intellect.

There has been continuous debate regarding the nature of the spirit mentioned in the above ayah. When the Makkans asked the Prophet ﷺ about it, the answer Allah gave him was, 'The spirit is at the command of my Lord and He has revealed only a little knowledge of it'. Allah tells us in the Qur'an that He orders things in two distinctly different ways – by creation or command (Qur'an 7:54). While Allah's command is immediate, creation is left to gradually evolve. In other words, while He commands without any concept of time, His creation is governed by both time and space.

Rūh al-Qūds is used in Qur'an 2:253, to indicate the spirit sent to assist Messengers to convey the messages entrusted to them. However, the word 'Rūh' is used in Qur'an 58:22 in reference to the spiritual and Divine power within believers which strengthens their faith. On the other hand, the Trustworthy Spirit – 'Rūh al-Amin' – is used in Qur'an 26:193 to indicate the Archangel who brings revelation to the Prophet ﷺ. It seems from the context of Ayah 85 that none of these issues was a matter of concern to the Makkans. Indeed, they only asked what it is that distinguishes human beings and makes them superior to other creatures.

Since the structure of the spirit is completely different to the structure of matter and none of its physical and chemical characteristics can be studied, Allah ordered the Prophet ﷺ to answer with the very brief statement, 'tell them that the spirit is at the command of my Lord' and, to avoid further discussion at that stage, the ayah continues, 'and He has revealed only a little knowledge of it.'

Although our spirit is our most essential element, we have different understandings regarding its reality and secret nature. People imagine, decide, comprehend, love, hate and have ability to acquire knowledge. The doing of such things highlights the essential difference between them and wood, stone and other inanimate objects. We refer to the distinguishing difference between people and plants and minerals as 'the human soul' or 'spirit'. Both spirit and soul are different faces of the same coin. When we trace the link between spirit and body and observe the interaction between them we refer to that as 'soul'. Whereas, in seeking the non-materialistic characteristics of our life we refer to it as 'spirit'.

In Muslim understanding, the soul has seven dimensions:

1) mineral
2) vegetable
3) animal
4) personal
5) human
6) the secret soul
7) the soul's 'secret of secrets'.

Each of us possesses these seven levels of consciousness and the goal of all spiritual exercise is for them all to operate together in balance and harmony.

Many spiritual systems stress only one or two of these levels; however, according to Islamic teaching, emotional well-being and healthy nourishing relationships are as essential for well-being as spiritual and physical health. The universe is meant to be the place for the search of Allah. This is derived from the hadith Qudsi, 'I was a hidden treasure, I longed to be known and so created Creation'. At one level this indicates that the universe mirrors the Divine and that Allah is Omnipresent,

> The East and the West belong to Allah and thus, wherever you turn, there is the Face of Allah.
>
> Qur'an 2:115

The East and the West mentioned here are not confined to the directions of the rising and setting sun, but refer, rather, to the whole cosmos which manifests Allah's omnipotence and absolute control over the universes. His Face is His manifestation because the word 'Wajh', which is used in the ayah, denotes the manifestational aspect of things.

Islamic teaching emphasises the development of the soul and spirit. The following lists the necessary means by which to achieve that:

1) **Initial awakening** The recognition that our spiritual search has far greater meaning and importance than any worldly ambition.
2) **Patience and gratitude** Both are essential for spiritual development. One scholar eloquently delivered a lecture on patience, with beautiful words of wisdom. While doing this a scorpion stung him repeatedly on the foot yet, despite the pain he must have felt, he continued his talk. When students, aware of what had happened, asked him why he had not reacted, he replied that it would have been shameful to have acted impatiently while delivering a lecture on patience.
3) **Fear and hope** Every human activity is based upon fear of one thing or hope for another. Imam 'Ali ﷺ tells us, 'Hope only for your Lord and fear only your disobedience'. The difference between fearing natural things and fearing Allah lies in our reaction. While our instinct is to run away from natural things, we instinctively try to approach Allah. That hope engenders optimism and indicates that, in spite of our shortcomings, we all can still make progress.
4) **Self-denial** Dedication to serve others rather than our own selfish desires and gratifications is an essential aspect of spiritual training.
5) **Trust in Allah** Imam Muḥammad al-Jawad ﷺ (the 9th Imam) said, 'Trust in Allah is the price of all that is precious and the ladder by which every quality He values is reached'. A true believer realises that everything they own comes from Allah.
6) **Sincerity and truthfulness** Concern and concentration on our underlying intentions, rather than on the forms of action to be observed by others. The clearer and purer our intentions, the more advanced we are in the eyes of Allah.
7) **Self-appraisal and self-assessment** Prepare one for the reckoning of the Day of Judgement.
8) **Remembrance of Death.** Helps one remain aware and work for the everlasting rather than for what is fleeting and temporal.

The above points lead believers to understand that a link exists between their remembering their Creator and their regard for themselves. Allah tells us that when people disregard Him, it follows that they also disregard themselves (Qur'an 59:19).

A 'wayfarer' may achieve inner wisdom and knowledge of spiritual truths through his/her inner heart. Heart and 'inner heart' have close links. The difference between them lies in that the heart 'knows' while the inner heart 'sees'. When knowledge and vision combine, the unseen becomes visible and certainty may be achieved. This was the goal of Ibrahim ﷺ when he saw the 'Malakut' of the heavens and the earth referred to in Qur'an 6:75 . There is no point in knowledge without vision, nor in vision without knowledge. This is analogous to visiting a foreign country without knowledge of its language, history, or customs. The Prophet ﷺ said,

> Worship Allah as if you see Him for even if you do not, He truly sees you.
>
> Bihar al-Anwar, Vol. 77, p. 74

15 Validation of the Message

86. And if We willed, We could certainly erase what We have revealed to you. Then you would have no one to petition Us on your behalf.

87. [You have only been spared] by the Mercy of your Lord. His favours to you are indeed great.

88. Say [O Muḥammad], 'If both humankind and jinn laboured to produce the like of this Qur'an they could not succeed, even if they managed to successfully co-operate with each other'.

89. Although We have provided them with multifaceted explanations in this Qur'an, most human beings are ungrateful and reject it.

As Allah created human creatures and promised to guide them to the successful fulfilment of their potential He sent, throughout the ages, a succession of prophets to guide them towards monotheism. The concluding link in this chain of gradually unfolding Divine guidance is represented by the Holy Prophet of Islam – Muḥammad ﷺ.

Other than Islam, we know of no other religion to warn that Divine Revelation will one day terminate, nor are we aware of any other heavenly sent personality claiming eternal validity for the 'message' that had been revealed through them. More than 14 centuries have passed since the lifetime of Muḥammad ﷺ and throughout that long period the Prophet of Islam has been acclaimed as the Seal of Prophethood. He perfected existing laws and, with the rich content of his own actions, demonstrated the supreme value of all the earlier prophetic missions.

The Qur'an itself depicts the characteristics and personality of the Prophet Muḥammad ﷺ as the perfect model for good action and moral conduct.

In the Divine revelation delivered and taught by the Prophet Muḥammad ﷺ – the Holy Qur'an – Allah tells us,

> It is We who have sent down this Qur'an and it is We who will protect it.
>
> Qur'an 15:9

This testifies that even though its phraseology was delivered by the Prophet ﷺ, the precise content and detail of the Qur'an emanated from Allah – Creator, Law-Maker and Guide. To assure us of the authenticity and validity of his Message, the Prophet ﷺ was required to convey what had been revealed about himself,

> If he had invented anything concerning what We had said, We would certainly have seized his right hand [cancelled his authority] and severed his jugular vein.
>
> Qur'an 69:44–46

This enormously strong statement regarding the validity of Allah's Message is included to elucidate Ayah 86 of this Surah.

With reference to the phrase, 'Erase what We have revealed to you', Allamah Tabatabai draws our attention to the previous ayah, 'The spirit is at the command of my Lord and He has revealed only a little knowledge of it', and points out that Allah has said that the spirit which reveals the Qur'an to you is part of His command and Authority. If He wished to erase this spirit, which is [His Revelation to you] you would have no one to petition Him on your behalf.

Challenge to bring the like of the Qur'an

> **88. Say [O Muḥammad], 'If both humankind and jinn laboured to produce the like of this Qur'an they could not succeed even if they managed to successfully co-operate with each other.**

To end allegation and speculation that the Qur'an – revealed to a person known not to have received any formal education – could possibly be the construct of the human intellect, Allah Almighty challenges human beings to compose even one Surah in the style and manner of His Divine Revelation.

In what respect then is the Qur'an an unchallengeable miracle, and how is it the proof of its own truthfulness? In answer to these questions the following opinions have been raised:

1) The Qur'an's universal message of guidance is in appropriate language and style, to address every aspect of human life and endeavour – individual and social, economic and political, physical and spiritual. Allah Almighty challenged the poets and orators of the Jahiliyyah to match the eloquent and unique rhetorical style of the Qur'an. In failing this challenge, some chose to confront Allah's final Messenger ﷺ and sacrifice their life and dignity.

2) The Qur'an's powerful and fascinating tone has the ability to touch the human mind and heart. This was acknowledged in the advice given by early opponents of Islam. They advised fellow citizens of Makkah not to go near the Prophet ﷺ for fear of being bewitched, for they claimed his Qur'anic recitation wove magical spells over people. Some tried to block their ears, but were not able to resist their hearts being touched and their lives transformed once they heard it.
3) Muḥammad's gift of prophecy, foretold, for example, the Roman victory over the Persians. Between 614 and 616 CE the Persians defeated the Byzantine Emperor Heraclius and gained many of his lands. While Muslims were saddened by this Persian victory, Makkan pagans were overjoyed that Fire Worshippers had overcome followers of Divine scripture and taunted Muslims that they would ultimately suffer the same fate. Allah, however, revealed in the Qur'an that Rome would gain ultimate victory. This was fulfilled when Heraclius defeated Persia in the year 624 CE and when, at the Battle of Badr, the Muslims defeated the disbelievers of Makkah.

   It is interesting to note the different reaction of the Emperors of Rome and Persia to Muḥammad's letters to them. The former received his graciously and returned valuable gifts in response – the latter is reported to have torn it up.
4) The extensive Islamic legal structure in which rulings, based on Qur'anic teaching, provide comprehensive, accurate and appropriate legislation to cover every aspect of human activity. This discipline is referred to as 'Principles of Jurisprudence'.
5) The scientific facts presented in many ayat of the Holy Qur'an that cover the order of the universe, celestial bodies, the laws of nature and other subjects that could not have been known during the Prophet's lifetime other than through Divine revelation.

   For example, in the Qur'an, Allah discloses the fact that everything that grows in the earth has a specific weight. If any change of weight were to occur in the parts of the plants, for example, it would form a different organism,

> The earth We have spread out, and placed therein firm hills and caused each thing to grow therein, well proportioned.

Qur'an 15:19

In another ayah Allah alludes to the need for various species to be pollinated by wind in order to blossom (Qur'an 15:22). Another, at the time unknown scientific fact unveiled by the Qur'an, is the movement of the earth. In this regard Allah Almighty tells us that, 'It is Allah who has appointed the Earth as a cradle' (Qur'an 20:53) – a cradle is a device that oscillates on rockers or swings on pivots to induce movement.

A further unknown fact disclosed in the Qur'an 14 centuries ago was the existence of another continent (Qur'an 55:17), in which Allah refers to the two easts and the two wests, where sunrise and sunset times are different.

To conclude, the Holy Qur'an is not any 'scripture' conceived by man, but a precise revelation. In Ayah 88 Allah tells us that even if humankind and jinn managed to unite to produce the like of the Qur'an they would not be able to succeed. In another ayah Allah reduces His challenge to the production of only ten Surahs: 'Do they say 'He has forged it'? Say, 'Bring then ten Surahs the like thereof and call to whomsoever you can, other than Allah, if you are truthful.' (Qur'an 11:13)

As the orators and disbelievers failed to meet either of His challenges, Allah reduced His challenge to their producing even one Surah. 'Do they say, he [Muḥammad] has forged it? Say, 'Bring then a Surah like this, and call on whomsoever you can other than Allah if you are truthful (Qur'an 10:38).

Allah's challenge remains open and valid to this day.

16 Outrageous Makkan demands

90. And they say, 'We will not believe you [O Muḥammad] until you make a spring of water gush forth for us from this [arid] land.

91. Or until you have a garden of palms and vines and make rivers suddenly surge through it.

92. Or you cause, as you threaten, the heaven to shatter and drop upon us; or you bring Allah and the Angels face to face before us.

93. Or you have a house of gold, or ascend into the heavens; and we will not believe you have been there unless you bring back a book which we may read'. Say then [O Muḥammad], 'Glory to my Lord. I am only a mortal who has been sent as a Messenger'.

The reason for the above ayat being revealed was because a group of well-known members of Quraish including Walid, the son of Mughirah and Abu Jahl, had gathered near the Ka'bah to request the Prophet Muḥammad ﷺ to hold discussions with them. The Prophet ﷺ attended in the hope of guiding them toward the right path. The Makkan spokesperson began by listing the many changes Muḥammad ﷺ had wrought to the traditions and customs of their tribe. He concluded, 'You have disrespected our gods, ridiculed our religion, annulled our ambitions and wrought disunity. If your purpose is to gain wealth, we are prepared to help you achieve that; if you are after political power, we are willing to establish you as the head of the tribe; if you are suffering from anything, we will assist you in any way we can'.

Muḥammad ﷺ responded, 'I seek none of these; the truth is that Allah has sent me as a Messenger and revealed His Divine scripture for me to deliver to you. If you accept it you will gain the prosperity of this life and the life hereafter. If you reject it, I will patiently persevere until Allah passes His judgement between us'.

The spokesman replied, 'If you persevere, you will not find a place more uncongenial than our city so ask your Lord to move these mountains and make rivers flow in our land like those of Syria and Iraq'.

The Prophet Muḥammad ﷺ responded, 'I was not sent to do such things'.

They said, 'Then ask your Lord to send down Angels to certify your status and to bestow you with castles of gold within lush gardens'.

The Prophet ﷺ said, 'I was not sent to do such things. I brought you what has been sent with me and what I have been ordered to deliver. If you do not accept this, I must leave the matter with Allah'.

They then said, 'Then cause, as you threaten, that the heavens shatter and drop down upon us'.

He ﷺ said, 'That is up to Allah.'

The Prophet ﷺ then left. Abdullah, the nephew of A'tikah and Abu Umayyah, went with him saying, 'O Muḥammad, they made you generous and fair offers yet you refused them. When they challenged you, you declined to accept their challenges so I will not believe you until you ascend into the heavens and bring us back a book to read'.

Abu Jahl threatened, 'If he does not cease disrespecting our gods and ridiculing the customs of our ancestors, I will have a boulder dropped on him when he prostrates himself'. The Prophet ﷺ who hoped they would follow the right path, was disturbed by the incident until the above ayat were revealed.

Their six outrageous requests are listed below:

1) Make a spring gush forth.
2) Make gardens of palms and vines with rivers through them.
3) Shatter the heaven and cause it to drop.
4) Bring Allah and the Angels face to face.
5) Have a house of gold.
6) Ascend into heavens to bring us a book.

If they thought all this would end the Prophet's claim to prophethood, he ﷺ disappointed them. The Prophet's twofold response to the Makkan suggestions, designed to safeguard idol worship and existing traditions, was:

1) Allah Almighty is glorified and above puerile requests.
2) That he, like them, was human while the supranatural incidents and miracles they demanded were under the sole control of Allah Almighty and could only be brought about by His permission.

Would Angels be appropriate beings to be chosen as Allah's messengers?

> **94. And when guidance came to them, nothing would have prevented them from accepting it other than their saying, 'Would Allah have sent a mortal as His Messenger?'**
>
> **95. Say to them, 'Had there been Angels walking at peace on earth, We would have sent an Angel to them as Our Messenger'.**

As cited above, many nations of earlier times had objected to and challenged Allah's other messengers. We read in the Qur'an:

> We sent Nūh to his people, and he said, 'O my people, worship Allah. You have no God other than Him. Will you not then guard yourselves against evil?'
>
> But the chiefs of those people who disbelieved said, 'This is only a man like you who wants to exalt himself over you; had Allah willed, He would certainly have sent down Angels'.

Qur'an 23:23–24

The people of Hud ﷺ behaved in a similar manner when they said,

> This is no more than a man like yourselves, he eats what you eat and drinks what you drink, so if you follow a man like yourselves, you will truly be the losers.

Qur'an 23:33–34

The Arabs reacted similarly to the Prophet Muḥammad ﷺ,

> They say, 'What sort of messenger is this who eats food and walks in the markets? Why has an Angel not been sent to him so that he may warn him? Or a treasure be thrown down to him, or a garden for him from which he could eat'. And those who are unjust say, 'You only follow a man who has been bewitched'.

Qur'an 25:7–8

The Holy Prophet ﷺ, sent as a teacher of humankind, shared their joys and sorrows, mingled with them and was acquainted with their doings. Angels, however, would not have been useful as messengers. Had they been sent, they would have caused confusion rather than understanding in the minds of people. The leader of society must match the nature of those who follow, a role model whose characteristics people can emulate. This is not possible unless feelings, emotions and desires have a similar basis. Had the Messenger of Allah no idea about anger, greed, jealousy, self-centredness, or other human emotions, how would he have been in the position to propose solutions for them?

Familiarity with the hardships, difficulties and sufferings of ordinary folk qualifies a leader to empathise with his people and make realistic proposals. To give an example, Imam ʿAli ﷺ wrote to his governor in Basra after he learned that he had attended a banquet,

> Remember, everyone emulates their role model. Be informed that your leader [himself] has contented himself with two shabby garments out of all the comforts of the world and two loaves for his daily sustenance. It is unlikely that you will be able to do the same, but at least support me by remaining pious, chaste and upright. By Allah, I have no treasure of gold in this world nor have I plentiful wealth . . . should I be content with being called Commander of the Believers, even if I do not share with them their lives' hardships . . . I try to keep myself engaged in piety so that I am secure on the Day of Judgement and steady on the slippery path. If I wished, I could have found my way to pure honey, fine wheat and silken clothing, but I dare not allow passions to lead me to greed.
>
> Nahj al-Balagha, Letter number 45

The understanding of the commentators varies regarding the part in the ayah in which Allah says, 'Had there been Angels walking at peace on earth'. Some consider this to refer to the belief of some pre-Islamic Arabs, that their lives had been peace and contentment before Muḥammad ﷺ came to ruin it. Allah tells them in the Qur'an that even peaceful Angels would have needed messengers similar to themselves to guide them. Others think the word 'peace' refers to absence of any restrictions whatsoever. However, we understand that the purpose of this ayah is to illustrate that all creatures are in need of leadership. Living in peace has no bearing on the need for Divine guidance delivered by one of Allah's Messengers.

Allah is the Witness

> **96. Say, 'Allah suffices as witness between us, He sees and knows what is in His servants' hearts'.**
>
> **97. And whoever Allah guides is indeed guided aright, and those whom He lets go astray can find no one except Him to protect them. We shall assemble them on the Day of Resurrection on their faces, blind, deaf and dumb; their destination Gehennam [Hell]; and whenever the blaze dies down We shall again increase its intensity.**

Having discussed the proofs and arguments regarding Divine Unity, prophethood and challenging the disbelievers, the above ayat conclude the discussion. First, Allah tells His Messenger that, if the Makkans do not accept the Oneness of Allah their Creator – tawḥid; Prophethood – nubuwah; and accountability – ma'ad, he ﷺ should say to them, 'Allah suffices as witness between us, He sees and knows what is in His servants' hearts'. This ayah serves two purposes: a) To threaten those who adamantly refuse to submit themselves willingly to their Creator; b) To underline that when people stick resolutely to their principles, the impact of their words resounds more strongly.

However, being convinced by argument is not sufficient to support strong faith. People still depend on Allah's grace for, 'whoever Allah guides is indeed guided aright'. Stepping on the right path or going astray are results of the choice of free will which Allah has granted human beings. However, when people insist on making choices with no regard to His guidance, He lets them stray in the sense that He withdraws His grace from them:

> . . . what does Allah mean by this parable? He causes many to err thereby, and guides many aright thereby, but He only permits those who wilfully transgress to stray.
>
> Qur'an 2:26

> Allah leaves transgressing wasters and doubters to stray.
>
> Qur'an 40:34

Allah eventually tells those who remain adamantly unwilling to submit, that on the Day of Resurrection He will drag them, face down, blind, deaf and dumb. One may ask how they may attend their reckoning and judgement in that condition? The response is that there are a variety of stages through which souls will have to pass on the Day of Resurrection. In some, those who were unwilling to submit will be raised blind, deaf and dumb as a punishment for not benefiting from Allah's bounties while they remained on earth.

However, as they pass through subsequent stages, they will again be given the ability to see, hear and respond to questioning.

The above ayah concludes with, 'their destination Gehennam [Hell], and whenever the blaze dies down We shall again increase its intensity'. The fires of hell are not extinguishable nor does Allah permit them to die down.

Those who deny Resurrection

98. That will be their recompense for disbelieving Our signs and questioning, 'When we [have perished] and our bones reduced to dust, shall we really be raised up and given a new existence?'

99. Can they not see that Allah, who created the heavens and the earth, is able to recreate their like? There is no doubt that He decreed an appointed time for them, but there are those who are unjust refuse to accept anything other than disbelief.

100. Say [to them], 'Even if you possessed the [limitless] treasuries of my Lord's mercy, you would hoard it for horror of spending; people are always grudging'.

In the previous ayat we are warned of the painful end for those who disbelieved and behaved mischievously. That is followed by the above ayat that discuss life after death. They say, 'How can we accept that rotten flesh and decaying bone distributed throughout the earth is able to be reassembled in its original form?' Allah's answer to this is that, 'Can they not see that He who created the heavens and the earth is able to recreate their like?' It is obvious that the Creator is able to recreate. Disbelievers do not recognise that it is Allah who created them from nothing and can create them again with memories of the lives they lived in this world, so that they will be able to render an account of their deeds to Him. The subject of the restoration of life was discussed in connection with Ayah 49 of this Surah.

Miracles of the Prophet Mūsa ﷺ

101. And We gave Mūsa [Moses] nine clear proofs [of Allah's sovereignty]. Ask the Children of Israel. When he came to them, Fir'awn [Pharaoh] said to him, 'Mūsa [Moses], I think you are possessed'.

102. Mūsa [Moses] said, 'You know very well that no one except the Lord of the heavens and the earth has sent these signs as clear proofs [to you]. [If you cannot see this] you are surely doomed.

103. At this, Fir'awn [Pharaoh] resolved to expel them from his realm, but We drowned him and those who accompanied him.

104. After that, We said to the Children of Isra'il, 'Dwell in that land. And when the promised day arrives We will gather your dispersed people together'.

The Holy Qur'an refers to many miracles brought about by the Prophet Mūsa ﷺ with the permission of his Lord:

1) His stick transformed into a serpent (Qur'an 20:20).
2) His hand came forth white and illuminated (Qur'an 20:22).
3) Tsunami (Qur'an 7:133).
4) Locusts destroyed all vegetation (Qur'an 7:133).
5) Lice affected plant life (Qur'an 7:133).
6) The plague of Nile frogs (Qur'an 7:133).
7) Blood, variously interpreted as noses bleeding or the Nile turning blood red (Qur'an 7:133).
8) The escape path though the sea (Qur'an 2:50).
9) The provision of both Manna and Quails (Qur'an 2:57).
10) Springs gushed forth from rocks (Qur'an 2:60).
11) The mountain split to conceal them (Qur'an 7:171).
12) The famine and dearth of fruits of Pharaoh's people (Qur'an 7:130).
13) The restoration to life of a human being (Qur'an 2:73).
14) The provision of clouds for protection (Qur'an 2:57).

Ayah 101 only mentions Mūsa ﷺ performing nine miracles which leads one to suspect that it refers to the events linked solely to Pharaoh and his people and does not include those which relate to the Children of Isra'il – e.g., Manna and Quails. Thus, Qur'an 7:133 refers to five miracles in addition to the transformation of Mūsa's stick and hand, making a total of seven. Where then are the other two? They must be references to the affliction of drought, famine and a dearth of fruits.

In conclusion, those nine miracles are: the stick, the illuminated hand, the tsunami, the locusts, the lice, the frogs, blood, drought and the dearth of fruits.

Did the Prophet ﷺ ask the Children of Isra'il?

After referring to nine miracles, in Ayah 101 Allah orders the Prophet ﷺ to speak to the Children of Isra'il about this to remind them of their ancestors' resistance to Mūsa's mission. Was there any specific need for the Prophet ﷺ to involve them? The answer is that the main people to be addressed were the disbelievers of Makkah who rejected Allah's signs and miracles He sent to support the Prophet Muḥammad ﷺ, as He did to Mūsa عليه السلام for the Children of Isra'il.

17 Revelation in stages

105. We revealed [the Qur'an] to guide you to truth and it has brought the truth! We sent you only as an encouragement and as a warning.

106. We revealed the Qur'an in stages and organised it so that sections may be regularly recited.

107. Tell them, 'Believe in it or not. Those who already innately knew [the truth] prostrated themselves as soon as the Qur'an's message was conveyed to them'.

108. Saying, 'Glory to our Lord! His covenant must be fulfilled'.

109. Humbled and with tears in their eyes, they prostrated themselves.

Once again, the Holy Qur'an illustrates the significance of this Divine Scripture in order to end all the disbelievers' arguments. Ayah 105 starts with 'We revealed [the Qur'an] to guide you to truth' and then immediately follows with the statement, 'It has brought the truth'. It concludes, 'We only sent you as an encouragement and as a warning'.' This clarifies that you have no right to change or alter any of the Qur'an's content.

The difference between the first and second statement:

1) The first statement refers to Allah's decree, the second, to its achievement.
2) The first statement refers to the content of the Qur'an to be the truth, the second to Allah's objectives and goals.
3) People sometimes begin projects, but do not finish them. In other words, not every beginning has a successful ending. However, this does not apply to the Qur'an because it begins with guidance to truth and continues to do so.

The next argument of disbelievers was that if the Qur'an was from a Divine source, why do they not have the complete scripture available to them? Allah tells us in the Qur'an that, 'We revealed the Qur'an in stages and organised it so that sections may be regularly recited'. A similar argument with response also appears in Qur'an 25:32, 'Those who disbelieve say, "Why was the complete Qur'an not revealed all at once?"' The answer is, 'That We may strengthen your heart therewith, and We have recited it to you in well-arranged gradual stages'. This points to the necessity of teaching people to understand the meaning of each and every ayah and become thoroughly familiar with its content.

To elaborate further:

4) Although the Holy Qur'an is a book, unlike those which assemble and present arguments throughout their content, the Qur'an refers to everyday social and spiritual life over a period of some 23 years. The events and vicissitudes of 23 years could obviously not be presented before they occurred. The Qur'an provides details of battles and delegations, as well as the reactions of a variety of different people including the hypocrites.
5) The process of education and purification is only established over a period of time. A child cannot, in one lesson, assimilate all they need to know to attend university. That takes them many years. Neither is the reform of a corrupt and ignorant society achieved without a great deal of patience. Each fruit must have time to ripen.
6) Gradual revelation also served to assure people of the Prophet's continued link to the source of revelation.

However, one learns from the above that education and purification need careful nurturing. Even though the Qur'an was revealed to the Prophet ﷺ on the Night of Measure – Laylat al-Qadr – it was sent down in a planned, precise and meaningful way over a period of 23 years.

Then, the subject matter of the Qur'an changes to the condemnation of those who disbelieve and to telling them that, if they believe in Islam and Qur'anic content or not, it is indeed the absolute truth. One of the signs that people have submitted to absolute truth is their prostration.

Indications for recommended prostration appear throughout the Qur'an, one of these in Ayah 109 of this Surah. Mandatory prostrations occur in Surahs 32, 41, 53 and 96.

One may easily differentiate between Surahs revealed in Makkah and those revealed in Madinah. The first group deals with the Oneness of the Creator, Prophethood and the Day of Resurrection, the second with rulings, regulations, rights and duties in the establishment of an Islamic society.

18 Allah's Most Beautiful Names

110. Say to them [O Muḥammad], 'Pray to Allah or to The All-Merciful, no matter which you choose, the Most Beautiful Names are all His. And do not be loud in your prayer nor hushed but be moderate'.

111. And say, 'Praise be to Allah who has no son, no one to share His sovereignty with, and who needs no aid. So extol Him and His limitless greatness'.

In *Majma al-Bayan*, Ṭabrisi quotes Ibn Abbas (regarded as the most learned of the Prophet's companions and known as The Sage of the Muslim Nation – Ḥabr al-Ummah) saying that when the Prophet ﷺ prostrated and recited, 'O Raḥman, O Raḥim', disbelievers accused him of inviting others to the belief in One God while he himself called upon two different Gods. At this, Allah revealed Ayah 110 to clarify that it is entirely proper and correct for Allah to be called upon by any of His attributes as all of the Most Beautiful Names indeed belong to Him.

Allah is perfect, pure and beyond limit in His Existence and Creation. No human being is able to imprison Him within the bounds of their imagination or comprehension. His names all manifest Omnipotence, Omniscience and Omnipresence. In whichever direction one turns, one has turned to face Him. That is precisely what is referred to in the Qur'an,

> To Allah belong all the Most Beautiful Names, so call on Him by them – Wa lilahil-Asma' al-Ḥusna faduhu biha.
>
> Qur'an, 7:180

Although there are other Qur'anic references to the Most Beautiful Names – Al-Asma'-al-Ḥusna – the above ayah is the most categoric in recommending that we use Al-Asma'-al-Ḥusna to call upon the Creator.

The six major Sunni hadith collections, referred to as *Al-Siḥaḥ as-Sittah*, all refer to Allah's Most Beautiful Names.

Imam al-Bayhaqi researched these for his book, *The Names and Attributes – Al-Asma' wal Sifat* – in which he presents the following references:

Abu Hurairah reported that he had heard the Prophet ﷺ say,

> Almighty Allah has 99 names, a hundred except one. Whoever counts them will enter paradise.

Ibn Abbas and Abd-Allah ibn Umar reported that they had heard the Prophet ﷺ say,

> Almighty Allah has 99 names, a hundred except one. Whoever counts them will enter paradise.

Ibn Abbas and Abd-Allah ibn Umar also reported that they had heard the Prophet ﷺ say,

> Almighty Allah has 99 names in the Qur'an, whoever counts them will enter paradise.

In his book *Al-Dur al-Manthur*, Jalal al-din Suyuṭi records the beautiful names of Allah which he found in both the ahadith and in the Surahs of the Qur'an. He presents evidence of 110 names.

As one might expect, the major Shi'ah collections of hadith, referred to as *The Four Books – Al-Kutub al-Arba'a* – also refer to Allah's Asma'-al-Ḥusna. In his scrutiny of the *Kutub al-Arba'a* for his work *The Oneness – Al-Tawḥid*, Sheikh Saduq provided the following references:

Imam Jaffar al-Sadiq ﷺ reported that 'Amir al-Muminin' – Imam ʿAli ﷺ, said that he had heard the Prophet ﷺ say,

> Allah has 99 names, a hundred except one. Whoever counts them enters paradise.

In *The Balance – Al-Mizan* – an extraordinarily erudite exegesis of the Qur'an, Allamah al-Sayyid Muḥammad Husayn al-Tabataba'i, presents evidence for 127 names.

The resources of scholars, from all schools of thought, contain authentic hadith which refer to 99 names some of which appear in the past or present tenses. Notwithstanding this, all scholars claim to have uncovered more than 99 names and agree that not all of the names are to be found in the Qur'an.

Even though lists of Asma' al-Ḥusna may vary in the inclusion or omission of one specific name or other, the significance of His Names lies not in which of His Beautiful Names we use, but in our remembering Him.

Muslims traditionally classify Allah's names in two groups; Names of Beauty – Asma' al-Jamal – and Names of Majesty – Asma' al-Jalal. Names of Beauty represent aspects of Divine Mercy and Forgiveness which includes the name 'Al-Raḥman', that Allah intimates in the Qur'an characterises The Divine Essence. It is understood that the whole of creation emanates from the Divine attribute – Al-Raḥman – as the Qur'an itself flows from the statement, at the begining of its first Surah, 'In the Name of Allah, Al-Raḥman, Al-Raḥim'. The names Al-Raḥman and Al-Raḥim represent aspects of Divine Mercy as, for example, do the names The Generous – Al-Karim and The Forgiver – Al-Ghafūr.

In contrast, names associated with justice, judgement and rigour, such as 'The Just' – Al-ʿAdl and 'Sari'al ḥisāb' – which indicate Allah's quickness to balance the accounts of humanity, represent aspects of Divine Majesty and are classified under Asma' al-Jalal.

Because life in this world is interwoven with rigour and mercy, names of both Majesty as well as those of Beauty are manifest. The religious life of Islam stresses the importance of Allah's Justice as well as of His Forgiveness. The significance of His Wrath is emphasised, in addition to His Love for His creatures. Thus, Allah sees and judges actions but is Merciful to those who repent and turn towards Him.

The Names and Qualities of Allah are arrived at when Divine Essence – Al-Dhāt – is combined, for example, with qualities such as Generosity – Karam – to form the name The Generous – Al-Karīm. An inextricable relationship thus exists between Divine Essence, Divine Qualities and Divine Names. Names such as 'The Merciful' and 'The Generous' reflect qualities or 'states of being' such as generosity and mercy.

Divine Names especially emphasised are sometimes referred to as 'mothers' – ummahāt – from which other names are derived. The ummahāt comprise names such as 'The Powerful' – Al-Qādir and 'The Merciful' – Al-Raḥmān. These themselves are in turn contained within the Supreme Name – Allah. Allah, which combines all the Divine Names, is at once the Name of Divine Essence, as well as the synthesis of all Divine Qualities and Names.

Many scholars refer to 'The Greatest Name' – Al-Ism al-A'ẓam – which, when used, answers all wishes and impacts upon everything. It is mentioned in some narrations that 'Bismillah al-Raḥman al-Raḥim' is as close to that great name as 'the pupil is to the eye' and in other narrations that this 'Greatest Name' appears in the Qur'an in the Ayat al-Kursi. It has been said that Āsif, son of Barkhia, the Prophet Sulayman's minister, called on Allah by this Great Name to enable him to bring the Queen of Sheeba's throne to Jerusalem 'in the blink of an eye'. However, we cannot accept that all events can follow from mere utterances of the human tongue. It is Allah's Divine Attributes which affect and control all things. Neither utterance nor concept in our mind about the beautiful names have any effect. It is only the will of Allah, in His Majesty, which is able to affect everything.

Allah tells us,

> At those times when my servants ask you concerning Me, I am truly near and answer the prayers of the supplicants who call on Me.
>
> Qur'an 2:186

In the following A–Z section, we trace the Most Beautiful Names, the number of times each is mentioned in the Qur'an and cite the reference for the first appearance of each.

We will try to give the literal meaning and root, followed by the interpretation of each and the description of its role in creation.

A–Z of Allah's Most Beautiful Names – Al-Asma' al-Husna.

A

Al-ʿAdl The Just

This name does not appear in the Qur'an as one of Allah's Beautiful Names.

ʿAdl is itself the root word from which al-ʿAdil – the One who is Just – is derived. Al-ʿAdl is He who is just and from whom all justice emanates – the justice which underpins peace, harmony and order from which balance flows. He gave all things existence, created everything perfectly and, with absolute justice and generosity, sited creation in a perfectly balanced environment. Each aspect of creation is fully equipped to fulfil its own special function. Al-ʿAdl represents absolute justice, the converse of tyranny – justice which represents right as opposed to wrong, order as opposed to chaos, and harmony as opposed to dissension.

Even though we are not able to observe things at every stage of their journey, or permitted to see their inner aspects, everything is treated justly and is 'as He likes it to be'. Everything has been created with purpose. If we see only clouds, we know that without them we would not appreciate clear skies. Without weakness we would not appreciate strength, without poverty, riches, etc. Allah knows His creation and it knows that He is just.

Humankind's share in the attribute Al-ʿAdl rests in allowing reason and religion to control the passions and anger which cause injustice. To behave justly towards ourselves, our families, relatives, neighbours, employers and employees, we must restrict ourselves within the parameters of the Divine Law. On no account may we bestow inappropriate advantages to disrupt order and balance.

Humankind's greatest benefit arises from accepting Allah Almighty's Justice, for His plans, decrees and actions are just, whether they correspond with our will or not. In the same way that patients accept the medication that doctors prescribe to alleviate their physical suffering, our acceptance of Allah's divine and absolute justice alleviates the suffering that stems from objecting to and resisting Allah Almighty. Absolute faith lies in acceptance of what He has ordained with absolute justice.

The Justice of Allah has become a matter of controversy among Muslims. The Shi'ah and Mu'tazalites believe that Allah is 'absolutely just' in the sense that it would be contrary to His nature to wrong anyone. The Asharite school consider it objectionable to regard Allah Almighty thus. 'Who are we', they ask, 'to place any stipulation on the will of Allah?' They are certain that no one has any right to an opinion on how Allah will decide any matter, even if He is to commit the righteous to hell and reward the criminal on 'The Day of Judgement'.

The Shi'ah and Mu'tazalites reject that view. They say that 'Allah Almighty Himself' promised to reward the righteous and to punish the criminal and, they claim, Allah never breaks His promises. Because of their support of Allah's justice, the Shi'ah and Mu'tazalites came to be known as 'Those who are Pro-Justice' – Al-ʿAdliyah. The Imamiyyah school consequently includes 'The Justice of Allah' as a 'Root of Religion' while the Asharite schools, the majority of Sunni Muslims, do not. (Compare with Al-Ḥakam on p. 198).

Al-ʿAfūw The Pardoner

Appears in the Qur'an five times, the first reference in 4:43,

> . . . Allah is pardoning, oft forgiving.
>
> Qur'an 4:43

"ʿAfw' is to pardon. The one who most frequently pardons is Al-ʿAfūw.

The sins of people do not affect Allah Almighty. To refrain from sin is to benefit oneself and to remove the filth and corruption that clutters the soul. Whenever Allah's disobedient servants repent and feel shame, they take comfort that their Lord erases their sins.

One of the recommended forms of remembrance – Dhikr – by which to seek purification and tranquility from one's Creator is, while in prostration, to repeatedly call upon 'al-Afūw'.

In Islamic teaching, there is a firm link between the concepts of pardon and repentance. Our share in this quality lies in our pardoning others. Thus, in one of his supplications, Imam ʿAli ibn Ḥusayn ﷺ says, 'O Allah, you ordered us to pardon those who have wronged us; we have now wronged ourselves and have no one other than You to pardon us'.

(*See* also Al-Ghafūr on p. 195).

Al-Aḥad The Unique

Appears in the Qur'an once in 112:1,

> . . . He is Allah the Unique.
>
> Qur'an 112:1

'Waḥid' is the Arabic for the number one. While number one is followed consecutively by numbers two, three, four, etc., that which is unique – 'Aḥad' – cannot, by definition, be preceded or followed.

In our commentary on Ayat 42 and 43 (*see* p.86), Allah's Oneness is discussed in detail and the name Al-Aḥad clarified.

Al-Ākhir The Last

Appears in the Qur'an once, in 57:3,

> He is the First and He is the Last.
>
> Qur'an 57:3

Because Allah is eternal and everlasting, He is beyond both time and space. The concept of time is related to motion, a characteristic of matter. However, as it is clear in Islamic theology that Allah Almighty is neither body nor matter, and that motion, change or alteration have no relevance to Him. Everything perishes for it is He alone who is everlasting, eternal. In this way He is The Last with none existing after Him. This attribute forms a pair with the name Al-Awwal (*see* p. 182) which means The First.

Al-ʿAlīm The Omniscient (All-Knowing)

Appears in the Qur'an 131 times, the first reference in 2:29,

> . . . He has perfect knowledge.
>
> Qur'an 2:29

ʿIlm is the root word for knowledge. The past tense ʿAlima means he knew (ʿAlimat, she knew) and anyone who is knowledgeable is referred to as an ʿAlīm. With unlimited and endless knowledge, Allah is thus Al-ʿAlīm.

Al-ʿAlīm is the One who comprehends and has perfect knowledge of all things: the first and the last; the manifest and the hidden; large and small; origin and culmination. His knowledge is the basis which preceded the infinity of things. Everything is simply a flowering of His inherent knowledge, the source from which all existence has been derived. Perfect knowledge is disclosed with perfect clarity, and it is not possible for human beings to conceive anything with such perfection.

Although humankind may reflect this attribute, our knowledge differs from the knowledge of Al-ʿAlīm in four distinct ways:

1) Our knowledge is derived from things. It is not knowledge from which things are derived. Allah's knowledge precedes creation while ours is the result of creation – e.g., while the acquired knowledge of those who devised the game of chess may be said to have been the 'cause' of that game, the fact that there is now a game called chess is itself the 'cause' for people acquiring 'knowledge' of that game.
2) Our knowledge is based on reflection while His is based on things being in His presence. He does not have to search for them.

3) Despite our knowledge being vast and wide-ranging, it is finite rather than infinite – e.g., while humanity has lived on this earth for thousands of years we are still studying and trying to understand its climactic, environmental, ecological and life forms. Nor do we know all that has happened in the past or is to happen in the future.
4) Despite being clear, the clarity of our knowledge is limited and not limitless – e.g., although it is clear to us that all creatures have to eat to live, we are not always clear about the result of eating a particular thing. The example of 'Mad Cow Disease' or Bovine Spongiform Encephalopathy is a clear illustration of this.

As knowledge is an attribute of our Creator, those who have knowledge derive distinction from it. The degree of distinction they attain relates to the degree of distinction of the subject of their knowledge. It is undoubtedly knowledge of Allah Almighty which secures the greatest distinction of all. The highest level of knowledge to distinguish humanity is knowledge of the actions of Allah Almighty that enable us to come closer to Him and to acquire even further knowledge of His actions.

Al-ʿAliyy The Most High

Appears in the Qur'an nine times, the first reference in 2:255,

> . . . He is the Most High . . .
>
> Qur'an 2:255

'ʿAla' is 'on' or 'upon'; 'ʿUluw' is 'height'; 'ʿAali' is 'high'; and 'ʿAliyy' is 'the highest'.

Being Most High – Al-ʿAliyy – refers to difference in rank rather than to differences in spatial height. Rational gradings are mere perceptions. One is above another in that it is the cause, the other below, in that it is contingent on the former. Thus, it is that the cause of all existence holds the highest rank. Everything in existence holds a lower or inferior rank than Allah the Most High – Allah al-ʿAliyy.

We can only reflect this aspect in relation to each other. Physical height or height above sea level play no part in our position in this life which is determined solely by the rank which we hold. The 'most high' rank achieved by a human being was that held by Allah's final Prophet, Muḥammad Mustafa ﷺ.

Another aspect of being Most High is being above and beyond comprehension or imagination. However precise we attempt to be in identifying Him, He remains beyond anything which we are able to imagine or describe. This is referred to in the following ayah,

> He is above what they attribute to Him.
>
> Qur'an 6:100

Allah Allah

Appears in the Qur'an 2697 times, the first reference in 1:1,

> In the name of Allah.
>
> Qur'an 1:1

'Aliha' is Arabic for 'meant', while 'ilah' is the objective of perfection sought by humanity. Allah is thus the name of the Almighty Creator in whom the whole of Creation finds its every bounty.

This is the greatest name of all – Al-Ism al-A'aẓam – that represents the very essence of divinity. Allah alone has a uniquely independent existence, while all other things, that owe their existence to Him, are ephemeral and perishable. The name 'Allah' represents the totality of the attributes that His Beautiful Names describe. Allah is the name for The Almighty – The Perfection of Existence who is alone worthy of worship. He is, always was and ever will be. He is unique, the cause of everything. He is the Creator with no resemblance to the created. He alone is self-existent and without need.

The names which unite to make this totality, describe attributes to which humankind should aspire.

'Allah' is the name for the One True God in the Arabic language. Used in preference to the word God, this term is singular, has no plural and is not associated with masculine, feminine, or neutral characteristics.

In many ayat in the Qur'an, Allah Almighty is referred to as 'Hu', which equates to the word 'He'. Calling upon Allah with the words 'O He' – Ya Hu – is similar to the name 'Jehovah' used by Jews.

Al-Awwal The First

Appears in the Qur'an once, in 57:3.

> He is the First, and He is the Last.
>
> Qur'an 57:3

Allah's is the Kingdom of the heavens and the earth. It is He who gives life and causes death. The beginning was established by His existence and to Him is the last return and destination. He is the Last stage for those with spiritual aspirations. As one author, Brian Leftow expressed it,

> God exists without beginning or end. He is eternal and timeless. A timeless God does not remember or forget. He has neither future nor past. He does not change, and there is no temporal gap between His forming a plan and executing it.
>
> *A Companion to Philosophy of Religion*, p. 257

By its very definition eternal is self-existent; it could never have been non-existent nor can it ever be terminated. It has no beginning because if we were to suppose a beginning for it, we would have to admit that it was non-existent before that. In the same way, eternal can neither be a compound nor a mixture, for compounds or mixtures depend for their existence upon their constituent parts. Therefore, if we accept that eternal is self-existent, we cannot accept that its existence is dependent upon any component or part.

The eternal cannot be subject to change, because change would render it either better or worse. If a change made it better it would imply that the eternal was not perfect prior to that change. We have, however, already concluded that that which is eternal is perfect and not in need of anything. Equally, if the change were for the worse, it would imply that the eternal had been in need of something to make it perfect.

Imam ʿAli ﷺ explained the above in the following way,

> He commences creation without any means or instruments. He measures without any recourse to thought or reflection. He is free of all need and derives no benefit from anything. Time and place do not accompany Him, tools and instruments do not aid Him. His existence precedes all time, and His pre-eternity precedes all beginning.

Nahjul Balagha, Sermon 186

We read in the Old Testament:

> God has made every thing beautiful in its own time . . .
>
> I know that, whatsoever God doeth, it shall be for ever: nothing can be put to it, nor any thing taken away from it . . .

Ecclesiastes, Chapter 3, Verses 11 and 14

Al-ʿAẓim The Tremendous (The Supremely Glorious)

Appears in the Qur'an seven times, the first reference in 2:255.

> . . . The most Tremendous in Glory.

Qur'an 2:255

'Aẓamah' means greatness or mightiness. "Aẓim' is derived from it and means the great or the mighty. Al-ʿAẓim, associated with Allah, is translated as tremendous in its sense of vastness. In terms of our visual perception, tremendous has two connotations: the first, of capturing attention and filling one's view, the second, of not possibly being able to see something in its entirety. Similar differences apply to intellectual perceptions. We may comprehend the essential reality of some objects but not of others. While a few intellects may comprehend the essential reality of these latter, most intellects will not. The essence of al-ʿAẓim is vast in precisely the sense that it is beyond the limit of humankind's intellectual comprehension.

The truly tremendous amongst humankind are Allah's Prophets and Imams, those who were ordered by Him to bring new laws and to teach people obedience. They are considered in this light because they had to be and to remain free of error, in order to discharge their duties accurately. While they are undoubtedly tremendous compared to us, Allah al-ʿAẓim is beyond all comparison for His tremendous vastness is absolute.

Al-ʿAziz The Eminent (The Almighty)

Appears in the Qur'an 92 times, the first reference in 2:129.

> . . . You are the exalted in might [Almighty] . . .
>
> Qur'an 2:129

While a scarce gemstone might be referred to as being precious or rare – Izzah or Nudrah – ʿAziz refers to one who is distinguished or noble. Al-ʿAziz, when associated with Allah, is translated as Eminent because it is the highest degree of nobility, preciousness and scarcity. To be al-ʿAziz requires four related qualities: being rare, being needed, being difficult to approach and being Almighty. Difficulty of access is related to greatness of need and remarkableness of quality. So, while all life depends on sunlight, sunlight is not considered eminent because it is readily accessible. And, notwithstanding the sun's uniqueness for earth, there are apparently millions of suns in the universes.

Absolute rarity lies in uniqueness in actuality as well as possibility. The ultimate degree of being needed lies in being needed by all creatures, both for their attributes and for their existence and survival. Only Allah Almighty fulfils these qualities. Being ultimately difficult to approach also rests with Him, for not only is it impossible to come near to Him through likeness, it is even impossible to obtain full knowledge of Him. Being Almighty, He is the ultimate in power. No force in the universe can overwhelm Him or oppose His Will. Indeed, there is nothing as perfect in eminence as al-ʿAziz the Almighty.

People are considered eminent when others need their guidance in matters which are important to them, namely their lives and eternal happiness. The most eminent are thus the Prophets and those Imams who are free from error. These are followed by scholars and teachers of rank who busy themselves guiding their Lord's creatures.

B

Al-Badīʿ The Originator (of Creation)

Appears in the Qur'an twice, first reference in 2:117.

> Wonderful Originator of the Heavens and the Earth!
>
> Qur'an 2:117

'Badaʿa' means original creation without the need to copy anything. Thus, 'Badīʿ' is the Originator of Creation. The other word linked with this root is 'Bida'ah' which means innovation and refers to something that is new and not part of the Sunnah.

The Genome Project to 'map' human genes, which pharmaceutical companies hope will assist them in the development of expensive patented cures for many diseases and ailments is, simply put, an exploration of the name Al-Badīʿ.

Great painters create works of art using their own intellect and creativity, while their pupils simply copy their 'masterpieces'. To the educated it is not terribly difficult to distinguish between the two. As Allah Almighty is The Creator and source of every 'arrangement and design', all scientific discovery merely uncovers and explains a small part of His original creation.

Al-Bāʿith The Raiser of the Dead – The Resurrector

Only appears in the Qur'an in the present tense of the verb – 'Yabaʿath' – the first reference in 6:36,

> . . . and as to the dead, it is Allah [Al-Bāʿith] who raises them up to be returned to Him.
>
> Qur'an 6:36

'Ba'th' is the verb to send, to delegate, or to resurrect. Since resurrection from the grave is a sort of despatch or arousal from dormancy, Allah, who will cause that to happen, is referred to as Al-Bāʿith.

On 'The Day of Resurrection' or 'Last Day', Allah [Al-Bāʿith] will raise the dead from their graves and revive from their life on this earth, the thoughts, feelings and deeds, for which they must account. Belief that the deceased will be returned to life after their death is central to the Islamic faith and Allah repeats it in many ayat of the Qur'an:

> The hour is certainly coming for Allah [al-Bāʿith] to raise those who are in graves.
>
> Qur'an 22:7

> We created you from [earth], will return you to it, and then bring you forth from it a second time.
>
> Qur'an 20:55

> It is Allah who created you, sustains you, causes you to die and then brings you back to life again . . .
>
> Qur'an 30:40

Such ayat clarify that souls do not disintegrate into 'nothingness' at death, that Allah created souls for eternity, and not to 'write them out' after one episode, that life on earth and in the grave are simply stages on a continuum of everlasting life. Allah tells us in the Qur'an,

> And do not reckon those who are slain in the way of Allah, to be dead. No, they are alive with their Lord and getting sustenance from Him. Rejoicing in what Allah has bestowed on them of His grace, rejoicing that their comrades who have not yet joined them are not afraid and are not grieving over them. They rejoice in the grace of Allah and His bounty, and truly Allah does not let the reward due to believers go to waste.
>
> Qur'an 3:169–171

A hadith relates that after the battle of Badr, the Prophet ﷺ addressed those who had died in their attack on the Muslim community,

> O Utbah, O Shaibah, O Umayyah, O Abu Jahl: did you find the promise of your lord true? Because I found true what my Lord promised me.

When Umar asked,

> O Messenger of Allah, are you talking to dead bodies without souls?

The Prophet ﷺ replied,

> By He who holds my soul in His hand, you are not a better listener than they, despite their inability to respond.
>
> Kanz al Uma'al, Tradition number 29874

But being raised from the dead does not imply that such rebirth will echo the last life, or that anything new will be brought forth. Allah makes clear that He – Allah al-Bāʿith – revives or re-creates souls many times in the process of their progression and purification. He refers to this frequently in the Qur'an.

> He created you from clay, decreed a term [of life], plus also another determined term . . .
>
> Qur'an 6:2

> It is Allah who creates you, takes your soul at death and returns some of you to a feebleness so that they know nothing after knowing much . . .
>
> Qur'an 16:70

> . . . changing your forms and creating you [again] in a form which you do not know.
>
> Qur'an 56:61

> . . . He has created you by various stages.
>
> Qur'an 70:14

Allah refers to our changing from one state to another as our various qualities and capacities develop. One change was the evolution of life from inorganic matter; another, when insignificant sperm and seed develop into a fertilised ovum, foetus and then baby. Change occurs, too, from infant to child of discernment, to youth with reason, to mature adult, and then to the retrogressive stages of old age and death. Allah Almighty tells us death is followed by life in the grave, the resurrection of 'The Last Day' and then, yet further life.

Each change is a stage of perfection. Each change follows the one that preceded it. Each is a stage of development that requires the creation of a new form. Every soul has the potential to progress towards perfection. Every soul is suspended between acceptance and rejection, between separation and attainment. Each is, as Hildegard von Bingen described it, 'Like A Feather on the Breath of God'.

While the concept of new cells replacing dying ones is not difficult to understand, the concept of new identities replacing dying ones is rather more difficult. And this is particularly so with changes beyond the grave. One can perhaps understand this best via analogy. A child, too young to understand, and who has not yet felt what it means to be burned, has no reason to believe that fire is hot. However, if it believes its mother and does not touch fire, it may remain a happy baby. Not surprisingly, our ultimate happiness also depends on what we believe. For it is belief in Allah's Messengers, and obeying the laws which they brought, that prepares our eternal soul for its cycle of death, rebirth and change of state on its journey towards purification and, hence, peace.

Those who would reflect the qualities of Al-Bā'ith must remain aware that death precedes re-creation. Ignorance has to pass before knowledge can emerge. Focus on the things of this world must end before anticipation of those of the next can begin. One reaps what one sows and good actions must replace bad if we are to crop a harvest which will sustain us in the future.

Al-Bāqī The Everlasting

Only appears in the Qur'an in the present tense – Yabqa, first reference in 55:27.

> But the Supreme Being of your Glorious and Gracious Lord will remain forever.
>
> Qur'an 55:27

'Baqeya' – the root of al-Bāqī – means to remain or to stay. With reference to the Most Beautiful Names, it means everything will perish except for He who remains.

Allah is the pure and perfect existent, whose existence is inherent and not acquired. He is beyond time, space and limits. He is the Creator of the whole universe and, since time is related to motion, it is easy to comprehend that before there was anything in the cosmos, there was no motion and, consequently, no concept of time.

While all physical and materialistic beings have an end, Allah, who is beyond time and material measure, is eternal and everlasting.

All creatures, including human beings, exist within the boundaries of their limitations while Allah Almighty exists without boundary. He is Omnipresent in the sense that the whole universe is merely the result of an act of His and an expression of His grace and bounty.

Compare this name to 'The Last' – Al-Ākhir (*see* p. 180).

Al-Bārī The Originator (The Producer)

Appears in the Qur'an three times, the first reference in 59:24,

> He is Allah, the Creator, the Originator [Producer], the Fashioner . . .
>
> Qur'an 59:24

Bārī – derived from the root 'Bara'a' – means to produce or create.

A specification, blueprint, or plan must exist before non-existence is able to emerge into existence. That which was previously non-existent must be originated and then fashioned to conform with what was envisaged. Allah is Creator – Khaliq – in that He devises the plan (*see* p. 210). He is Originator – Bārī – in that He initiates existence and He is Fashioner – Muṣawwir – in that he fashions the form of what He has created (*see* p. 222). An analogy might describe the work of an architectural practice with consultants to design, quantify and specify materials; a building contractor to provide materials and manage the labour of erecting the fabric of the building; and specialist contractors who install the services, final decor and furnishings.

It is the knowledge that Allah Almighty 'has' of a form that enables this form to exist in one's heart. And it is this existence in one's heart that enables the soul to realise it.

We are not able to 'produce' anything out of nothing; we require raw materials for whatever we wish to make. Had we been able to produce raw materials from any other part of creation we might then have been tempted to claim the title of true producer. We have no access to this name other than metaphorically. That which we 'produce' can only be said to have been grown, extracted, fabricated, built, constructed, or supervised.

We, however, derive benefit from knowing the meaning of the name Al-Bārī when, by acquiring this attribute in our soul, we become producers, even if that is only metaphorically. However, such cognitive forms only occur when we strive to be exposed to the mercy of Allah Almighty.

Al-Barr The Benign (The Source of All Goodness)

Appears in the Qur'an once, in 52:28,

> . . . He is the Benign, the Merciful.
>
> Qur'an 52:28

'Birr' means kindness, especially in actions and manner. 'Barr' describes devoted kindness and at the same time indicates a person who is full of every type of goodness. This attribute may apply to Allah as well as to His honourable messengers. This is why 'Isa's behaviour towards his mother is described in Qur'an 19:32 as being Barr and, in Qur'an 19:14, the same is said of Yahya's conduct towards his parents.

However, in Qur'anic terminology the plural of Barr – i.e., 'Abrar' – is used to indicate those who are righteous,

> Truly, the righteous shall drink a cup tempered with camphor which contains water from the spring which Allah's servants drink . . .
>
> Qur'an 76:5–6

Allah is the source of every type of goodness, and humanity shares this attribute by doing good to all His creatures regardless of their being deserving or not.

Al-Baṣīr The All-Seeing

Appears in the Qur'an 43 times, the first reference in 2:96,

> . . . Allah sees all the things they do.
>
> Qur'an 2:96

'Baṣar' is the verb 'to see'. When this is in a physical context, the past and present tenses 'Abṣara' and 'Yubṣeru' are used. However, when the context refers to 'inner sight', the verb 'Baṣirah' is applicable. Baṣīr is used to cover both aspects.

The attribute that Al-Baṣīr represents is the perfection of seeing and witnessing all things. For Al-Baṣīr, everything is visible, be it as yet undisclosed, distant, secreted, concealed, or in the future. His sight, without eyes, pupils, or lenses, is free from distortion and with such clarity that both the inner as well as the outer appearance of things are obvious to Him.

In comparison, human sight is deficient and sometimes fails us completely. Our sight, concerned only with the outer appearance of things, is not equipped to glimpse that which is interior and secret or even, at any distance, the detail of things.

The subtle contemplative works of simplicity and quietude of one of the most admired painters of the 20th century – Georgio Morandi (1890–1964) – are exhibited around the world and represented in many public and private collections. In the words of Morandi, whose work has been described as 'a celebration of what is both familiar and unique about a particular moment':

> We know that what we can see of the objective world as human beings never really exists as we see and understand it.
>
> I believe that nothing can be more abstract, more unreal, than what we actually see.
>
> Georgio Morandi, 1958

An example of this is what is perceived by all as light, which is indeed the complexity of seven different colours easily proven in physical experiment.

However, those who remain ever conscious of Him are sometimes rewarded with glimpses of the 'core' of one matter or another. Such information is also referred to as 'insight'. Awareness of Al-Baṣīr provides the awareness that it is He who gives us the sight by which to observe and reflect on His signs. It also reminds us that whatever we do, we are always within His vision. This means that everything, seen as well as unseen, is merely a mirror which reflects Allah's full knowledge.

Al-Bāsiṭ He Who is Open-handed

Only appears in the Qur'an in the present tense – 'Yabsot', the first reference in 13:26,

> Allah open-handedly increases the sustenance of whomsoever He wills.
>
> Qur'an 13:26

'Basṭ' means open-handedness or generosity. Referring to Allah's attribute, Bāsiṭ means oft-giving. Since the sustenance of the whole of creation depends on Allah's provision, Bāsiṭ is linked to His open-handedness. Al-Bāsiṭ is comprehended most clearly as one of a pair of contrasting aspects. It is Al-Bāsiṭ who increases provision and provides abundantly – but Al-Qābiḍ – who decreases provision and withholds (*see* p. 227). Thus, Al-Qābiḍ extracts souls from the dead while Al-Bāsiṭ extends souls to new life in the womb. Al-Qābiḍ appropriates alms from the rich; Al-Bāsiṭ gives abundantly to the poor. Al-Qābiḍ withholds sustenance to further weaken those who are weak, while Al-Bāsiṭ extends abundance. His bounty surpasses every need of the wealthy. Al-Qābiḍ's might and awesomeness contracts hearts in fear, Al-Bāsiṭ's divinity, forgiveness and mercy instils hearts with peace. Amongst those who remain ever conscious of Allah – who have 'Taqwa' – a few inspired, eloquent and wise people have the ability to reflect the aspects of Al-Qābiḍ and Al-Bāsiṭ. As they infuse awareness of Allah Almighty's abundant mercy and blessings, people's hearts expand in peace and joy. But when they recount warnings of punishment, their audience's hearts contract and shrink in fear.

Al-Bāṭin The Hidden

Appears in the Qur'an once, in 57:3,

> He is the first and the last, the manifest and the hidden.
>
> Qur'an 57:3

'Bāṭn' is the noun for abdomen or stomach. However, Bāṭin is the opposite of Ẓāhir the manifest or self-evident (*see* p. 246). The concept of existence is the most obvious concept known to humankind. If, however, one asks scholars and academics about the essence of existence they can give no clear answer. This is why philosophers regard existence and its qualities as the main subject of their research. Allah Almighty is the purest and most absolute existence from which all other existence stems. It is correct to say that He is manifest even though His essence is unknown and hidden. In our life, a thing cannot be both manifest and hidden, for things are manifest and hidden only in relation to modes of perception. However, according to Allah Almighty, He remains hidden while He is sought by sensory perceptions or resources of imagination. Only by using the sources of reason and insight, which are the illumination of guidance, does the Almighty become manifest. Imam Ḥusayn ﵇ – in his supplication on the day of Arafah (9th of Dhul Hijjah) – prayed, 'O Allah, were you hidden that we need to prove your existence? Or was it the evidence which guided us that was stronger than You? No, it is You who are the stronger.'

D

Al-Ḍārr The One Who Disadvantages

Appears in the Qur'an once, in 48:11,

> . . . who then has any power to intervene with Allah on your behalf, if He should wish to disadvantage or grant you an advantage.

Qur'an 48:11

'Ḍarar' is a disadvantage and 'Nafʿa' a benefit or advantage. Ḍārr is the One who disadvantages in the sense that loss or disadvantage is the result of His so willing it to be.

This attribute is paired with Nāfi' (see p. 225) to convey belief in Allah's ultimate authority and that nothing ever benefits or harms anyone without His permission. Natural causes do not operate independently or in isolation. They are merely channels through which Allah's will is directed. Allah created fire with its characteristic burning and gives poison the ability to kill. Yet without specific permission from Him, fire was not able to burn Ibrahim ﷺ, nor on many occasions was poison able to affect the well-being of the Imams of the Ahl al-Bayt. In one incident Allah reproaches those Christians who believe that ʿIsa ﷺ is God.

> Truly those who say that the Masi'a son of Maryam is Allah, are infidels. Who then would be capable of challenging Allah's authority if He wished to destroy the Masi'a and his mother along with the whole of humanity?

Qur'an 5:17

Dhul-Jalāl wal-Ikrām The One Full of Majesty, Bounty and Honour

Appears in the Qur'an twice, the first reference in 55:27.

> But the Supreme Being of Bounty and Honour is everlasting . . .

Qur'an 55:27

According to Islamic Theology and Creed – ʿIlm al-Kalam – Allah Almighty's attributes are of two types: attributes of affirmation such as knowledge, power, wisdom and life; and attributes of negation such as not having a body, not having any needs and not occupying space. For Qur'anic reference for these types of attributes some theologians refer to the above mentioned ayah. Here, Al-Jalāl refers to His negative or negating attributes and Al-Ikrām to His affirmative or affirming attributes. 'Dhu' in Arabic simply indicates ownership. Dhul-Jalāl wal-Ikrām thus refers to Allah Almighty possessing both affirmative and negative attributes. On the affirmative side He is the owner of bounty and honour; on the negative He is so beyond imperfection as to be truly Majestic. Here, negation of His imperfection affirms His perfection. In other words, His is the most perfect existence.

F

Al-Fattāḥ The One Who Opens

Appears in the Qur'an once, in 34:26,

> Our Lord will gather us together and will, in the end, open [reveal] the truth to us. He is the Opener, the All-Knowing.
>
> Qur'an 34:26

'Fatḥ' means to open, to grant victory or success. Thus, Fattāḥ is the opener of the gates to sustenance and profit. Surah number 48 is called al-Fatḥ – Victory. The word 'Miftāḥ' derives from the same root and names the tool for opening – the key. At the discretion of Al-Fattāḥ, that which was closed is opened, and that which was unclear is clarified. It is He who lifts the veil from the hearts of the pious to reveal vistas of His majesty. Al-Fattāḥ is, thus, an appropriate title for the keyholder to the invisible world.

> None can withhold Allah's mercy to humankind, nor grant them that which He withholds . . .
>
> Qur'an 35:2

Those who aspire to reflect the quality of 'Al-Fattāḥ' should strive to attain levels at which Divine mysteries are revealed to them. Such knowledge might enable them to 'open' windows of understanding for others and to grant them a share in this quality.

Muslims are advised to inaugurate every project with the name of Allah. Thus, even praise of Allah should precede all one's prayers. The first surah in the Qur'an, called al-Fatiha, begins with the words, 'Praise is due to Allah, the Lord of the Universes – Al Hamdu lilahi Rabbil Alamin'. The first words of the 'Iftitah' prayer that is recited every night of the Month of Ramadan are, 'O Allah, I begin with your praise'.

In one tradition this name is linked with Allah as the Provider so believers call upon Allah, by repeating the name O Provider – Ya-Fattāḥ 70 times after the dawn – Fajr prayer.

G

Al-Ghaffār He Who is Full of Forgiveness (The Forgiver)

Appears in the Qur'an five times, the first reference in 20:82,

> Truly, I forgive again and again . . .
>
> Qur'an 20:82

'Ghafara' is to forgive or to pardon, 'Istighfar' is to seek forgiveness; thus, 'Astaghfir Allah' means, 'I seek Allah's forgiveness'.

Al-Ghaffār prefers that He and His creatures see only that which is beautiful. He, therefore, covers over and conceals all that is unpleasant. He prefers to conceal the ugliness of sin in this world and to refrain from seeking compensation for it in the next.

Seeking forgiveness from Al-Ghaffār means, therefore, to seek that He erase and conceal the things of which we are ashamed. He made our innermost hearts a secret hiding place for our ugliest thoughts and intentions. If our deceptions, hatred, bad thoughts and betrayals were not hidden in our consciences but were seen by all, outraged reaction might destroy us. It is the Mercy of Al-Ghaffār that allows our weaknesses to remain hidden.

Assurance of forgiveness is related in the Qur'an,

> For those who repent, believe and do good, He will change their evil deeds to good deeds.
>
> Qur'an 25:70

We reflect the attributes of this name when we conceal faults and weaknesses of others and refer only to their good characteristics. The Prophet ﷺ said that,

> On the Day of Judgement Allah will conceal the faults of those who concealed the weaknesses of others.
>
> Musnad of Ibn Hanbal IV, 159
>
> Sahih al-Bukhari, Mazalim 3

As an illustration of this, a story is told about 'Isa ﷺ and his companions passing the decaying remains of a dead dog. 'What a stench', one remarked. 'Isa ﷺ responded, 'What beautiful white teeth this creature of Allah has'.

In the second book of *Les Misérables, 'Intestine of Leviathan – The Earth Impoverished by the Sea'*, Victor Hugo provides an example of filth being rendered wholesome. Referring to the Parisian sewer, he asks readers what the foetid stream of subterranean slime hidden by the pavement is? He then explains that, spread on the earth, 'It is the flowering meadow, it is the green grass, it is the marjoram and thyme and sage, it is cattle, it is the satisfied low of huge oxen at evening, it is the perfumed hay, it is golden corn, it is the bread on your table, it is warm blood in your veins, it is health, it is joy, it is life'. This is all brought about by the will which causes transformation upon earth and transfiguration in heaven.

Al-Ghafūr The All-Forgiving

Appears in the Qur'an 91 times, the first reference in 2:173'

> . . . If their behaviour is not excessive, those who are driven by necessity, with no intention of being wilfully disobedient, are not guilty of sin. For Allah is All-Forgiving.

Qur'an 2:173

While 'Al-Ghaffār' refers to the readiness, frequency and all-encompassing nature of Allah's forgiveness, 'Al-Ghafūr' refers to the characteristic flawlessness and totality of Allah's forgiveness.

We share in the attributes of this name to the extent that we truly forgive and forget the transgressions of others.

The most courageous and bold is not the one who takes revenge, but rather the one who is able to ignore transgressions against him/her and excuse them completely.

Al-Ghanī The Self-Sufficient (For whom everything is readily available)

Appears in the Qur'an 18 times, the first reference in 2:263,

> . . . and Allah is self-sufficient and forbearing.

Qur'an 2:263

'Ghanī' is the state of being free from want, with everything available. Because Allah Almighty is Himself the source of all that is good, He is self-sufficient and needs nothing from any other source. No other being provides Him with existence, power, knowledge, etc. It is He who is the source of everything.

Describing something as incomplete is to evidence its need for something else to complete it. Describing people as being poor implies that they have a shortage of finance and need funds. Only He who is self-sufficient is not in need of anything:

> While Allah is free of all need it is you who are needy.

Qur'an 47:38

> O humankind, it is you who stand in need of Allah. Allah is He who is free of all needs.
>
> Qur'an 35:15

This name illustrates the permanent relationship between the Creator and His creatures who, for their very existence, depend entirely and absolutely on their Creator.

H

Al-Hādī The Guide

Appears in the Qur'an twice, the first reference in 25:31.

> . . . but your Lord is sufficient as a guide and helper.
>
> Qur'an 25:31

'Hadā' means to lead people to the right way, to guide them. When this verb is associated with faith, it is to guide to true faith. 'Hudā' and 'Hidāya' both refer to guidance, thus Hādī is The Guide and Mahdi, the rightly guided.

Allah tells us in the Qur'an,

> This Book, with no doubt in it, [is] a guidance to those who guard [against evil], those who believe in the unseen . . .
>
> Qur'an 2:1-2

It is thus clear that those who guard against evil, believe in Allah, believe in the unseen and are pious. The first four ayat in Surah Al-Baqarah enumerate five characteristics of piety: believing in the unseen, maintaining the prayer, spending benevolently of His gifts, believing in what has been revealed and being sure of the hereafter. The next ayah clarifies that those with these characteristics, '. . . are on guidance from their Lord'. He guides them to be pious and guides them to guard themselves from evil. Once they achieve this first stage they may, with the guidance of the Qur'an, make further progress.

There is thus clearly initial guidance that leads or points to the right way, after which there is further guidance from the Qur'an.

The simplest level of guidance is that which helps every creature meet the requirements of life. Thus, it is He who guides the infant to the breast once it has left the womb, the chick to peck for food when it emerges from the egg and the bee to build hexagonal combs without any of them needing to learn these things.

We need guidance, not only to obtain knowledge of the theory and practice of the doctrines we believe in, but also to perceive the extraordinary truths which open new and wider spiritual horizons.

Al-Ḥāfiẓ The Best Preserver

Appears in the Qur'an once, in 12:64.

> . . . But Allah is the best preserver; and He is the Most Merciful of the merciful.
>
> Qur'an 12:64

'Ḥafiẓa' means to preserve, to protect, or to memorise; thus, Ḥāfiẓ is the protector, and describes a person who knows the Holy Qur'an by heart.

Allah, Al-Ḥāfiẓ, preserves all that is in the heavens, the earth and everything that lies between them. He preserves and perpetuates existence by:

1) **Sustaining**: Preserving, as in sustaining the heavens, earth and all therein.
2) **Safeguarding**: Preserving by safeguarding orderly arrangement and identity – e.g., water from being permanently transformed into steam or ice, fresh water from being permanently transformed into salt water.
3) **Reconciling**: Preserving by reconciling the balance between inimical forces – i.e., between heat and cold, moisture and dryness, etc.
4) **Reinforcing**: Preserving by reinforcing to overcome a condition – i.e., when coldness or moisture are overtaken by heat and dryness, cold moist rain is sent to reinforce, revive and re-establish those conditions.
5) **Equipping**: Preserving by equipping creatures with protective instincts, senses, limbs and memory so that they may perceive danger, learn how to defend themselves, fight or escape and acquire and accumulate knowledge to promote their progress and survival.

In similar manner, plant life is equipped with shells, husks, thorns, prickles, and even venoms and symbiotic partnerships.

Water is equipped with characteristic surface tension, which enables each droplet to remain suspended until surrounding moisture is gathered to it. It may then drop without warm air overcoming and evaporating all of it.

We may reflect this attribute in as far as we are able to preserve our limbs, tongue, heart and faith, from the assault of anger, desire, self-deception and other perils which would result in our downfall. We also reflect this attribute by committing Allah's guidance to memory and keeping it constantly in our hearts.

When Yusuf's brothers returned to their father they said, 'O Father, a further portion has been denied to us, so send with us our brother that we may get our full entitlement, truly we will look after him well'. Their father said, 'Can I trust you with him as I previously trusted you with his brother? Allah is the best Preserver'. This ayah illustrates that the Prophet Yaqub ﵇ did not trust his sons to take care of Benyamin after they had thrown Yusuf ﵇ into the well. Almighty Allah alone is to be trusted to take care of all things.

Al-Ḥakam The Arbitrator (The Judge)

Appears in the Qur'an five times, the first reference in 7:87,

> . . . then have patience until Allah judges between us; and He is the best of all judges.
>
> Qur'an 7:87

'Ḥakama' means to rule, to pass judgement, or to give a decision. 'Ḥikma' is wisdom, while 'Ḥakam' is an arbitrator, umpire, or referee. When we compare the different levels of judgement passed by a judge and a referee, the necessity for justice and remaining without bias is obvious.

Having created everything with the utmost precision and established clear rulings to ensure justice, Allah causes [predestines] everything to happen in its own appointed time. As Judge – Al-Ḥakam – He assesses our behaviour in the light of His rulings and determines the precise harvest each one of us must reap from our actions. Only then is the crop of each allotted, be that reward or punishment. None can oppose His decree nor delay its execution.

From the examples of His rulings below, it is clear that He has left each and every one of us the opportunity to change our condition and to merit happiness or hell-fire. Examples of His rulings are:

> Humankind get only what they strive for and their efforts will soon be seen.
>
> Qur'an 53:39–40

> The righteous will earn happiness, the wicked hell-fire.
>
> Qur'an 82:13–14

> . . . He will not change the condition of a people until they change that which is in themselves . . .
>
> Qur'an 13:11

> . . . Allah does not withdraw a favour He has bestowed upon people until they change themselves . . .
>
> Qur'an 8:53

We reflect the quality of Al-Ḥakam when we consider the possible result of our actions before we act. While we remain aware that 'He made [us] [His] vicegerents . . . so that He may try [us] in what He gave [us] . . .' (Qur'an 6:165), and realise that no matter what happens, anxiety is unnecessary because the only choices open to us are obedience or disobedience. This alone is what will be judged.

In so far as the judgement of others on this earth is concerned, only those who are just and learned enough to judge by Allah's decrees should presume to try.

Al-Ḥakīm The Wise

Appears in the Qur'an 97 times, the first reference in 2:32.

> . . . Glory be to You. We have no knowledge other than that which You taught us. Truly You alone are the All-Knowing, The All-Wise.
>
> Qur'an 2:32

Since 'Ḥikma' is wisdom, Al-Ḥakīm is The Wise. In the Qur'an, this Beautiful Name of Allah is combined with Al-ʿAlīm (The Omniscient) 38 times and with Al-ʿAziz (The Eminent) 47 times. It also appears with Al-Khabīr (The Most Aware) four times. (*see* pp.180, 184 and 209, respectively.)

Al-Ḥakīm represents the perfection of unlimited wisdom – wisdom of the highest rank that uniquely comprehends Allah and all His attributes; wisdom which is all-seeing, all-hearing and all-knowing. Perfect wisdom that ensures absolute justice is all-encompassing and entirely independent. It is the wisdom that originated and sustains universes; that understands the function, purpose and interrelation of every atom and element; that maintains the mind, body and soul of His creatures; and the wisdom which knows who is faithful and who is faithless.

Only those with knowledge of Allah, the Highest and Most Sublime, may be considered to be truly wise. They alone benefit from the reflection of His knowledge. Those who are wise do not concern themselves with temporal advantage but with the benefits of the world to come.

With regard to ethical values, the one who is wise is the one who behaves in a proper and appropriate manner. The Wise – as one of the Beautiful Names of Allah – refers to the fact that his decisions to give or withhold are based on the appropriateness of His doing so.

Al-Ḥalīm The Tolerant

Appears in the Qur'an 11 times, the first reference in 2:225,

> Allah does not call you to account for your thoughtless oaths but for the intentions in your hearts; and Allah is tolerant and gentle.
>
> Qur'an 2:225

'Ḥilm' in Arabic means forbearance and tolerance. Those who tolerate atrocities or injustice perpetrated against them, and yet are able to overcome anger and hatred, are referred to as Ḥalim.

Al-Ḥalīm is never overcome by anger, disobedience, or rebelliousness. Neither does He react with haste or recklessness nor rush to take vengeance. We are told in the Qur'an that,

> If Allah were to punish human beings for their wrongdoing, He would not leave a single creature moving on earth.
>
> Qur'an 16:61

Thus, He prefers to afford them time to recognise their guilt, to regret, to repent, to make recompense and become good servants. For, being mild, gentle, indulgent and forgiving, He prefers to pardon rather than to punish.

We reflect this attribute in as far as we are able to retain mild dispositions and remain gentle and indulgent of the foibles of others.

Al-Ḥamīd Worthy of All Praise

Appears in the Qur'an 17 times, the first reference in 2:267,

> . . . and know that Allah is . . . worthy of all praise.
>
> Qur'an 2:267

'Ḥamd' means to praise or extol; 'Aḥmad' is 'The Commendable' or 'Laudable'; and Maḥmūd and Muḥammad, both names of Allah's final Prophet ﷺ, mean 'praised'. The opening Surah is also referred to as Surah al-Ḥamd. Thus, Ḥamīd as a beautiful name of Allah means 'Worthy of All Praise'.

It has been said that the word 'al-ḥamd' is used to praise people for something good that they themselves strove to achieve and eventually acquired. 'Al-Madḥ', also translated as 'praise', is more generally used to praise people or things for something good that they have acquired without exerting any particular effort. Thus, either al-ḥamd or al-madḥ may, for example, be used to praise someone's benevolence. It is inappropriate to praise a pearl for its lustre with the word 'al-ḥamd' but correct to use 'al-madḥ', because a pearl does not acquire lustre from its own will, effort, or power. The 'al' in al-ḥamd and al-madḥ is used for both types of praise and may, therefore, be translated as 'all'.

In the Qur'an, Allah tells us about Himself:

> He is Allah, your Lord, the Creator of everything.
>
> Qur'an 40:62

> He who made all things which He created excellent.
>
> Qur'an 32:7

Because everything has been created by Him, is attributed to Him and has been made excellent by Him, it follows that everything is good, that everything is beautiful:

> He is Allah, the One, the Subduer.
>
> Qur'an 39:4

> And faces are humbled before the Ever-Living, the Self-Subsisting . . .
>
> Qur'an 20:111

It is clear from this that Allah was not coerced or compelled to create anything, but did so of His own volition, with His knowledge, power and will. The above ayat reflect His actions; those that follow refer to His names. We are told in the Qur'an:

> He is Allah: there is no God but He. To Him belong the Most Beautiful Names.
>
> Qur'an 20:8

> The Most Beautiful Names belong to Allah; so call on Him by them and shun those who profane them.
>
> Qur'an 7:180

Allah is, thus, praised for the qualities reflected in His Beautiful Names, as well as for His action of creating everything excellently. It follows that, no matter what the source, every praise is ultimately directed to Allah alone. This is obvious because all that is good (and thus the object of praise) emanates from Him alone. In short, Allah is worthy of all praise.

The dictionary describes 'praise' as the ascription applied to perfection. But He tells us in the Qur'an that,

> Glory be to Allah, far above what they ascribe to Him.
>
> Qur'an 37:159

This declaration of praise is found in many ayat as an act of Allah, His Prophets and the people of Paradise. For example, He addresses Nūḥ عليه السلام in these words,

> When you are settled . . . say, 'All praise is due to Allah who has delivered us from unjust people'.
>
> Qur'an 23:28

He quotes Ibrāhīm عليه السلام as saying,

> Praise be to Allah who has given me Ismāīl and Isḥāq in spite of my old age.
>
> Qur'an 14:39

He told His final Prophet Muḥammad ﷺ several times,

> And say, 'Praise be to Allah . . .'
>
> Qur'an 27:93

He says about Dāwūd and Sulaymān عليهما السلام,

> And they both said, 'Praise be to Allah' . . .
>
> Qur'an 27:15

He tells us that the people of Paradise will end their prayer,

> All praise to Allah, Lord of the worlds.
>
> Qur'an 10:10

In the Holy Qur'an, all other creatures are described, not as praising, but as glorifying Allah with His praises. To glorify is to exalt to a state of glory, to illuminate, to make splendid by light. He tells us that:

> . . . the Angels celebrate His glory with the praises of their Lord.
>
> Qur'an 42:5

> . . . thunder glorifies Him by repeating His praises.
>
> Qur'an 13:13

> The seven heavens and the earth, and whatever is in them, glorify Him; there is not a single thing that does not glorify Him with His praises.
>
> Qur'an 17:44

In these ayat, 'praise' is preceded by glorifying; 'glorifying' is the main verb and 'with praise' a clause attached to it.

None but Allah can fully comprehend the beauty and perfection of His work, nor can any fully understand the beauty and perfection of His names or attributes. He tells us in the Qur'an that,

> . . . they do not comprehend Him with [their] knowledge.
>
> Qur'an 20:110

If we do not comprehend Him with our knowledge, our praises cannot shower adequate or sufficiently resplendent light on His glory. Our limited understanding and comprehension thus restricts our ability to offer appropriate praise (i.e., He is worthy of all praise but our limitations renders us unable to accomplish that). In all the examples from the Holy Qur'an, creation is careful to ensure that His glory is not restricted by any limitation of comprehension. For Allah tells us,

> . . . Allah knows and you do not know.
>
> Qur'an 16:74

Only the praise of servants who have been purified and freed from the defects of sin, are regarded by the Almighty as being equivalent to those He Himself utters. It is clear, therefore, that the appropriate words of praise for His servants to use are those which He has chosen for Himself. No deviation from them can possibly be acceptable. In a universally accepted hadith, the Prophet ﷺ said,

> I do not enumerate Your praise, You are as You have praised Yourself.
>
> Al-Mizan, by Allamah Tabatabai, Vol. 1, p. 29

The Divine words, 'All praise is due to Allah', thus serve to guide us as to how we should refer to Allah Al-Ḥamīd.

Al-Ḥaqq The Ultimate Truth

Appears in the Qur'an six times, the first reference in 22:62:

> . . . because Allah is the Ultimate Truth . . .
>
> Qur'an 22:62

> . . . because Allah is the Ultimate Truth, and that which they invoke other than Him is false.
>
> Qur'an 31:30

'Ḥaqq' means truth, perfection and rights (as in Human Rights). The first meaning is the opposite of falsehood, the second refers to thoroughness and preciseness – 'Fahima Ḥaqq al-Fahm' means to have precise understanding or thorough comprehension. The third meaning refers to jurisprudence and legal science. Thorough and ultimate true existence belong to Allah Almighty, which completely overshadows all other references to truth.

Allah al-Ḥaqq is the ultimate Truth in that He is the sole, constant, unchanging reality in the universes. All souls begin, change, disappear and reappear. Their characteristics and forms alter as they move from life through death, barzakh and resurrection to further life. Allah alone is constant, unchanging, reliable and true.

Only by concentration on Al-Ḥaqq – the unchanging reality – is it possible to elude error, imprecision and the inaccuracy of all things which are inconstant.

Al-Ḥasīb The Reckoner

Appears in the Qur'an three times, the first reference in 4:6,

> . . . and Allah is sufficient as a Reckoner [taking account of].
>
> Qur'an 4:6

'Ḥisab' is arithmetic and 'Ḥasib' and 'Ḥasīb' are those who keep account of or calculate anything. Thus, Muḥasib is an accountant.

Allah al-Ḥasīb has warned us that He keeps records of the way His creatures behave on earth. On the Last Day – also called the Day of Judgement or Day of Reckoning – all will be obliged to account for their actions and He will mete out reward or punishment. At that time, none will be able to undo what they have done, even if they spend the rest of eternity trying to do so.

If we regard the span of our lives as a capital loan from Him, we can readily understand that one day we must be required to account for how we spent every second of that loan. Every moment not spent remembering, glorifying, thanking, or being of service to His creation, is a moment wasted.

We may reflect this attribute to the extent that we remain aware of, focus our lives on, trust completely in and worship only our Creator.

Al-Ḥayy The Ever-Living

Appears in the Qur'an five times, the first reference in 2:255,

> Allah! There is no god save He, the Ever-Living, Self-Subsisting.
>
> Qu'an 2:255

'Ḥayāh' is life or to live; thus, 'Ḥayy' means alive, lively, active, or energetic.

Two types of thing exist: one type whose condition does not necessarily change while it exists, for example, stone and other mineral matter; the other type which develops and changes, such as plant and animal life. After some time this second group also deteriorates. For everything of this type, a specific moment is reached when its life on this earth comes to an end. As animals such as human beings sometimes lose consciousness while they are still alive, we realise that there is something other than our senses that keeps us alive, something which is the source of all our senses and perceptions. Its presence is referred to as 'life' and its absence as 'death'. It is that which is the source of perception and power.

If we go a step further, we realise that 'real' life, as opposed to temporary life, is life which 'cannot' be overtaken by death. That the life of the hereafter is not overtaken by death unless Allah so wishes, shows that real life is that for which non-existence is impossible. It is, in other words, 'essential being'. Allah says,

> And rely on the Ever-living who dies not.
>
> Qur'an 25:58

Ever living, as a Divine attribute refers to pure, perfect and unlimited existence for which non-existence is impossible.

J

Al-Jabbār The Compeller

Appears in the Qur'an once, in 59:23.

> He is Allah, there is no god save He, the King, the Holy, the Peace-loving, the Bestower of conviction, the Guardian, the Ever-prevalent, the Compeller . . .
>
> Qur'an 59:23

One of the meanings of 'Jabr' is force, power and might. Although the word 'Jabbār' is used ten times in the Holy Qur'an, it only once refers to the Beautiful Names of Allah. The other nine uses refer to tyrants and oppressors. As a Beautiful Name of Allah, Al-Jabbār is the All-Mighty whose force is unchallengeable. It is Al-Jabbār whose will prevails over all and whom none are able to overcome or resist. Allah 'Al-Jabbār' is truly without peer.

Those who aspire to reflect the quality of Al-Jabbār are those who are themselves followed, not those who follow. They are exemplars because the nobleness of their character and conduct compels the respect and emulation of others. They benefit, influence and lead Allah's creatures, without themselves being led, influenced, or rewarded. Such quality is possessed by Prophets and error-free Imams. The Prophet Muḥammad ﷺ – Master of Men – epitomised this quality.

Al-Jalīl The Majestic

Appears in the Qur'an twice, the first reference in 55:27,

> But the Supreme Majesty of Bounty and Honour is everlasting . . .
>
> Qur'an 55:27

The Arabic word 'Jalla' means to be exalted and sublime. When 'Jalla' is associated with anything, it indicates that it is far above and beyond everything else. For example, to afford a King or Queen the highest respect within society, he or she is referred to as Sahib al-Jalalah (his or her majesty). Thus, the most appropriate translation for Al-Jalīl is 'The Majestic'.

Every attribute of majesty is distilled in Al-Jalīl, the Supremely Majestic Being. For Al-Jalīl is immeasurable in might, dominion, knowledge, wealth, power, space, time and existence. He has power over every atom in the universes of His creation. His mercy, generosity, compassion and treasures are without limit.

The majestic amongst humankind are the intelligent and learned who are distinguished by their generosity, discernment, compassion and nobility of spirit, despite their not having temporal power.

The name 'The Great' – 'Al-Kabir' (*see* p.208) – refers to the perfection of the Divine essence, while the name 'The Majestic' – 'Al-Jalīl' – refers to the perfection of attributes. Intellectual insight combines these two into the name 'The Tremendous' – 'Al-Aẓim' (*see* p. 183).

He is both beautiful and majestic and every beautiful thing is loved and desired by those who perceive that beauty. For that reason Allah is both Great and Glorious and loved by those who know His eternal and beautiful forms. This is obviously only possible for those who see and not for those who are blind.

We reflect this name in our lives when we acknowledge that everything beautiful in this life is from Allah Almighty and overshadows any deficiency we perceive in it.

Al-Jāmi' The Gatherer

Appears in the Qur'an twice, the first reference in 3:9,

> Our Lord, truly you will be the Gatherer of humanity on a Day about which there is no doubt.
>
> Qur'an 3:9

On the Day of Judgement, as a sign of resurrection, Allah will unite the bones, veins, muscle, brain, skin, blood, and all other constituent parts of the bodies of each and every human being. Bodies will precisely and accurately combine with their own souls to prepare for their accountability and reckoning. Although this concept might appear strange and unacceptable to those who deny the restoration of life, Allah tells us in the Holy Qur'an that He will re-assemble even fingertips with their unique markings:

> He questions us about resurrection and has forgotten his own origin. He says, who will put life in bones when they have decayed? Say [O Muḥammad], He who created them the first time will grant them life again.
>
> Qur'an 36:78–79

> Does man think that We shall not assemble his bones? We certainly have the power to re-form even his fingertips.
>
> Qur'an 75:3–4

Allah Almighty will unite the heavens, stars, air, earth, plants and diverse minerals, different shapes and colours, tastes and properties, to bring them together on earth to establish one united world and be a sign – ayah – of His existence and omnipotence.

In ethical and spiritual teachings of Islam, it is highly recommended to bring people together and not to divide them. In court, it is the duty of a judge to encourage couples to reconcile their differences rather than to divorce. And it is the duty of every Muslim to work for harmony and unity in the community rather than to divide it by dispute and disunity.

K

Al-Kabir The Unsurpassable in Greatness

Appears in the Qur'an six times, the first reference in 13:9,

> He is the Knower of the unseen and the seen, the Unsurpassable in Greatness, the Ultimately exalted.
>
> Qur'an 13:9

The word 'Kabir' is the opposite of 'Sagheer'. While the latter refers to something that is small in size or capacity, the former refers to something that is large. These obviously cannot apply to Divine Existence because He is beyond both time, space and measure. He is not a material being, so largeness of size is a meaningless concept by which to refer to Him.

Al-Kabir, as one of the Most Beautiful Names of Allah, means that He is Unsurpassable in Greatness because 'Perfection of Essence' is 'perfection of existence', that is everlasting, eternal and constant, unmarred by any possibility of non-existence. Al-Kabir is also 'Unsurpassable in Greatness' in that all other existence emanates from His existence.

We reflect this quality only in so far as attributes of our perfection, reason, piety and knowledge, flow from us to others. The greatest among us are undoubtedly those who guide and serve as exemplars to their own and succeeding generations.

Al-Karim The Generous, The Noble

Appears in the Qur'an four times, the first reference in 23:116,

> Lord of the Most Noble Throne.
>
> Qur'an 23:116

The word 'Karuma' in Arabic may stem from two distinctly different roots. Drawn from one it means, 'To be generous, open-handed and munificent'. Drawn from the other, it indicates someone 'Of noble and pure descent or origin'. It is with the sense of this second meaning that Muslims say, 'May Allah honour him' – 'Karrama Allah Wajhah' – after mentioning Imam 'Ali ﵇. In a variety of Surahs in the Qur'an, Allah refers to 'Karim' as being,

> The Most generous.
>
> Qur'an 82:6

'Al-Karim', thus, represents infinite generosity and infinite nobility – infinite generosity in that He generously grants His creation absolutely everything it requires for its existence; infinite nobility in that He has originated all Creation.

Our generosity is limited to those to whom Allah – The Most Generous – has specifically granted this quality. They are not content when unable to give to or assist others. It is Allah,

Lord of the throne of honour, who determines who is born of noble and pure lineage and who will work justly and tirelessly out of love for Him. It is not those who lay claim to the illusory status of inherited wealth, land owned, or their connection with those in ruling positions, but those to whom Allah has granted that quality, who are truly honourable and noble.

Al-Khabir The Thoroughly Aware

Appears in the Qur'an 45 times, the first reference in 2:234,

> . . . Allah is thoroughly aware of the things you do.
>
> Qur'an 2:234

'Khabar' in Arabic means 'The News', the past tense 'Akhbara' means 'informed' or 'made aware'; thus, 'Khabir' means one who is an expert. In relation to the Most Beautiful Names of Allah it may be translated as He who is thoroughly aware and from whom no secret information remains hidden. This name is, in some ways, similar to 'The Omniscient' but, in this case, the knowledge referred to is hidden and, for this, the word awareness is more appropriate.

Allah tells us in the Qur'an,

> No one can explain it to you as an expert does.
>
> Qur'an 35:14

People normally reject advice of which they are unsure. However, when advice is given by a fully qualified and competent expert on matters concerned with their own field of study, advice is likely to be heeded.

Who other than Allah is thoroughly aware of what is both manifest and hidden in this world and that to come?

Al-Khafiḍ The Abaser

Although this name does not appear in the Qur'an, it is used to refer to 'The Lord of the Day of Resurrection'. (*See* Qur'an 56:3.)

'Al-Khafiḍ' is another of the Most Beautiful Names – Al-Asma'a al-Ḥusna – which is comprehended most clearly as one of a pair of contrasting aspects. While Al-Khafiḍ is the aspect by which infidels are abased and condemned to hell, the opposite aspect – Al-Rafi' – is the aspect by which the faithful are exalted and elevated to paradise (*see* p.231). Allah exalts by drawing to His presence and abases by sending away from His presence. The possibility of being debased exists for those who aspire to gratify their passions and base desires, while the possibility of being exalted exists for those whose aspirations rise above passion and base desire. It is Allah Al-Khafiḍ who abases and exalts.

People who reflect these qualities, condemn falsehood and praise truth; reproach those in the wrong and support those in the right; seek the company of those inspired by faith and avoid the company of those who reject faith.

On the Day of Judgement many prominent and respected people will be abased as the result of their mischief and disobedience to the commands of their Lord. Thus, the Lord Himself is the ultimate abaser. Although human beings were originally created in the best of forms, some earn for themselves the rank of 'the lowest of the low'. (*See* Qur'an 95:5.)

Al-Khaliq The Creator

Appears in the Qur'an 8 times, the first reference in 6:102,

> . . . there is no Divinity other than Him, the Creator of everything.
>
> Qur'an 6:102

Creation means bringing something into existence out of nothing. Philosophically, only Allah Almighty is the necessary existent; all others are only 'possible existents' in that they may or may not exist. Allah is the ultimate source of existence from whom everything else emanates.

Allah is Creator and Law-Giver. He creates everything, from sub-atomic particles to galaxies. If the Almighty Creator withdraws His favour and grace from anything in the universe it no longer exists and immediately becomes nothingness.

However, guidance is always combined with creation,

> Glorify the name of your Lord Most High, who creates, gives shape, ordains [laws] and provides guidance.
>
> Qur'an 87:1–3

In a dialogue between Pharaoh, Mūsa and Harun عليهما السلام we read,

> Pharaoh said, 'Who is the lord of you two, O Mūsa?' Mūsa replied, 'Our Lord is He who gave to everything its natural form, and then guided it aright'.
>
> Qur'an 20:49–50

People may assemble particles to complete an object; however, the combining of sperm and egg within a tube is not creation. The Holy Qur'an admits the possibility of such an occurrence and thus provides a clear understanding of the concept of creation:

> It is We who created you, so why do you not admit the truth?

1) Look at semen, 'Is it you or We who created it'?
2) Look at what you sow, 'Is it you or We who cause it to grow'?

3) Look at the water that you drink. 'Is it you or We who send it down from the clouds'?
4) Look at the fire that you kindle, 'Is it you or We who cause it to burn'?

Extrapolated from Qur'an 56:57–72

Life is not able to continue to exist without the above four elements which are provided by Allah.

L

Al-Latif The Most Subtle

Appears in the Qur'an six times, the first reference in 6:103,

> . . . He is the Most Subtle, thoroughly aware.

Qur'an 6:103

Al-Latif is He who discerns and is perceptive. His perspicacity comprehends subtlety and hidden meaning. He meets the needs of humanity with gentleness of action and consideration.

He protects the growing foetus within its mother's womb and sustains it through the umbilicus; inspires it to suckle nourishment from its mother's breast; and delays the development of teeth until these are needed to crush food. At that stage, teeth are differentiated into those that break, that cut and that crush, and the tongue is taught to direct food – all this to nourish His creature. In addition, He established a food-supply chain, a co-operation of creatures to prepare the land, plant the seed, water, harvest, sift, grind, kneed, bake, deliver, etc. Such subtlety, knowledge, planning and behaviour is inconceivable for any, other than the Creator Himself. Other examples of consideration for His creatures are: His providing them with more than they require and demanding less from them than they are able to give; facilitating their attainment of an eternity of happiness within a relatively short life span; and supplying them with resources such as honey from bees, silk from worms and pearls from oysters and mussels.

We reflect this attribute by behaving with gentleness and consideration to all of His creation. By guiding His creation gently, without rebuke, harshness, or fanaticism and remaining of benign and pleasing disposition.

M

Al-Majid The Glorious

Appears in the Qur'an twice, the first reference in 11:73,

> . . . truly He alone is praiseworthy, glorious.
>
> Qur'an 11:73

The glory of humanity is insignificant compared to that of Allah. His Majesty and Glory encompass the whole of the universe. Flowers, rivers, oceans and all beautiful gardens and valleys are the work of the glorious painter who exhibits His omnipotence in every corner. Everything glorifies Him – the song of the nightingale, the iridescent colour and rapid movement of the hummingbird, the agility and awesomeness of a raptor. All creatures, on land, in the air, or in water, glorify the Lord in the manner prescribed by Him. Even thunder is glorification of Him (*see* Qur'an 13:13).

Mālik-al-Mulk The Owner of the Kingdom

Appears in the Qur'an once, in 3:26,

> Say [O Muḥammad], 'O Allah, owner of the kingdom! You give kingdoms to whoever you like and take them from whoever you like'.
>
> Qur'an 3:26

Pure and complete belief in the oneness of Allah – 'tawḥid' – requires appreciation that every source of power emanates from Him. It is He who provides both 'mulk' and 'melk' explained below.

Al-Malik The King – (Sovereign)

Appears in the Qur'an 5 times, the first reference in 20:114,

> High above all is Allah, the Sovereign and the Truth.
>
> Qur'an 20:114

The Arabic root for both this name and the one immediately above is 'M-L-K', which may indicate several different meanings:

1) Malik – refers to the King or supreme authority.
2) Mālik – refers to the owner of something.
3) Malak – refers to an Angel and its plural, Mala'ikah.
4) Melk and Mulk – both refer to land, property or other material things owned.

The common thread behind all the above is power and authority.

Al-Malik is the one who is sovereign of all that is in the universe, who does not need any of His creation, despite all of it needing Him.

It was thought that humans who claimed sovereignty submitted to Allah's rule alone and needed nothing other than Him. History, however, records few kings who served Allah in preference to their own egos. Now, at the dawn of the twenty-first century, it is clear to most that kings, queens and rulers are themselves dominated by politico/economic powers at home or abroad.

Examples of those ruled by Allah alone may, thus, only be found amongst the Prophets and error-free Imams who, guided by Him, in turn guided others.

To aspire to the quality of Al-Malik is to focus one's life on Allah alone and not to be ruled by the desire for any of the things of this world.

Al-Maniʿ He Who Grants Immunity

This does not appear in the Qur'an as one of Allah's Most Beautiful Names; however in Qur'an 59:2, Allah tells us that those who did not believe, 'Imagined their forts would protect them against Allah'. By negating such physical symbols of protection He indicates that the sole protector to grant immunity is Allah Himself.

The Arabic word 'Manaʿa' has the following meanings:

1) To prevent.
2) To obstruct or to bar access.
3) To deprive.
4) To guard or to protect.

Thus, Maniʿ is the one who undertakes any or all of the above. It is the context of the sentence that clarifies which of the above is meant. Thus, 'Manāʿah' is the immune system of an organism.

As a name, referring to Allah Almighty, Al-Maniʿ is The One who counters the causes of destruction and diminishment of religious and temporal affairs through defensive and protective systems that grant immunity and prevent 'contagion'. In this way, this name is related to the name Al Ḥafiẓ, which has already been discussed (*see* p. 197). Everything that preserves may also be said to protect. However, none who protects can grant immunity other than The One who is the Absolute Protector.

Al-Matīn He Who is Secure in Power

Appears in the Qur'an once, in 51:58,

> It is Allah who provides sustenance, the Lord who is secure in His power.
>
> Qur'an 51:58

'Al-Matīn' indicates perfect power which cannot be challenged. Allah Al-Matīn possesses the utmost power, perfect in every aspect. Al-Matīn may be translated as the One who is Firm, to denote the strength which is discussed under the name Al-Qawiyy (*see* p. 229).

Al-Mu'akhkhir The Delayer

This occurs six times in the Qur'an, but only in the present tense Yu'akhkhir,

> Do not think that Allah remains headless of what the unjust do. He only gives them respite until the day when all eyes will stare aghast.
>
> Qur'an 14:42

People sometimes suppose that Allah's chastisements have to be prompt and immediate. When they are not able to perceive a prompt response, many imagine that Allah's warnings need not be taken seriously. However, the fruits of any action may appear at the same time as the action or they may be delayed for a long period. In the above ayah, Allah tells us that there certainly will be a Day of Reckoning during which all human beings are to be held accountable for their actions. On that day, the transgressors and the mischievous are scheduled to reap the fruits of their deeds.

Al-Mubdi The Originator of Creation

Only occurs in the Qur'an in the present tense – 'Yubdi' – and this three times.

> Can they not see how Allah has originated creation . . . ?
>
> Qur'an 29:19

Life is a gift from the Almighty Creator to all creatures in the universe. He bestows life and, thus, is The Originator of Creation. The verb 'yubdi' is frequently combined with the verb 'yu'id' to indicate both original creation as well as His ability to raise life from death.

Al-Mudhill The Humbler – Humiliator

Only occurs in the Qur'an in the present tense – 'Yudhill' – and this only once,

> O Allah, owner of the kingdom! You give kingdoms to whoever you like and take them away from whoever you like. You exalt whom you like and humble whom you like.
>
> Qur'an 3:26

Al-Mudhill is another of Allah's Most Beautiful Names – Asma' al-Husna – comprehended most clearly as one of a pair of contrasting aspects. While Al-Mudhill is the aspect through which Allah humbles, Al-Mu'izz, the opposite (*see* p. 218) – is the aspect through which He honours. Allah grants and removes supremacy as He wills. To honour us on this earth He grants us supremacy over need, passions and ignorance, removes the veil from our hearts and lets us behold the beauty of His presence, grants us the perspicacity to free us from creation, and provides the power and support to help us take control of our own souls. He tells us in the Qur'an that in the next life He will honour the righteous by saying,

> O you soul who has gained tranquillity, return to your Lord well-pleased [with Him] and [He] well pleased [with you]; enter among My worshippers, enter paradise.
>
> Qur'an 89:27–30

On the other hand, those who preoccupy themselves with earthly matters inevitably are so overcome by greed that no quantity is able to satiate their 'needs'. Captivated by worldly affairs they remain ignorant. Allah tells us in the Qur'an that their ultimate humility will occur on the Day of Judgement when they will be reminded,

> . . . then you let yourself be tempted . . . doubting [Allah's warning] your own vain desires deceived you till Allah's decree came to pass and you were deceived by the arch deceiver. So no ransom will be accepted from you on this day . . .
>
> Qur'an 57:14–15

Only those whose speech or actions are decent and honourable are able to reflect this aspect.

Al-Mughni The Enricher

Only appears in the Qur'an in the present tense – 'Yughni' – and this four times,

> If you fear poverty, through His grace, Allah will enrich you, if He so wills . . .
>
> Qur'an 9:28

Under the name 'Al-Ghanī' (*see* p. 195) the concept of everything being available to Allah Almighty was explained. He is the source of all grace, bounty and wealth, the One who is truly rich, who has everything at His disposal and who extends access to His riches to whomever He pleases.

Al-Muhaymin The Overall Controller

Appears in the Qur'an once, in 59:23,

> He is Allah, there is no Divinity save Him, The King, The Holy, The Peace-Loving, The Bestower of Faith, The Overall Controller . . .
>
> Qur'an 59:23

The Overall Controller – Al-Muhaymin – is in complete command and control. It is He who is prepared, willing and able to oversee His creatures' actions and grant them protection and sustenance from birth through to the time of their death. The concept 'command' implies knowledge, possession of power and protective action. Only Allah Almighty combines such qualities absolutely and perfectly.

Those who aspire to reflect the quality of al-Muhaymin must have the strength and will-power to protect their hearts. They need to comprehend its nature and have the will-power to shield it from the wiles of their egos' desires. The Overall Controller supervises, protects and guards their progress along the 'Right Path'. And if they also help Allah's other servants in this, their reflection of this quality is even greater.

In the Arabic language, Allah is defined as the name which encompasses all aspects of perfection. That is to say that each of the 98 other Beautiful Names refer to only one aspect of perfection while the name Allah encompasses all of them. That is why it is correct and safe to say that the name Allah is the name with overall control over all the other names.

Al-Muḥṣi The Precise Recorder

Appears five times in the Qur'an in the past tense – 'Aḥṣa' – the first reference in 58:6,

> On the day when Allah will raise them up together, He will inform them of what they did. Allah's records are precise and comprehensive.
>
> Qur'an 58:6

In the past it was difficult to imagine how it could be possible to maintain records of the trillions of actions and deeds of billions of people and present a precise account of them. However, in these days of IT when almost every household owns a computer and every CD is able to store megabytes of information, this no longer appears bizarre. Who endowed people with the ability to conceive and achieve such things other than He who created them?

Fourteen centuries ago the messenger of Allah ﷺ explained the above to the illiterate people of the Arabian peninsula in the following manner,

> When the Book of Deeds shall be presented, then you will see the guilty and criminal fearful of what is contained therein, and they will say, 'Woe to us! What a book this is. It does not omit anything, small or great and has even elaborated on it'.
>
> Qur'an 18:49

Al-Muʿid The Reproducer (of Creation)

Only appears in the Qur'an in the present tense – 'Yuʿid' – the first reference in 21:104,

> As it is We who first created you, so shall we recreate you. It is a promise binding upon us.
>
> Qur'an 21:104

During the early years of prophethood the Prophet ﷺ concentrated on the concept of resurrection so that people would be aware that life does not end with death. Death is merely movement from one level to another. This was a difficult concept for the average person to comprehend. A bedouin once brought a human skull and asked, 'Are you telling me that this will again turn into a live being?' The reply was 'As We first created you, so shall we re-create you'.

As we have already noted in this Surah, the same question was frequently posed to the Prophet ﷺ and we quote:

> They ask, 'When we [have perished] and are bones reduced to dust, shall we really be raised up and given a new existence?' (Ayah 49)

> That will be their recompense for disbelieving Our signs and questioning, 'When we [have perished] and our bones reduced to dust, shall we really be raised up and given a new existence?' (Ayah 98)

Al-Mu'izz The Honourer (The Granter of Honour and Glory)

Appears once in the Qur'an, in the present tense 'Yuezz' only,

> O Allah, owner of the kingdom! You give kingdoms to whoever you like and take them away from whoever you like. You exalt whom you like and humble whom you like.
>
> Qur'an 3:26

'Al-Mu'izz' is another of the Most Beautiful Names – Al-Asma' al-Ḥusna which is most clearly understood as one of a pair of contrasting aspects. Al-Mu'izz is the aspect through which Allah honours, while Al-Mudhill, the opposite (*see* p. 215) is the aspect through which He humbles. Allah grants and removes supremacy as He wills. To honour us on this earth: He grants us supremacy over need, passions and ignorance; removes the veil from our hearts to allow us to behold the beauty of His presence; grants us tranquillity to free us from creation; and provides us power and support to help us control our own souls. He tells us in the Qur'an that in the next life He will honour the righteous by saying,

> O you soul who has gained tranquillity, return to your Lord well-pleased [with Him] and [He] well-pleased [with you]; enter among my worshippers, enter paradise.
>
> Qur'an 89:27–30

On the other hand, those who preoccupy themselves with earthly matters are eventually so overcome with greed for them that no quantity is able to satiate their 'need'. Deceived by worldly affairs they remain ignorant.

Allah tells us in the Qur'an that their ultimate humility is to come on the Day of Judgement when they will be reminded,

> . . . then you let yourself be tempted and . . . doubting [Allah's warning], your own vain desires . . . and the arch deceiver deceived you with regard to Allah. So no ransom will be accepted from you on this day . . .
>
> Qur'an 57:14-15

Only those whose speech and actions contribute to decency and honour share this aspect,

> Allah is The Eminent – 'Aziz – and the source of every honour – Mu'izz.

Al-Mujīb The Responsive

Appears in the Qur'an twice, the first reference in 11:61,

> . . . for my Lord is [always] near and ready to respond.
>
> Qur'an 11:61

Knowing His creation, Al-Mujīb attends to and provides for His creatures' every need. The manner of His response, which precedes requests, points the way to how we should respond to the needs of others. And in situations where we are inattentive to the needs of others and they have to ask us for help, we may follow Allah Almighty's own example. He tells us,

> . . . I am very near and I answer the prayers of those who beseech Me . . .
>
> Qur'an 2:186

Those who share in this quality do so to the extent in which they worship Allah Almighty by responding to and obeying His command and prohibitions, and by responding to the needs of His creation. He tells us,

> And do not drive away those who ask . . .
>
> Qur'an 93:10

Al-Mu'min The Bestower of Faith

Appears once in the Qur'an, in 59:23,

> He is Allah, there is no Divinity save Him, The King, The Holy, The Peace Loving, The Bestower of Faith, The Overall Controller . . .
>
> Qur'an 59:23

'Amn' means peace. 'Aman' means conviction. 'Iman' means faith. Thus, Mu'min may be derived from Aman to convey that Mu'min is a giver of conviction and peace or may also be derived from faith to mean faithful.

The One who is Faithful – Al-Mu'min – is the one upon whom we can depend. Al-Mu'min is He who provides nourishment and means of security and safety: who quells our fears; provides remedies to cure our sicknesses; provides food to satisfy our hunger; drink to slake our thirst; limbs to protect us; and senses to warn us. Ever faithful, He provides protection for us from our greatest fear of all – eternal damnation. He tells us that protection lies in our professing faith in the unity of Allah, 'there is no Divinity but Allah', which is His fortress, and He says, 'Whoever enters My fortress is safe from My punishment'. (Hadith Qudsi)

Not only are all creatures safe from those who aspire to the quality of Al-Mu'min, those who are fearful, may expect protection from them. The faithful are, thus, those who protect others from Allah's punishment by leading them to the 'Right Path'.

Every believer – mu'min – reflects this aspect when he or she ensures that their hands and tongues are not employed in attacks on others.

Al-Mumit He Who Brings about Death

Appears 16 times in the Qur'an, but only in the present tense – 'Yumit' – the first in 2:258,

> Ibrahim said, 'My Lord is He who gives life and brings about death'.
>
> Qur'an 2:258

Both life and death are in the ultimate authority of Allah. No life springs from any source other than Him and no death can be authorised by any other than Him.

Al-Muntaqim The Avenger of Evil

Appears in the Qur'an three times, the first reference in 32:22,

> . . . truly We shall exact appropriate retribution from those who are evil.
>
> Qur'an 32:22

When recommendation and admonishment are no longer effective in drawing people to the right path, the only strategy left is to be severe towards those who break the law and destroy community safety and well-being. These are not acts of revenge but means to protect society from those who make mischief.

This theological and ethical concept has nothing to do with the application of criminal law in Islamic jurisprudence, which some critics regard as 'inhumane'. There are, however, only four recorded cases in the first 200 years of the history of Islam, in which thieves were sentenced to having their hands cut off. From this we learn the efficacy of such severity in protecting property and wealth.

Al-Muqaddim The Advancer

Although this does not appear in the Qur'an at all, it is, nonetheless, linked to the Delayer – Al- Mu'akhkhir – which has already been discussed (*see* p. 214).

Al-Muqit The Provider of All Energy and Food

Appears in the Qur'an, once in 4:85.

> . . . and Allah is the provider of all energy and food.
>
> Qur'an 4:85

Al-Muqit describes the One who provides 'Quwwah' and 'Qūt' – energy and food.

The forces below the earth's tectonic plates and those generated as these move; the pressures of the air in the Stratosphere, Troposphere and denser Boundary Layer in which life abounds; the temperatures on earth as it revolves and circles the sun; the oceanic and air currents established by differentials in temperature and geography; the condensation and precipitation of water; the climatic condition; mineral and vegetable nutriment; and the fertility of soil, are all controlled by Allah Al-Muqit. It is He who holds power over the above and every elemental force which affects the atmosphere, climate and environment. It is Allah, Al-Muqit who controls and has power over the soil's quality, nourishment, fertility, and every condition for which a flourishing life depends.

Allah, Al-Muqit provides the means of sustenance for all His creatures. Humanity has the ability to earn and the choice between lawful or illegal means. Those who understand that Allah is The Provider, opt for the lawful; those who do not, sometimes try to obtain more via illegal means. The latter, however, only endanger themselves here and in the Hereafter. But those who remain aware of, and remember the needs of others, share in this attribute to the extent that they anticipate and meet those needs. (*See* also the name Al-Razzaq on p. 233).

Al-Muqsiṭ The Impartial

Appears in the Qur'an 15 times, the first reference being 7:29,

> Say, 'My Lord has enjoined justice and impartiality'.
>
> Qur'an 7:29

Appears in the Qur'an as the One who orders us to behave with impartiality – Qisṭ. Impartiality, an application of justice has been fully discussed under the name Al-ʿAdl (*see* p. 178).

Al-Muqtadir The Determiner of All Things (The All-Powerful)
Appears in the Qur'an four times, the first reference in 54:42.

> Warners were also sent to Pharaoh's people but when they denied all Our signs we seized them with all Our power and might.
>
> Qur'an 54:41–42

Both Al-Qādir and Al-Muqtadir mean 'one who possesses power', philosophically referred to as Omnipotent. However, to emphasise this quality, we have translated the latter as The Determiner of all things. (*See* the names Al-Qādir and Al-Qawiyy, on pp. 228 and 229, respectively.)

Al-Muṣawwir The Fashioner
Appears in the Qur'an once, in 59:24,

> He is Allah, the Creator, the Producer, the Fashioner.
>
> Qur'an 59:24

The Arabic root for this Most Beautiful Name is – 'Ṣurah' – which means picture or photograph. Allah tells us in Qur'an 7:11 that the shape of human beings was only determined after their creation; however, He also tells us that He regards humankind as being the best of His creation,

> He has shaped you in the most noble form and provided pure things for your sustenance. He is Allah, your Lord, so praise be to Him, the Lord of the worlds.
>
> Qur'an 40:64

The Fashioner – Al-Muṣawwir – describes the aspect of the Almighty that orders the quality and finish of individual components, as well as their integration and co-ordination so that they work together to fulfil their function and discharge their obligations.

So fine is the order of everything in the heavens and earth that if any part is altered, all order is abolished. This applies on both a macro-cosmic and micro-cosmic scale. The greater one's understanding of its detail, the greater one's comprehension of the organisation of the universe, its arrangement and the name Al-Muṣawwir.

As all knowledge exists in a form that corresponds to the thing known, those souls who aspire to the quality of Al-Muṣawwir must, according to their ability, acquire the disposition, organisation, arrangement and 'form' of all material and spiritual things that exist in the heavens and earth.

For it is the knowledge which Allah Almighty has of any form which enables it to exist in one's heart. And it is the existence of that in one's heart which enables the cognitive to be realised by one's soul.

Share in the name Al-Muṣawwir derives from the acquisition of the cognitive forms which correspond to existential forms. We benefit from knowing the meaning of the name Al-Muṣawwir by acquiring this form in our soul through which we, too, become fashioners, be that only metaphorically.

Al-Muta'ali The Most Highly Exalted

Appears in the Qur'an once, in 13:9,

> It is He who Knows both the seen and the unseen, the Great, the Most Highly Exalted.
>
> Qur'an 13:9

As we indicated under the name Al-ʿAliyy (*see* p. 181), Allah is far above humankind's comprehension and imagination. It refers to the highest possible rank or status that has nothing to do with physical qualities but everything to do with His being exalted far above the might and majesty of this world.

Al-Mutakabbir The Splendid

Appears in the Qur'an once, in 59:23,

> He is Allah, there is no Divinity save Him, The King, The Holy, The Peace-Loving, The Bestower of Faith, The Overall Controller, The Ever-Prevalent, The Supreme and the Splendid.
>
> Qur'an 59:23

The proud regard their own position as the most august and elevated, and others as being less important, less worthy and less valuable than themselves. Pride, other than for Allah Almighty, may He be praised and exalted, is incredibly blameworthy, vain and false. While pride refers to arrogance, imperious behaviour, haughtiness and other foolishness, it is used here to refer to Allah being both The Splendid and The Supreme Authority.

Those who aspire to the quality of Al-Mutakabbir, know that it is only when they have rejected and disdained all things which could possibly distract their hearts from the ultimate Truth, that they will be able to attain an elevated status. Those who remain shackled to food, sex and other earthly distractions, even if they claim to have renounced them, remain slaves unworthy of any status, distinction, or pride.

Al-Muḥyi The Giver of Life

Appears in the Qur'an twice, the first reference in 30:50,

> Look at the signs of Allah's mercy, how He gives life to the earth after it appears dead. Truly, He is the Giver of Life and it is He who has power over all things.
>
> Qur'an 30:50

We have already discussed the name 'Ḥayy' (*see* p. 205). Both the past and present tense for 'giving life' are used in the Qur'an 43 times. Physical and spiritual life are gifts of the Almighty Creator. He gives life to animals and vegetables as well as to tiny microbes. Life according to Islam is His sacred gift. None may touch or take it. This is why abortion, infanticide, genocide and all other categories of murder are prohibited.

The Prophet Ibrahim ﷺ requested his Lord to show him how He gives life and how He restores that after death,

> Ibrahim said, 'My Lord, let me see how you give life to the dead'. He said, 'What? Do you not believe?' Ibrahim said, 'I do, but my heart needs to be at ease'. Allah said, 'Take four birds and train them to follow you, then cut their throats and place a small part of each on various mountains, before you call them. They will fly to you, . . .
>
> Qur'an 2:260

In the Qur'an, Allah contrasts and compares a pure life with one full of destruction. Both are based on deeds and behaviour. This shows that although life is the gift of the Creator, the manner in which it is lived is the result of free will:

> We shall certainly let believers who do good, whether they are male or female, live a good and pure life . . .
>
> Qur'an 16:97

> But whoever turns away from My admonishments will have their livelihoods restricted . . .
>
> Qur'an 20:124

N

Al-Nafi' The Benefactor

Appears in the Qur'an once, in 48:11,

> Who can possibly challenge Allah once He intends to either benefit or harm you?
>
> Qur'an 48:11

Every good and every benefit comes from Allah even when He acts via the actions of Angels, men, inanimate matter, or other thing. True believers do not regard water as the only element that quenches thirst but rather, that it is Allah who achieves this via water. In the same way, a visit to a physician and taking the medicine prescribed can be of no benefit without Allah willing a cure to be effected via this channel. No king, emperor, or influential business person is able to benefit another without Allah's permission.

When the Prophet 'Isa ﷺ produced miracles, such as reviving the dead and curing the deaf and dumb, he would first say, 'I do this with the permission of the Creator'. This clarifies that even the highest level of humanity – Allah's prophets and messengers – recognised that every benefit is only derived from the 'Origin' who is Allah. When people take the opportunity to effect charitable work, it is Allah who enables it to come to fruition.

Al-Naṣīr The Helper

Appears in the Qur'an 11 times, the first reference in 4:45,

> Allah knows best who your enemies are. Allah is a sufficient Protector and Helper.
>
> Qur'an 4:45

Although it is normal for people to seek the help and protection of those who are physically, socially and financially better off than themselves, Islam teaches that human beings should place their hopes only with Allah. In *Nahj al-Balaghah*, Imam 'Ali ﷺ gives believers five extremely important pieces of advice. The first of which is, 'Do not hope for anything from anyone other than your Lord'.

As all power, wisdom and provision come from Allah Almighty, none other is able to independently benefit others.

Al-Nūr The Light

Appears once in the Qur'an, in 24:35,

> Allah is the light of the heavens and the earth; the similitude of His light is as a niche wherein a lamp is lit. The lamp is shielded by glass which appears as though it were a shining star lit from a blessed tree, the olive, which is neither of the East nor of the West, whose oil glows forth of itself though fire has not touched it. Light upon light. Allah guides to His light whomever He wills and Allah sets forth parables for people.
>
> Qur'an 24:35

Light is an attribute of Allah and a symbol of guidance. It is manifested in both creation and legislation. Allah is the light through which every creature comes into existence and through which every creature is guided towards its final goal. This goal – the fruit of true guidance – is salvation, bliss and satisfaction. In the above ayah, 'light' illuminates the surroundings. 'Niche' – 'mishkat' – refers to the point at which Allah's names and attributes become manifest. The mishkat is a recess in the wall, high above the ground, and the Divine light, according to this parable, is located in it above everything that has been created (i.e., above all the universes). The lamp, the core of real illumination, is inside glass and protected from all outside interference.

Like a bright star, this illumination shines in a world in which all understand that illumination depends upon a power source. To indicate the source of that light, the above ayah refers to it being generated from the oil of a blessed olive tree.

The Qur'an is the light of wisdom protected within the breast of the last and final Messenger ﷺ, as the lamp is by its glass. When we combine this ayah with Qur'an 33:33 we conclude that the prophet's progeny – Ahl al-Bayt عليهم السلام – are indeed 'light upon light'.

Light is understood by all to be the means of illumination. Both existence and light are interrelated in that, coming from nothingness into being, they are both sometimes referred to as moving from darkness into light. When Allah Almighty is referred to as light it indicates that everything in the universe has been created and introduced by Him, the source of all light and existence. His light equates to guidance, mercy and every good. It is illuminating to trace those ayat that relate light to Him:

> Non-believers attempt to extinguish the light of Allah by blowing it out, but Allah will not permit that.
>
> Qur'an 61:8

> Are the ones who are dead, but raised to life and provided with the light to walk amongst people, equal to those who remain in utter darkness, unable to find their way out?
>
> Qur'an 6:123

> O you who believe, fear Allah and believe in His Messenger. Allah will grant you twice as much of His mercy and will appoint for you a light by which to safely walk on the straight path.
>
> Qur'an 57:28

The fruits of faith and good deeds are bathed in the illumination of His light.

Q

Al-Qabiḍ He Who Withholds

Appears once, in the present tense – 'Yaqbeḍ' – in 2:245,

> Who is ready to provide Allah a loan without interest so that He may multiply it many times over? It is Allah who withholds or permits . . .
>
> Qur'an 2:245

Al-Qabiḍ is comprehended most clearly as one of a pair of contrasting aspects: Al-Qabiḍ who withholds and Al-Bāsiṭ (see p. 191) who provides abundantly. Thus, Al-Qabiḍ extracts souls from dead bodies, while Al-Bāsiṭ extends souls to new life in the womb. Al-Qabiḍ appropriates alms from the rich, Al-Bāsiṭ gives abundantly to the poor. Al-Qabiḍ withholds sustenance to further weaken the weak, Al-Bāsiṭ extends in such abundance that His bounty surpasses the every need of the wealthy. Al-Qabiḍ's might and awesomeness contracts hearts in fear, Al-Bāsiṭ's divinity, forgiveness and mercy expand hearts in peace.

Amongst those who remain ever conscious of Allah – those with 'Taqwa' – a few inspired, eloquent and wise people have the ability to reflect the aspects of Al-Qabiḍ and Al-Bāsiṭ. As such people infuse awareness of Allah Almighty's abundant mercy and blessings, their audience's hearts expand in peace and joy. But when they recount warnings of punishment and tell them about Mālik (the Angel in charge of hell) and the Zabaniya (Angels who assist Mālik) who, when it is said to them, 'take him, fetter him, then roast him in hell', hasten to accomplish their orders without respite, their audience's hearts contract and shrink in fear.

Al-Qādir The Omnipotent

Appears in the Qur'an 11 times, the first reference in 6:37,

> Truly Allah is Omnipotent and able to send a sign, even though most of them know it not.
>
> Qur'an 6:37

Both Qādir and Qadīr appear in the Qur'an as attributes of the Almighty. Even though the latter appears 45 times, it is the former that is regarded as one of Allah's Most Beautiful Names. Both omniscience and omnipotence have been known to philosophers and theologians throughout history as attributes of the Divine. There is no limit to Allah Almighty's power and, as we noticed from the attribute Mālik al-Mulk (*see* p. 212), the source of every sovereignty and effectiveness is The One who is Omnipotent. The Omnipotent is the One who acts as He wills, or not if He so wills.

As far as humanity is concerned, no power can be possessed, even within the bounds of possibility, without Allah, the sole Creator of human power.

After the battle of Badr, the first Muslim victory, Allah addressed His Messenger as follows,

> You did not shoot the arrow, rather Allah did so that He could grace believers with a great achievement.
>
> Qur'an 8:17

When Muslims pray, they are recommended to recite the following remembrance – dhikr – while standing between prostrations – rakaats,

> I only stand and sit by the power of Allah – Bi hawl lilahi wa quwwatehi aqumu wa aqu'ud.

In Qur'an 18:39 Muslims are enjoined to say,

> As Allah wills, there is no power other than from Him – La quwwata illa billah.

Al-Qahhar He Who Dominates

Appears in the Qur'an six times, the first reference in 12:39,

> O my two fellow-prisoners! Are many Lords who argue with each other better, or One True God who Dominates everything.
>
> Qur'an 12:39

Al-Qahhar represents the One who is able to dominate and destroy the power of all enemies. No power exists that He is not able to overcome. To remain dominant, human beings must have the power to subdue their enemies. And their greatest enemy is their ego's desire. Only those who are able to dominate their ego are able to conquer the passions and lusts which lure others to ruin. To dominate passion and lust is to be free, for it means that the shackles of their influence have been cast off. Even if one is killed, the spirit – 'rūh' – lives on. Allah tells us in the Qur'an,

> And do not think that those slain in the way of Allah are dead. No, they are still alive with their Lord [and] receiving sustenance [from Him].
>
> Qur'an 3:169

The clearest proof of this attribute of the Almighty is that He Dominates and subdues every living thing at the time of death, which none may escape.

In the Qur'an Allah tells us about the Day of Resurrection,

> The Day when they shall come out of their graves, with nothing hidden from Allah. Whose is the Kingdom on this day? It is Allah's, the One who Dominates.
>
> Qur'an 40:16

Al-Qawiyy The Strong

Appears in the Qur'an nine times, the first reference in 8:52,

> . . . truly Allah is Strong . . .
>
> Qur'an 8:52

This name is related to the other two names, Al-Qādir and Al-Muqtadir (*see* pp. 228 and 222, respectively). However, in the Qur'an Al-Qawiyy is invariably combined with 'Al-Aziz'. (*see* Qur'an 11:66, 22:40; 22:74; 42:19; 57:25; 58:21 and 33:25.)

Al-Qayyum The One Who Maintains the Existence of All Reality

Appears in the Qur'an three times, the first reference in 2:255,

> Allah, there is no Divinity save He, the Ever-Living, the One who maintains the existence of all reality.
>
> Qur'an 2:255

In precisely the same way that gravity maintains planets in their various trajectories, it is Allah who maintains the existence and function of all reality. When a mind full of thoughts ceases to concentrate, all thought dissipates. Similarly, if Allah were to withdraw His attention from the universe, everything manifest would disappear. This is the concept behind the name Qayyum. Many translators infer that the name Qayyum means The Self-Subsistent, by whom all subsist. However, The Self-Subsistent does not convey the spirit of this name.

Al-Quddus The Holy

Appears in the Qur'an twice, the first reference in 59:23,

> He is Allah, there is no Divinity save He, the King, the Holy . . .
>
> Qur'an 59:23

Al-Quddus represents the One who, despite being referred to, is indescribable because He transcends the quality and description that the human intellect and imagination are able to conjure. Al-Quddus is free from, and not limited by, the perfection and imperfections which affect human perception.

To aspire to the quality of Al-Quddus is to free oneself of the tangible and the imagined, to free oneself of the pleasures of desire, anger and the input of the senses which we share with animals. To aspire to this quality is to target all attention on Allah Almighty alone.

R

Al-Ra'uf The Compassionate

Appears in the Qur'an eleven times, the first reference in 2:143,

> . . . Allah is compassionate and merciful towards humanity.
>
> Qur'an 2:143

(*see* the names Al-Raḥman and Al-Raḥim on the next pages.)

Al-Rafi' The Exalter

Although it does not appear in the Qur'an as one of the Most Beautiful Names, it does appear in the Qur'an in reference to 'The Day of Resurrection' (*see* Qur'an 56:3).

Al-Rafi' is another of the Most Beautiful Names – Al-Asma' al-Ḥusna – which is best understood as one of a pair of contrasting aspects. While Al-Rafi' is the aspect by which the faithful are exalted and elevated to paradise, its opposite – Al-Khafiḍ – (*see* p. 209), is the aspect by which infidels are abased and condemned to hell; Allah abases His creatures by sending them from His presence and exalts them by drawing them to Him. While it is Allah Almighty who abases and exalts, the possibility of being exalted exists for all those who aspire to levels above passion and base desires. Conversely, the possibility of being debased exists for those whose only aspiration is to gratify their passion and desires.

People who reflect the qualities of Al-Rafi' praise truth and condemn falsehood; support those who are in the right and reproach those who are in the wrong; and seek company inspired by faith and avoid the company of those who reject faith.

All human beings naturally seek promotion and elevation of rank. For example, a clerk who aspires to become the head of the office, works assiduously towards that end, as must politicians who aspire to the prime ministership, etc. However, believers know that the only power with ability to exalt and distinguish them is Allah, Al-Rafi'.

Al-Raḥim The Most Merciful

Appears in the Qur'an 95 times, the first reference in 1:3,

> Praise be to Allah, Lord of the worlds, The Beneficent, The Most Merciful.
>
> Qur'an 1:2–3

Al-Raḥim represents the perfection of mercy in both this world and the next. Allah is prepared to extend mercy to the deserving as well as to the undeserving, and it is only He, the Most Merciful of the Merciful, who is able to meet every need.

To aspire to reflect the quality of Al-Raḥim is to intend to be merciful to those in need, even when one is not able to meet their need; it is to aspire to, not turn from; it is to help all to the extent of one's ability.

Al-Raḥman The Beneficent

Appears in the Qur'an 57 times, the first reference in 1:3,

> Praise be to Allah, Lord of the worlds, The Beneficent, The Most Merciful.
>
> Qur'an 1:2–3

Al-Raḥman is the epitomy of mercy – raḥma – which embodies the promise of good in the hereafter. This is beyond the ability of human beings because only Allah is Infinitely Good. The name Al-Raḥman sometimes also functions as the proper name of Allah as is expressed in the following Ayah,

> . . . Call upon Allah, or call upon Al-Raḥman . . .
>
> Qur'an 17:110

To aspire to reflect this quality of goodness may lead us to attempt to protect others from the potential consequences of their actions. Such desire to be of service requires one to behave with consideration, not contempt, and to offer wise and gentle counsel.

Al-Raḥman relates to the 'all-encompassing' mercy bestowed upon believer and unbeliever alike. This is the most frequent meaning of this word in the Qur'an and the reason for the prayer taught by Imam ʿAli ﷺ to Kumayl, beginning, 'O Allah, I beseech you by Your Mercy which encompasses all things'.

Mercy when used as one of the Most Beautiful Names of Allah, has nothing to do with the emotional feelings that people possess but is rather an encouragement for humanity to accept His invitation to seek Him. When Allah in His wisdom shuts one door, out of His mercy He opens another door for His servants.

Al-Raqīb The Ever-Vigilant

Appears in the Qur'an five times, the first reference in 4:1,

> . . . verily Allah keeps Ever-Vigilant watch over you.
>
> Qur'an 4:1

Al-Raqīb remains alert and ever-vigilant over His creatures. He maintains constant surveillance and scrupulously observes each and every act of His Creation, for He has promised that obedience to Him will be rewarded and disobedience penalised. He, thus, observes how easily Satan – Shaytan – ever alert for weaknesses, exploits our insatiable egos.

Those who would reflect this attribute may do so to the extent that they remain vigilant, stay in control and do not forget, disobey, or grant their egos access to their hearts. In this way they avoid overstepping the limits set by Allah Almighty, in the knowledge that He is Omnipresent and that the whole universe is observed by Him at all times.

Al-Rashīd The Guide to Integrity and Sensible Conduct

Does not appear in the Qur'an as one of the Most Beautiful Names of Allah.

However, in Qur'an 72:2, the Holy Qur'an is described as being a guidance towards integrity – 'rushd' – and sensible conduct. As the Qur'an is the word of Allah Almighty, His words and actions present the utmost integrity and sensibleness.

The name Al-Rashīd can be derived either from the Arabic root word 'Rushd', which implies right guidance and sensible conduct, or from the root word 'Rashad' which implies straightforwardness and integrity of conduct. However, 'Irshad', which means guidance, stems from the latter root word. When Rashīd refers to human beings, it refers to the integrity of their conduct.

Al-Razzaq The Provider

Appears in the Qur'an once, in 51:58,

> It is Allah who is secure in His power, who is the provider of sustenance.
>
> Qur'an 51:58

Al-Razzaq is the Creator of sustenance and of all whom He sustains (i.e., He is the source of sustenance as well as of the creatures that benefit from it). Sustenance may serve to nourish a body while it is on earth, or nourish a soul for eternity,

> He increases or restricts sustenance to whomever He wills . . .
>
> Qur'an 42:12

The ability to reflect this attribute stems from knowing its essential reality, comprehending that all sustenance comes from Allah Almighty alone, and that we cannot rely on any other than Him. Following this, Allah grants knowledge to guide us, speech to teach us and hands to write and do good. When Allah loves someone, He makes His other creatures depend on them to the extent that those whom He loves become intermediaries between Him and His creation. It is in enabling His sustenance to reach people that we may reflect this attribute. Thus, when a father financially supports his dependants, the actual provider is Allah because it is He who uses the family breadwinner as the channel for His provision to his dependants.

S

Al-Ṣabur The Most Patient

Does not appear in the Qur'an as one of the Most Beautiful Names of Allah.

Patience is one of the virtues recommended in many Qur'anic ayat. Allah loves those who are patient, especially in times of distress and hardship. Imam ʿAli عليه السلام linked patience with faith, describing their relationship as similar to that of a head and a body. Just as there is no value in a body without a head, there is no complete faith without patience.

It is safe to conclude that Ṣabur is supposed to be one of the characteristics of the virtuous and pious believer rather than being one of the Most Beautiful Names of Allah. However, to include this as a Divine attribute is not very different from the inclusion of the attribute of He who is tolerant – Al-Ḥalīm (*see* p. 200).

Al-Salām Giver of Peace

Appears in the Qur'an once, in 59:23,

> He is Allah, there is no Divinity save He, the King, the Holy, the Giver of Peace.
>
> Qur'an 59:23

Al-Salām represents the purest essence, free of all imperfection. Allah, Al-Salām, is the One who is untouched by evil and whose deeds are without flaw.

Those who aspire to the quality of Al-Salām need to be pure hearted, unadulterated by deceit, hatred, envy, or malice and unblemished by any sin. Their passions and anger must be sublimated by their intellect for none can aspire to flawlessness who are not freed from their lower selves. There can be no well-being when emotions rule the head, nor can there be well-being in 'Islam' without the speech and action of one equipped to protect Islam. How could anyone, not free of their lower self, be flawless or a protector?

The peace of Al-Salām is universal. Described on the Night of Measure – Laylat al-Qadr – as 'peace till the break of dawn and better than a thousand months' (Qur'an 97:3–5).

Al-Ṣamad The One Who is Able to Satisfy All Needs

Appears in Qur'an once, in 112:2,

> . . . He is Allah, The One. Allah is the only One able to satisfy all needs.
>
> Qur'an 112:1–2

The word Ṣamad originally meant 'to approach a reliable person who has the ability to satisfy one's wishes'. Most Qur'anic commentators mention a variety of meanings for the word Ṣamad but all lead back to satisfying all of one's needs.

Allah is The Creator and Originator; all others need to approach Him through His Attributes and signs for continuance of their existence:

> His is the Creation and the Command.
>
> Qur'an 7:54

> To your Lord is the final goal.
>
> Qur'an 53:42

In Arabic, 'al' is a prefix that has a variety of usages:

1) It is the definite article equivalent to 'the' in English.
2) It can also be used to refer to something that is understood between a speaker and listener.
3) It may also indicate 'exclusivity', as it does in the case of Al-Ṣamad, in Qur'an 112:2.

It follows that He does not beget nor is begotten because He is not in need of anything, while all else depends on Him.

Al-Sami' The All-Hearing

Appears in the Qur'an 43 times, the first reference in 2:127,

> Remember when Ibrahim and Isma'il raised the foundations of the House, praying, 'Our Lord, accept this service from us, truly You are the All-Hearing, The All-Knowing.
>
> Qur'an 2:127

The attribute of the All-Hearing – Al-Sami' – represents the perfection in awareness of all things disclosed. He is the One for whom every sound is audible, no matter how faint, secret, or concealed. Hearing with clarity, free of distortion, He hears and rewards all praise and responds to all entreaties. Yet, He hears without ears, acts without limbs and speaks without any tongue.

Human hearing is deficient for it sometimes fails completely. Not everything audible is heard clearly or distinctly. However, awareness of Allah's perfect hearing cautions us to mind our words and remember that it is only His teaching that is worth listening to.

It is said that when Aristotle met the Prophet Mūsa عليه السلام the following dialogue took place:

> Aristotle: Do you claim that the First Cause spoke to you?
>
> Mūsa عليه السلام: Yes indeed.
>
> Aristotle: From which direction did you hear His voice?
>
> Mūsa عليه السلام: I felt that my Lord's voice was addressed from both right and left, front and back, from above and below.
>
> Aristotle: Then you may be right.

Minhaj Al-Bara'ah, Vol. 19, p. 128

Such dialogue illustrates that Allah does not communicate via senses or physical direction.

Al-Shahīd The One Who Witnesses

Appears in the Qur'an 18 times, the first reference in 3:98,

> Say O Muḥammad, 'O people of the Book, why do you reject the signs of Allah, while He Witnesses all that you do?'

Qur'an 3:98

This name is identical to the name Al-Raqīb (*see* p. 232).

Al-Shakur The One Who Responds when Pleased

Appears in the Qur'an four times, the first reference in 35:30,

> He recompenses those who establish prayer and spend generously, and by His Grace, grants them greater reward. Truly, He is oft forgiving, and responsive when pleased.

Qur'an 35:30

When pleased by obedient response to His demand for good action and behaviour, Al-Shakur grants His creatures unconstrained rewards. He promises great recompense to:

> . . . believing men and believing women
>
> obedient men and obedient women
>
> truthful men and truthful women
>
> patient men and patient women
>
> humble men and humble women
>
> charitable men and charitable women
>
> fasting men and fasting women . . .

Qur'an 33:35

And Allah tells us in the Qur'an that our good actions, even for short periods, may yield an eternity of bliss in Paradise,

> [It will be said] Eat and drink to your satisfaction [as a reward] for the good you sent in the past.

Qur'an 69:24

Thus, those who use reason spend their lives in striving to gratify their Lord by being worthy servants. One part of this servanthood is pleasing His creation, another is thanking His creation. The Prophet Muḥammad ﷺ said,

> Whoever does not thank humankind does not thank Allah.

Bihar al Anwar, Vol.71, p. 44

As our ability to express thanks to Allah falls far short of the praise and thanks due to Him, our most appropriate response is to please Him with obedience rather than displease Him by disobedience. Allah tells us in the Qur'an that,

> Those who express their gratitude will have their provision increased.
>
> Qur'an 14:7

When the Prophet Sulayman ﷺ reached the valley of the ants and heard one of them warn the others to take cover because of his approach, he smiled and, laughing at its speech, said,

> O my Lord, arouse me to be thankful for the facilities you bestowed on me and my parents.
>
> Qur'an 27:19

Although Al-Shakur is one of Allah's Most Beautiful Names, in the Qur'an He describes some of His Messengers as being 'Shakur' which, in this context, means a truly grateful servant, e.g.,

> You are the offspring of those We delivered [in the Ark] with Nūh [Noah], a truly grateful servant.
>
> Qur'an 17:3

T

Al-Tawwab He Who Accepts Repentance

Appears in the Qur'an eleven times, the first reference in 2:37,

> Adam received word from his Lord who had turned in mercy to him, truly it is He who accepts repentance . . .
>
> Qur'an 2:37

One of the most important spiritual concepts is to refrain from sin and to repent when one has not been successful in so doing, an issue frequently referred to in the Qur'an:

> Say to My servants, whose sins have endangered their own souls, 'Do not despair of the mercy of Allah. Truly He forgives all sins. He is Oft-Forgiving, Most Merciful'.
>
> Qur'an 39:53

> O believers, turn together in repentance to Allah in order that you may become successful.
>
> Qur'an 24:31

It is He who accepts repentance from His servants and forgives sins, and He knows what you do.

Qur'an 42:25

O you who believe! Turn to Allah Almighty with sincerity, maybe your Lord will wipe your sins from you and admit you to gardens beneath which rivers flow.

Qur'an 66:8

Do they not know that it is Allah who accepts repentance from His servants and receives alms, and that it is Allah who is the Oft-Returning, the Merciful.

Qur'an 9:104

Truly I forgive again and again whosoever repents and believes and does good, and then continues to follow right guidance.

Qur'an 20:82

Similarly, the Prophet ﷺ and the error-free Imams عليهم السلام emphasise the significance of repentance:

The Conditions for Repentance outlined by Imam ʿAli عليه السلام:

Someone said, 'I ask Allah's forgiveness – Astaghfiru'llah – in Imam ʿAli's hearing.' He responded, '. . . Do you have any idea of the significance of "Istighfar"?''

The deserving status of 'Istighfar' has to be underpinned by six supports:

The first is sincere regret for past deeds.

The second, firm resolve never to repeat such misdeeds.

The third, to come to Allah unblemished, having fulfilled all the rights of others, with nothing left undone.

The fourth, to fulfil and do justice to every previously ignored obligation.

The fifth, for the remorse of repentance to extend to eliminating from one's body, all growth which has been nourished from unlawful earnings, until skin and bone meet and only uncontaminated flesh separates them.

The sixth, is to submit one's body to the rigors of obedience, as it savoured the sweetness of disobedience.

Only then may one genuinely plead, 'astaghfiru'llah'.

Nahj al-Balaghah, Maxim number 417'

Imam ʿAli ﷺ said,

Refraining from sin is far easier than repenting after sinning.

Bihar al Anwar, Vol. 73, p. 364

The Holy Prophet ﷺ said,

There is a medicine for every illness and the medicine for sin is repentance.

Wasa'il al Shi'ah, Vol. 11, p. 354

Imam Sadiq ﷺ said,

Delay in repentance is arrogance and deceit, continued delay results in confusion. Making excuses to Allah Almighty is total destruction.

Bihar al Anwar, Vol. 73, p. 365

Imam Baqir ﷺ said,

After repentance, one is as though one has never sinned.

Al Kafi, Vol. 2, p. 435

Imam Baqir ﷺ said,

Allah Almighty's happiness at seeing a sinner repent is greater than the joy of a lost traveller journeying alone on a dark night, who recovers his missing luggage and transport.

Al Kafi, Vol. 2, p. 436

Imam Sadiq ﷺ said,

When a servant turns to Allah in pure and sincere repentance, Allah Almighty loves him and erases his past sins. The narrator asked, 'O son of the Prophet ﷺ how are sins erased?' He replied, 'The two Angels responsible for recording sin erase them while Allah orders the sinner's body and all the places on earth which witnessed them, never to disclose them'. Thus, the soul can meet Allah Almighty in a state where there are none to witness their sins.

Al Kafi, Vol. 2, p. 436

From all the above quotations we may conclude:

1) In Qur'anic terminology, repentance is descriptive of a twofold process, that of the servant's repentance and that of his Lord's acceptance.
2) A person who has been poisoned rushes to hospital without the slightest delay because he/she knows that any hesitation might result in his/her death. Yet sin is more toxic to a soul than the strongest toxin is to the human body.

   As poison threatens worldly life, sin threatens eternal life. Poison may terminate all connection with relatives and friends while sin may terminate closeness and all connection with the Almighty. Repentance and return to Allah is of far greater importance than anything else.
3) The Almighty tells us in the Qur'an,

   > Allah will return to those who, after their iniquity reform and turn in repentance to Him.
   >
   > Qur'an 5:39

   The importance of repentance is clear and that is why Allah loves those who repent.
4) Throughout human history, Messengers and saints have continuously encouraged people to repent. In many Qur'anic ayat the Most Compassionate Lord invites all who have gone astray and sinned, to return to Him and promises that He will accept their repentance, this to the extent that after repenting, sinners are to be considered as never having committed any misdeed.

   Repentance is possible and available at all times and one need never despair of the mercy of Allah.
5) Sincerity is vital for repentance to be accepted. There is no point in articulating with one's tongue 'I seek Allah's forgiveness', if the heart does not repent.

W

Al-Wadūd The Loving

Appears in the Qur'an twice, the first reference in 11:90,

> . . . my Lord is indeed merciful and loving.
>
> Qur'an 11:90

The responses of mercy and love are well-intentioned and of benefit to recipients. While extensions of mercy have concern for the well-being of a weak recipient, extensions of kindness and generosity do not. Nor are they necessarily considered expressions of love. Allah, Al-Wadūd manifests infinite, fundamental and unconditional love by honouring, blessing and favouring His creatures.

And first amongst the favours He granted is our ability to reciprocate His love, an ability which permits us to penetrate beyond the intellect to arrive at Truth. Another of His favours is faith, through which we are permitted to express devotion and worship. It is through worship that our awareness of the temporary nature of this world and all its treasures develops. Unique in not being temporary are the Eternal One and the souls that He has loaned us. Realisation then dawns that our Creator has favoured us with the greatest honour and blessing, greater than He would had He given us the whole world and all therein. It is then that Allah becomes the sole focus of our souls.

To reflect this quality is to desire for Allah's creatures whatever one desires for oneself and at a higher level, to give preference to their needs above one's own.

Al-Wahhab The Bestower

Appears in the Qur'an three times, the first reference in 3:8,

> Our Lord, do not suffer our hearts to go astray after You have rightly guided us, and grant us Your Mercy, for truly, You and You alone are the Bestower.
>
> Qur'an 3:8

He who frequently bestows generous gifts, giving without seeking, expecting, or anticipating, directly or indirectly, tangibly or intangibly, any recompense or benefit whatever, is described as the Bestower – Al-Wahhab.

Anything which is bestowed in anticipation of benefit is accurately described as a transaction undertaken for recompense. A gift, by definition, is something given or conferred, without desire for recompense. As illustrated below, it is not possible for creatures programmed to do everything for reward, to bestow anything, generously or bountifully.

The only ones who can correctly be described as generous, are those who, without hope of future gain for themselves or their families, sacrifice everything, including life, for the sake of Allah Almighty alone.

Those whose sacrifices are motivated by the desire to enter paradise, or avoid the pain of hell, cannot accurately be said to value Allah Almighty's pleasure. In this respect they are no different to those who pursue wealth in order to obtain goods and services.

People who do not understand the purpose of, or anticipate the pleasure and delight of, drawing close to Allah, do not long for Him. And if they do not long for Him they cannot conceivably expect to be rewarded with that for which they do not yearn. In this respect they are like labourers who work only for the money they need to satisfy their immediate needs. They do not appreciate or anticipate the rewards of growing closer to the Almighty.

The concept of being free from gain is impossible for humanity to comprehend as long as everything they do is done to reap some or other material reward. This is an exceedingly difficult quality for humankind to reflect.

It is reported by the Imams of the Prophet's progeny that to call on Allah by this name 14 times while in prostration – 'sajdah' – after each daily prayer, will lead to an increase in worldly wealth.

Al-Waḥid The One

Appears in the Qur'an 19 times, the first reference in 2:163,

> Your god is One, there is no Divinity other than Him.
>
> Qur'an 2:163

Although in Arabic 'Waḥid' indicates the numeral one, it is also used to refer to Allah as the One Divinity.

During the battle of Jamal, a bedouin asked Imam ʿAli عليه السلام , 'Do you say that God is One?' Some companions, uncomfortable about this being asked while the Imam was fighting, rebuked him. However, Imam ʿAli عليه السلام said, 'Do not disapprove of his question, because what he asked is the very object of this battle. We are demanding the true answer to this question from our enemy'. Then he explained, 'Oneness, in essence, does not correspond to any limitation. Since He is unlimited, a second, an equal, or an opposite to Him is not conceivable.'

Imam ʿAli's reference to the objective of the battle clarified that, as the source of creation, law and authority are One; the head of state, successor to the Messenger ﷺ, Allah's appointed vicegerent on earth, is also only one. The challenge to this was the background of that battle. (Refer to the name Aḥad on p. 179).

Al-Wājid The Resourceful

Appears only in the past tense – 'Wajada'.

Wajada in Arabic means 'found'; however, as Al-Wājid is the One who lacks nothing, He is described as being resourceful. In its general meaning Wājid is the opposite of 'one who is in need'. We have already shown that Allah is beyond all need and rich in every possible aspect. True servants are filled with strength and confidence after having communicated with their Lord, while those who have severed all links with Him have none and remain empty within.

Al-Wakīl The One Who is Trusted

Appears in the Qur'an 13 times, the first reference in 3:173,

> That is Allah, your Lord; there is no Divinity but He, the Creator of all things; therefore, worship Him. He is the One who is trusted by all.
>
> Qur'an 6:102

Believers are strengthened in their faith by the knowledge that nothing is able to challenge Allah's power. With this knowledge they rely entirely and absolutely on Him. In Arabic, reliance on Allah is called 'tawakkul' and Allah tells us in the Qur'an:

> Allah is sufficient for those who rely on Him.
>
> Qur'an 65:3

and

> Allah loves those who rely on Him.
>
> Qur'an 3:159

When the Prophet Ibrahim 🕊 was almost burnt in Nimrud's fire, the Archangel Jibra'il offered to help him, but Ibrahim 🕊 declined saying, 'As He already knows my situation, I can rely on Him – that is sufficient for me'. This illustrates the highest degree of reliance in the One who is trusted. (Safinat al-Bihar, Vol. 1, p. 192).

Al-Waliyy The Ultimate Authority

Appears in the Qur'an 23 times, the first reference in 2:257:

> Verily, verily, those who have Ultimate Authority over you are Allah, His Messenger and those who believe, establish the prayer and give the poor their due while bowing in submission.
>
> Qur'an 5:55

> Allah is the Ultimate Authority [Waliyy] over those who believe. He delivers them out of darkness into light. The authority of those who disbelieve are the false gods, who guide away from light into darkness . . .
>
> Qur'an 2:257

Both 'Waliyy' and 'Mawla' are homonyms, that is, words which can be used to denote different things. A search for the various meanings of the word 'Waliyy' in Arabic lexicons lead us to the following:

Owner (Lord of); Master; Slave; the one who frees; the freed; who favoured (benefactor); has been favoured (beneficiary); lover; friend; companion; protector; neighbour; lodger; guest; partner; relative; follower; helper; one who has authority.

These 19 different meanings clearly illustrate that the meaning of this word can only be understood in the context in which it is used. With reference to the two above-mentioned ayat it is manifestly evident that the word 'Waliyy', used in the context of Divine attributes, indicates The Ultimate Authority.

Theologically, 'Wilayah' refers to the concept of the succession to Allah's Final Messenger ﷺ – Imamah.

Those who reflect this attribute promote the knowledge that guides humanity towards enlightenment, and away from the darkest desires of their egos. Such are the patrons and protectors among people.

Al-Warith The Heir

Appears in the Qur'an three times, the first reference in 15:23,

> It is We who give life and cause death, and We are the Heir.
>
> Qur'an 15:23

Inheritance in all legal systems deals with property, wealth and the entitlement of heirs to an estate. However, its use as a Divine attribute indicates that He alone is the true owner of all property and wealth. Because He is the First and the Last, it is He who ultimately inherits everything.

Al-Wāsiaʿ The All-Encompassing

Appears in the Qur'an eight times, the first reference in 2:115,

> Allah's is the East and the West, wherever you turn, you turn towards Him, truly Allah is All-Encompassing, All-Knowing.
>
> Qu''an 2:115

Al-Wāsiaʿ is the unlimited resource of the infinite variety of attributes and qualities, *viz.*, understanding, knowledge, charity, generosity, mercy, power, tolerance, compassion, gentleness, etc. There is no hiding from His boundless power other than in His endless tolerance and forgiveness.

The ability to reflect this quality is limited by knowledge and good character.

Z

Al-Ẓahir The Self-Evident

Appears in the Qur'an once, in 57:3,

> He is the First and the Last, the Manifest and the Hidden.
>
> Qur'an 57:3

Light is evident and permits visual things to become evident and apparent. It is itself light and illumination for its surroundings. We have already discussed the concept of Allah being the Light of the heavens and the earth – Al-Nūr (*see* p. 226). We once again emphasise that even though His essence is not possible for any to comprehend or compare, He is self-evident.

Alphabetical list of Allah's Most Beautiful Names – Al-Asma' al-Ḥusna

A Al-ʿAdl. *The Just*
Al-ʿAfūw. *The Pardoner*
Al-Aḥad. *The Unique*
Al-Ākhir. *The Last*
Al-ʿAlīm. *The Omniscient (All-Knowing)*
Al-ʿAliyy. *The Most High*
Allah. *Allah*
Al-Awwal. *The First*
Al-Aẓīm. *The Tremendous (The Supremely Glorious)*
Al-ʿAzīz. *The Eminent (The Almighty)*

B Al-Badīʿ. *The Originator (of Creation)*
Al-Bāʿith. *The Raiser of the Dead – The Resurrector*
Al-Bāqī. *The Everlasting*
Al-Bārī. *The Originator (The Producer)*
Al-Barr. *The Benign (The Source of All Goodness)*
Al-Baṣīr. *The All-Seeing*
Al-Bāsiṭ. *He Who is Open-handed*
Al-Bāṭin. *The Hidden*

D Al-Ḍārr. *The One Who Disadvantages*
Dhul-Jalāl wal-ikrām. *The One Full of Majesty, Bounty and Honour*

F Al-Fattāḥ. *The One Who Opens*

G Al-Ghaffār. *He Who is Full of Forgiveness (The Forgiver)*
Al-Ghafūr. *The All-Forgiving*
Al-Ghanī. *The Self-Sufficient (For whom everything is readily available)*

H Al-Hādī. *The Guide*
Al-Ḥāfiẓ. *The Best Preserver*
Al-Ḥakam. *The Arbitrator (The Judge)*

Al-Ḥakīm. *The Wise*
Al-Ḥalīm. *The Tolerant*
Al-Ḥamīd. *Worthy of All Praise*
Al-Ḥaqq. *The Ultimate Truth*
Al-Ḥasīb. *The Reckoner*
Al-Ḥayy. *The Ever-Living*

J Al-Jabbār. *The Compeller*
Al-Jalīl. *The Majestic*
Al-Jāmiʿ. *The Gatherer*

K Al-Kabīr. *The Unsurpassable in Greatness*
Al-Karīm. *The Generous, The Noble*
Al-Khabīr. *The Thoroughly Aware*
Al-Khafiḍ. *The Abaser*
Al-Khaliq. *The Creator*

L Al-Latīf. *The Most Subtle*

M Al-Majīd. *The Glorious*
Mālik-al-Mulk. *The Owner of the Kingdom*
Al-Malik. *The King – (Sovereign)*
Al-Maniʿ. *He Who Grants Immunity*
Al-Matīn. *He Who is Secure in Power*
Al-Mu'akhkhir. *The Delayer*
Al-Mubdi. *The Originator of Creation*
Al-Mudhill. *The Humbler – Humiliator*
Al-Mughni. *The Enricher*
Al-Muhaymin. *The Overall Controller*
Al-Muḥṣi. *The Precise Recorder*
Al-Muḥyi. *The Giver of Life*
Al-Muʿid. *The Reproducer (of Creation)*
Al-Muʿizz. *The Honourer (The Granter of Honour and Glory)*
Al-Mujīb. *The Responsive*
Al-Mu'min. *The Bestower of Faith*

Al-Mumit. *He Who Brings about Death*
Al-Muntaqim. *The Avenger of Evil*
Al-Muqaddim. *The Advancer*
Al-Muqit. *The Provider of All Energy and Food*
Al-Muqsiṭ. *The Impartial*
Al-Muqtadir. *The Determiner of All Things (The All-Powerful)*
Al-Muṣawwir. *The Fashioner*
Al-Mutaʿali. *The Most Highly Exalted*
Al-Mutakabbir. *The Splendid*

N Al-Nafiʿ. *The Benefactor*
Al-Naṣīr. *The Helper*
Al-Nūr. *The Light*

Q Al-Qabiḍ. *He Who Withholds*
Al-Qādir. *The Omnipotent*
Al-Qahhar. *He Who Dominates*
Al-Qawiyy. *The Strong*
Al-Qayyum. *The One Who Maintains the Existence of All Reality*
Al-Quddus. *The Holy*

R Al-Rafiʿ. *The Exalter*
Al-Raḥim. *The Most Merciful*
Al-Raḥmān. *The Beneficent*
Al-Raqīb. *The Ever Vigilant*
Al-Rashīd. *The Guide to Integrity and Sensible Conduct*
Al-Ra'uf. *The Compassionate*
Al-Razzaq. *The Provider*

S Al-Ṣabūr. *The Most Patient*
Al-Salām. *Giver of Peace*
Al-Ṣamad. *The One Who is Able to Satisfy All Needs*
Al-Samiʿ. *The All-Hearing*
Al-Shahīd. *The One Who Witnesses*
Al-Shakūr. *The One Who Responds when Pleased*

T Al-Tawwab. *He Who Accepts Repentance*

W Al-Wadūd. *The Loving*

Al-Wahhab. *The Bestower*

Al-Wāḥid. *The One*

Al-Wājid. *The Resourceful*

Al-Wakīl. *The One Who is Trusted*

Al-Waliyy. *The Ultimate Authority*

Al-Wārith. *The Heir*

Al-Wāsia'. *The All-Encompassing*

Z Al-Ẓāhir. *The Self-Evident*

Selected list of English references

Amuli, Sayyid Haidar, *Inner Secrets of the Path*. Trans. by Assadullah ad–Dhaakir Yate. One Vol. Element Books, Shaftesbury, 1989

Cohen, Morris R, *A Preface to Logic* London, 1946

de Vaux, Roland. OP. *Ancient Israel: Its Life and Institutions*. Trans. by John Mc Hugh. One Vol. Pbk Edn. Darton, Longman & Todd Ltd, London, 1973

JPS. *Hebrew-English Tanakh*. One Vol. Second Edn. The Jewish Publication Society, Philadelphia, 1999

Lieber, David L. Snr. Ed. *Etz Hayim' – Torah and Commentary*. One Vol. The Rabbinical Assembly of The United Synagogue of Conservative Judaism, New York, 2000

Leftow, Brian. Chapter on 'Eternity' in *A Companion to Philosophy of Religion*, One Vol. Blackwell Publishers Ltd., 1999

Prior, Michael, CM. *The Bible and Colonialism: A Moral Critique*. One Vol. First Edn. Sheffield Academic Press, Sheffield, 1997

Prior, Michael, CM. *Zionism and the State of Israel: A Moral Enquiry*. One Vol. First Edn. Routledge, London, 1999

Prior, Michael, CM. Exec. Ed. *Holy Land Studies: A Multidisciplinary Journal*. A Continuum Imprint of the Sheffield Academic Press, Sheffield, 2002

Rushkoff, Douglas. *Nothing Sacred: The Truth About Judaism*. One Vol. First Edn. Crown Publishers, New York, 2003

Selected list of Arabic references

Amidi al-, Abd al-Wahid, *Ghorar al Hikam – Glorious Words of Wisdom The Aphorisms of Imam ʿAli* ﷺ One Vol. Beirut, 1987

Amin, al-, Muhsin. *Miftah al-Jennat – The Key to Paradise*. One Vol. Najaf, 1942

'Ayyashi, al-, Muḥammad bin Masoud, *Tafseer – Exegesis of the Qur'an*. One Vol. Tehran, 1380 AH

Bayhaqi, al-, Imam Ahmad bin Husain. *Al-Asma' wal Sifat – The Names and Attributes*. One Vol. Beirut, ND

Hadid, al-, Izzudin Ibn abi, *Sharh Nahj al-Balaghah – Commentary on Nahj al–Balaghah*. 20 Vols. Cairo, 1965

Hamawi, Yaqut, *Mujam al-Buldan – The Encyclopaedia of Cities*. Five Vols. Cairo, 1323 AH

Harrani, al-, ibn Shoubah. *Tohaf al-Oqul – A Treasury of Intellect*. One Vol. Qum, 2001

Hindi – *see* Muttaqi, Mulla ʿAli

Hisham, Ibn-, Abd al-Malik. *Sirah – Biography of the Prophet Muḥammad* ﷺ. Four Vols. Beirut, ND

Howaizi, Abd ʿAli bin Jumu'a. *Tafseer Nur al-Thaqalain – Exegesis of the Qur'an*. Five Vols. Qum. 1382 AH

Hurr al-Amili, al-, Muḥammad bin Hasan. *Wasa'il al Shi'ah – Shi'ah Resources for the elucidation of Shari'ah*. 30 Vols. Qum, 1993

Ibn Sa'ad. *Tabaqatul Kubra – Classification of Narrators*. Beirut, ND

Isphani, al-, Al-Ragheb. *Mufradatu'l–Qur'an – Celebrated Qur'anic Terminology*. One Vol. Tehran, 1983

Koleini, al-. Muḥammad bin Yaqub. *Al Kafi – The Sufficient*. Eight Vols. Beirut, 1990

Majlisi, Muḥammad Baqir. *Bihar al Anwar – Oceans of Light*. 110 Vols. Beirut, 1983

Musawi al-, Sayyid al-Radi. *Nahj al-Balaghah – The Peak of Eloquence*. Beirut, 1990

Muttaqi, Mulla ʿAli, also known as 'Hindi', *Kanz al Uma'al – Treasury of Labours*. 16 Vols. Beirut, 1989

Naraqi, Muḥammad, Mehdi. *Jami' Al-S'aadat – Collector of Happiness*. Three Vols. Najaf, 1958

Noori, al-, Husayn. *Mustradak al Wasa'il – The Conclusion of Wasa'il al-Shi'ah*. 18 Vols. Beirut, 1986

Qortubi, Muhdem bin Ahmad. *Al-Jamia – Exegesis of the Qur'an*. Beirut, ND

Qummi, Al-, Abbas. *Safinat al-Bihar – Concise collection of the contents of Bihar al-Anwar*. Four Vols. Islamic Research Foundation, Mashad, 1416 AH

Razi, al-, Fakhr al-Din. *Al-Tafseer al-Kabeer – The Great Exegesis of the Qur'an*. 30 Vols. Cairo, 1984

Saduq, Sheikh Muḥammad bin ʿAli bin Babawayh *Al-Tawḥid – The Oneness*. One Vol. Tehran, 1374 AH

Suyuti, Jalal al-Din. *Al-Durr al-Manthur – Presentation of Pearls*. Six Vols. Qum, 1404 AH

Tabataba'i, Muḥammad Husayn. *Tafsīr al-Mizan – The Balance*. 20 Vols. Beirut, 1983

Tabrisi, Al Fadhl bin al-Hasan. *Majma al-Bayan – Centre of Clarification*. 10 Vols. Beirut, 1988

Zayn al-ʿĀbidīn, Imam ʿAli ibn al-Husayn عليه السلام. *Al–Sahifat al–Kamilat al–Sajjadiyya – The Psalms of Islam*. One Vol. London, 1986

Glossary

ʿAāli high.

Abrar in Qur'anic terminology, those who are virtuous.

Abşara the past tense (i.e., saw in the physical context).

Abu Hurairah the attributed source of a large number of ahadith, many of which are questioned by scholars.

Abu Jahl a prominent disbeliever at the time of the Prophet ﷺ.

Ahadith (pl) see hadith.

Aḥmad commendable or laudable.

Ahl al-Bayt the progeny of the Prohet Muḥammad ﷺ

Akhbara informed or made aware.

ʿAla on or upon.

Al-Asma' al-Ḥusna the Most Beautiful Names.

Asma' al-Jalal the Names of Majesty.

Asma' al-Jamal the Names of Beauty.

Al-Dhāt the Divine Essence.

Al-Ḥamd praise for something good achieved.

Al Ḥamdu lilahi Rabbil Alamin praise is due to Allah, the Lord of the Universes.

Al-Kutub al-Arba'a the Four Books of Traditions. Four major Hadith references that refer to the ahadith of the Holy Prophet ﷺ and his progeny ؑ: *Al-Kafi – The sufficient*, compiled by Muhammad bin Yaqub al-Koleini; *Man la Yahdhurohu al Faqih – Everyone is his own Lawyer*, compiled by Shaykh Sadūq; *Al Tahzeeb – Rectification*, compiled by Shaykh Tūsi; and *Al Istibsar – Acquisition of Inner Sight*, compiled by Shaykh Tūsi.

ʿAli ؑ cousin and son-in-law of the Prophet Muḥammad ﷺ.

Aliha meant.

ʿAliyy the highest.

Al-Ism al-A'aẓam the Greatest of Allah's names.

Al-Madḥ praise for something acquired without effort.

Al-Quds al-Sharif the city of Jerusalem.

Al-Raḥman the Beneficent.

Al-Siḥaḥ al-Sittah the Six Books of Traditions. Six major Hadith references that refer to the ahadith of the Holy Prophet ﷺ: *Sahih Bukhari – The Authentic Book of Hadith*, compiled by Muhammad ibn Isma'il al-Bukhari; *Sahih Muslim – The Authentic Book of Hadith*, compiled by Abul Husayn Muslim ibn al-Hajjaj; *Sunan abi Dawud – Traditions*, compiled by Abu Dawud; *Sunan al Tirmidhi – Traditions*, compiled by Tirmidhi; *Sunan al Nisa'i – Traditions*, compiled by Nisa'i; and *Sunan ibn Majah – Traditions*, compiled by Ibn Majah al-Qazwini.

Amān conviction.

Amn peace.

ʿAṣr, Ṣalat al-ʿAṣr afternoon prayer.

Astaghfir Allah I seek Allah's forgiveness.

Ayah (*pl.* **Ayat**) lit, a sign. In Qur'anic terminology, a verse.

Ayesha a wife of the Messenger Muhammad ﷺ.

Aẓamah mightiness.

Badaʿa original creation without copying anything.

Bani Aws an Arabian clan.

Bani Hashim the descendents of Hashim, the Prophet's great grandfather.

Bani Khazraj an Arabian clan.

Bani Thaqīf an Arabian clan.

Baqeya to remain or to stay.

Bara'a to produce or create.

Barr a person that displays every type of goodness.

Barzakh the period between death and resurrection.

Baṣar the verb to see.

Baṣirah inner sight.

Basṭ open-handedness or generosity when refering to Allah's attribute, Bāsiṭ.

Ba'th the verb to send, to delegate, or to resurrect.

Bāṭn abdomen or stomach.

Bida'ah innovation.

Birr kindness, especially in actions and manner.

Ḍarar disadvantage or harm.

Dawūd عليه السلام David.

Dhikr rembrance of Allah.

Dhu owner.

Dhuḥr, Ṣalat al-Dhuḥr midday prayer.

Du'ā prayer, supplication.

Fahima Ḥaqq al-Fahm to comprehend thoroughly.

Fajr, Ṣalat al-Fajr the prayer offered at dawn.

Faqih jurist.

Fatḥ to open, to grant victory.

Fir'awn Pharoah.

Gehennam Hell.

Ghafara to forgive, pardon.

Ghanī free of need, self-sufficint.

Ha her/them: the Arabic pronoun used for a single female or inanimate objects.

Hābil Abel.

Ḥabr al-Ummah the Sage of the Muslim Nation.

Hadā to lead or guide people to the right way.

Hādī guide.

Hadith a report of a saying of the Prophet Muḥammad ﷺ and the error free Imams عليهم السلام

Ḥadith Qudsī Sacred Hadith (i.e., communications revealed by the Almighty to the Prophet Muḥammad ﷺ, but expressed in his own words). In contrast to the Qur'an, revealed by the Almighty to the Prophet Muḥammad ﷺ but communicated verbatim.

Ḥāfiẓ the protector; also descriptive of a person who knows the Holy Qur'an by heart.

Ḥafiẓa preserve, protect, or memorise.

Ḥakam arbitrator, umpire, or referee.

Ḥakama to rule, pass judgement, or give a decision.

Ḥamd to praise or extol.

Ḥaqq truth, perfection and rights (e.g., human rights).

Ḥasīb those who keep account of or calculate anything.

Ḥatam al-Tai a non-Muslim from the Jahiliyyah, renowned for his generosity.

Ḥayāh life.

Ḥayy alive, lively, active, or energetic.

Hidāya guidance.

Ḥikma wisdom.

Ḥilm forbearance and tolerance.

Ḥisab arithmetic.

Hūd عليه السلام a prophet mentioned in the Qur'an.

Hudā guidance.

Hum them: the Arabic pronoun for live and rational beings.

Iblis the Devil

Ibn Abbas a cousin and the most learned of the Prophet's companions (*see* **Ḥabr al-Ummah**).

Ilah the objective of perfection sought by humanity.

Ilm al-Kalam scholastic theology and creed.

Imamah leadership.

Imamiyyah followers of the authentic Qur'anic teachings of the Prophet's progeny عليهم السلام.

Imān faith.

Injil the Bible

Irshad Lit. to point the way. Technically used for admonishment.

ʿIsa عليه السلام Jesus.

Isha, Ṣalat al-Isha the prayer offered after full darkness of night has set in.

Ismah being free from error.

Isra'a night journey.

Istighfār to seek forgiveness.

Izzah dignity

Jabr force, duress.

Jahiliyyah the Days of Ignorance, the pre-Islamic age.

Jalla to be exalted and sublime.

Jinn beings created by Allah from fire.

Juhamiyyah followers of Juham ibn Safwan who espoused pre-destination.

Kab'ah 'House of God' in Makkah.

Kabil Cain.

Kabir is something large in size or capacity.

Karamites followers of Muḥammad ibn Kerām, an anthropomorphist who limited the nature of Allah Almighty by claiming that He literally sat upon His throne.

Karrama Allah Wajhah May Allah honour him.

Karuma to be generous and open-handed, or a person of noble or pure origin.

Khabar news.

Khabīr expert.

Lāt the name of a pre-Islamic idol.

Laylat al-Qadr the Night of Measure.

Liwaa al-Hamd the Standard or Banner of Praise and Glory

Ma'ad return or hereafter.

Madinah city, Islamically used for the city where the Prophet ﷺ lived and died.

Maghrib, Salat al-Maghrib the prayer offered after sunset.

Mahdi the Rightly Guided One. The Holy Prophet's descendant, the 12th error-free Imam now in occultation.

Maḥmūd praised: one of the names by which the Propher ﷺ is referred.

Makkah the holiest city in Islam.

Mala'ikah angels.

Malak angel.

Malakut the Divine Kingdom.

Mālik the owner of something. (also the name of the Angel in charge of Hell)

Malik King.

Mana'a to prevent, to obstruct, to deprive.

Masīh Messiah

Masjid al-Aqsa the Holy Mosque in Jerusalem.

Masjid al-Haram the Holy Mosque in Makkah.

Masorah added notes of clarification to ancient Jewish manuscripts.

Masoretic texts Hebrew Bibles which accord with the masorah.

Mawla guardian, being in charge, and Master

Melk property

Miftāḥ key.

Mishkāt niche (for a lamp); pendent lamp.

Muḥammad ﷺ the name of the Prophet of Islam, Allah's final Prophet.

Muḥasib an accountant.

Mulk ownership.

Mu'min believer.

Mūsa ﷷ Moses.

Mu'tazilites distinguished from Asha'rites by their exercise of intellectual reasoning in the interpretation of theological issues.

Nafʿa a benefit or advantage.

Nimrūd a despotic ruler of the military capital of Assyria, near Babylon in today's Iraq.

Nubuwah prophethood.

Nudrah rarity.

Nūh Noah

Pharisees a religious party or school among the Jews at the time of Christ.

Polytheism belief in more than one deity.

Qiblah the direction of the Kab'ah.

Qist equity

Qunut devoutness and humility before one's Creator.

Quraish a famous Arabian clan.

Qūt food.

Quwwah energy or power.

Raḥma mercy.

Rak'ah (pl. Raka'at) cycles for standing, bowing and prostrating during prayer.

Rashad straightforwardness

Rūh the spirit.

Rūh al-Amin Trustworthy spirit, the Archangel who delivered revelation to the Prophet ﷺ.

Rūh al-Quds the Holy Ghost.

Rushd sensible conduct

Sages a general term for Rabbis and Jewish teachers of the 2nd century BCE to the 7th century CE.

Sagheer something small in size or capacity.

Sajdah prostration.

Sari'a al-ḥisāb Allah's quickness to balance the accounts of humanity.

Salah or Salat method of praying in Islam.

Shayṭan Satan.

Shirk associating or ascribing divine qualities to other than Allah.

Septuagint third-century BCE Greek translation of the Bible.

Subḥan I glorify.

Sunnah Lit. practise, in hadith terminology, the Prophet's sayings and way of life.

Ṣurah picture or photograph.

Surah a division of the Qur'an.

Tafsīr commentary, exegesis of the Qur'an.

Tahajjud the prayer offered at midnight.

Ṭair bird.

Tajassum al-ʿAmal the Embodiment of Deeds.

Tanakh the sacred book of Judaism that incorporates the Torah (the five books of Moses), the Nevi'im (the prophets) and the Kethuvim (the writings).

Targums third-second-century BCE Aramaic interpretations/paraphasings of Hebrew scripture.

Taqwa piety

Tasbiḥ glorification.

Tawakkul reliance on Allah

Tawḥid Divine Unity, Oneness of Allah.

Tawḥid al-Afa'al the Unification of Actions.

Tawḥid al-Ṣifat the Unification of Attributes.

Tawrāt the Torah.

Torah she-be'al peh rabbinical explanations of the Torah, referred to as the Oral Torah.

Torah she-bikhav the Written Torah.

ʿUluw height.

Umayyah a branch of the Quraish clan.

Ummahāt mothers.

URL Uniform Resource Locators (i.e., Internet addresses).

ʿUzair عليه السلام Ezra.

Vicegerent successor.

Vulgate fourth-fifth-century CE Latin translation of the Bible.

Wāḥid the numeral one.

Wajada found.

Wajh face.

Wasilah approach.

Wilayah authority, assistance, love, guardianship.

Ya Hu O He (Jehovah).

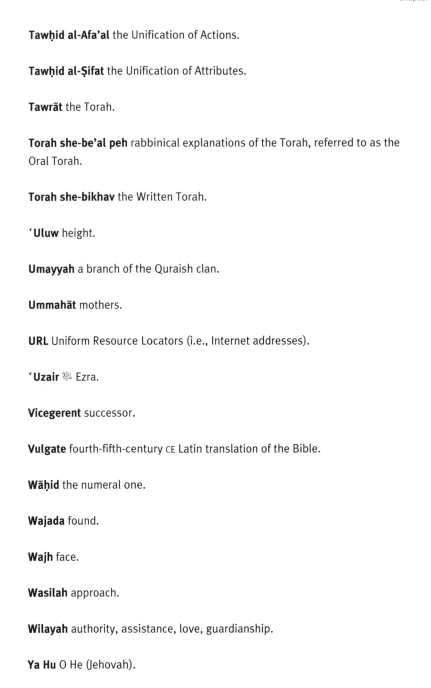

Yathrib the old name for Madinah.

Yubşeru to see.

Yu'id to repeat, to bring back.

Zabaniya angels in charge of hell, led by Malik.

Zabūr Psalms.

Zakah or **Zakat** religious tax.

Zaqqūm a bitter-tasting tree with stinging leaves.

Zaydiyyah followers of Zayd ibn ʿAli ibn Ḥusayn, who feel that he was eligible for Imamah rather than his brother Muḥammad al-Baqir عليه السلام.